"Indescribably Grand"

Diaries and Letters from the 1904 World's Fair

Edited and with an Introduction by Martha R. Clevenger

To Dan – my one-time "fearless leader." Thanks for all that discretionary time to work on this little project! With fond regards, Martha

PRESS
MISSOURI
HISTORICAL
SOCIETY

Missouri Historical Society Press

Saint Louis

©1996 by the Missouri Historical Society Press
Published in the United States of America by the
Missouri Historical Society Press,
P.O. Box 11940, St. Louis, Missouri 63112-0040
5 4 3 2 1   00 99 98 97 96

Library of Congress Cataloging-in-Publication Data

"Indescribably grand" : diaries and letters from the 1904 World's Fair / edited and with an introduction
by Martha R. Clevenger.
     p. cm.
    Based on the collections of the Missouri Historical Society.
    Includes bibliographical references and index.
    ISBN 1-883982-14-6 (cloth : alk. paper). — ISBN 1-883982-09-X (pbk.)
    1. Louisiana Purchase Exposition (1904 : Saint Louis, Mo.) 2. American diaries. 3. American letters.
I. Clevenger, Martha R. II. Missouri Historical Society.
T860.B1I53 1996
907.4'778'66—dc20   96-12981
                                                  CIP

Cover Image:
World's Fair, Palace of Liberal Arts. *Oil painting by John Ross Key, 1904.*

All illustrations in this book are from the collections of the Missouri Historical Society.

Designed by: Robyn Morgan
Printed by: Rose Printing Company, Inc.

∞ This paper meets the requirements of the American National Standard for Permanence of Paper for
Printed Library Materials, Z39.48, 1984.

The Missouri Historical Society thanks Deutsche Financial Services for its generous contribution to the
exhibit, *Meet Me at the Fair: Memory, History, and the 1904 World's Fair,* and related programming, of which
this publication is a part.

"Indescribably Grand"

For Mark

Contents

Acknowledgments

Although research, writing, and editing are often solitary endeavors, history is never written in isolation. This is particularly true when one works in public history and when one's work is shaped, at least in part, by the mission and initiatives of a larger institution. Thus this publication owes its appearance to the Missouri Historical Society and its staff, with whom I have worked since 1982. Of course, the list of individuals below does not include everyone who deserves thanks, but suffice it to say that I am indebted to every last one of my coworkers, colleagues, and comrades at MHS, whether they are listed individually or not.

The idea of publishing a collection of 1904 St. Louis World's Fair diaries and letters from the Missouri Historical Society's collections originated in a bull session several years ago, attended by my former boss, Peter Michel, and the former editor of the Missouri Historical Society's quarterly magazine, Martha Kohl. When they mentioned the idea to me in passing, I immediately decided that it was something I wanted to undertake. Eventually, that germ of an idea gave rise to this publication. To both of them, I owe immeasurable thanks.

I also owe deep gratitude to MHS president Dr. Robert R. Archibald and to vice-presidents Karen M. Goering and Marsha S. Bray for their support of the project and their faith in my ability to execute it. I owe a comparable debt of gratitude to Lee Ann Sandweiss, Director of Publications, for her enthusiasm as well as for her help in shepherding my initial proposal through the approval process. Special thanks also go to Duane Sneddeker for his assistance with photo editing, Tim Fox for his text editing, Robyn Morgan for her creative design, and David Schultz for his skill in reproducing historic photographs.

Peter Michel assisted me in many ways during the development of the manuscript, and Dan Baldwin, his successor, supported the project and allowed me to put other matters on the back burner. My fellow archivists, Dina Young, Dennis Northcott, and Kirsten Hammerstrom are the best colleagues one could have. Each assumed extra responsibility and ran interference for me so that my research and writing time was not disturbed. In addition, each funneled new information and sources my way on multiple occasions. Thanks also go to my intern, Damien Farwell, for his help in tracking down some of the annotations and for assisting with proofreading, and to my volunteer, Sue Schweitzer, and library assistant Sherrie Evans for their last-minute research assistance. Finally, the archives assistant, Mariana Salinas, kept the photocopy machine humming, producing copies as I needed them without complaint.

Several colleagues offered me their professional advice and insight on a number of occasions. Dina Young, Duane Sneddeker, Castle McLaughlin, Kirsten Hammerstrom, and Kathy Corbett all read the Introduction and gave me useful feedback and large doses of encouragement. Their intellectual power and readiness to be engaged by this project proved most gratifying and made my work even more rewarding. Others, including John Wolford, Mark Tebeau, Mary Ann VanPoelvoorde, and Jack Gillingham, suggested possible lines of inquiry and sources I might consult, as well as sharing my enthusiasm for the topic and for my approach to it. Special thanks also go to the many researchers who have made use of the resources in the Missouri Historical Society Archives and who have shared their ideas and methodologies with me over the years; one of the perks of being an archivist is that one is privy to new ideas long before they are in print.

Most importantly, I owe a very special thanks to my dear husband, Mark. He is my best booster and my best friend as well as my life-long companion.

Final thanks go to Edward V. P. Schneiderhahn, Edmund Philibert, Florence McCallion, and Sam P. Hyde for creating the manuscripts included in this publication. Thanks are also due their families and descendants for preserving these manuscripts and ensuring their survival for posterity. I have tried to do them justice. Where I have failed, the failure is mine alone.

Martha R. Clevenger
April 1996

Editors' Note

Because this work hopes to attract both popular and scholarly audiences, editing the texts has presented some dilemmas. While the editors have been committed to maintaining the integrity of the original texts, they have also been concerned with their readability. Thus, editing these documents has entailed some compromises. Fortunately, all four authors wrote well, despite their varied backgrounds and often limited formal education. Therefore, the editors have not had to alter language or syntax, except on a very few occasions. In those cases, additions and deletions have been noted with ellipses and brackets.

A few cosmetic changes have also been made, but only to insure the readability of the texts. Proper names and the first words of sentences have been capitalized, and the improper use of capitals following semi-colons and colons have been corrected. Idiosyncratic capitalization, as with the names of buildings or monuments, for example, has been left as originally written. Periods have been added at the ends of sentences where needed, commas have been added on occasion to break up run-on sentences, and improper uses of apostrophes have been corrected. Simple misspellings have also been corrected, though British spellings have been retained. Otherwise, every effort was made to retain the character of the original texts.

For researchers interested in examining the original texts prior to their editing, photocopies of the original manuscripts from which this publication was prepared may be obtained from the Archives of the Missouri Historical Society.

Martha R. Clevenger, Archivist
Tim Fox, Book Editor

"Indescribably Grand"

Diaries and Letters from the
1904 World's Fair

Southeast Corner of the Palace of Varied Industries. *Photograph, 1904. This view, featuring the Grand Basin in the foreground and the Louisiana Monument to the right, is one of the many "Indescribably Grand" views of the 1904 St. Louis World's Fair.*

Introduction

by Martha R. Clevenger

The view across the lagoon . . . was simply indescribably grand. But it is impossible for language to express the actual reality. We have become so addicted to the use of superlatives in common speech, that when we are taxed for resources of speech, as in this instance, we are at a loss what to do.

—Edward V. P. Schneiderhahn[1]

"Indescribably Grand" was a phrase that Edward V. P. Schneiderhahn used to lament the fact that the experience of visiting the 1904 St. Louis World's Fair could not be reduced to words on lined paper. "Beauty indescribable," "It cannot be even hinted at by words," and "Wish that you[2] could describe it" are three additional phrases he employed as he tried to capture the impact of the Fair's Main Picture in his post-Fair memoir of December 1904.

Schneiderhahn, an avid diarist throughout his youth and young adulthood, wrote beautifully lyrical passages that today seem to capture the immensity and beauty of the world's largest ever international exposition. Yet his most lyrical passage of all, a three-page description of "The Fair in General," is replete with evidence of frustration. Elsewhere in his World's Fair diary are similar expressions of disappointment—not only with the inadequacies of language, but also with the fact that the Fair would soon close and be given up to history. Never to be experienced and enjoyed again, the event itself engendered immediate nostalgia in the minds of Fair visitors. Elements of this immediate nostalgia, and of frustration with it, permeate the diaries and letters written by St. Louis area residents on the occasion of the 1904 St. Louis World's Fair that have survived in the archives of the Missouri Historical Society in St. Louis—diaries and letters that today attract the interest of researchers seeking to analyze the Fair from the visitors' perspective.

The 1904 St. Louis World's Fair has engaged the attention of historians and nonhistorians alike. Among local and regional students of St. Louis history, the Fair has provided subject matter for numerous theses and articles.[3] Within the community at large, it has elicited an urban fascination with a piece of history in an ahistorical age. When asked to name three significant events in the city's history, St. Louisans invariably include the 1904 World's Fair, while generally failing to mention the founding of the city, the Lewis and Clark Expedition, or Charles Lindbergh's New York to Paris flight.[4] The World's Fair is seen as the high point of St. Louis history—a time when "The World Came to St. Louis"[5]—and has become part of St. Louis' popular culture. Accordingly, it has fed the current mania for collecting popular culture: collectors of 1904 World's Fair artifacts abound in St. Louis.[6] It has spawned an organization, the 1904 World's Fair Society, consisting of lively and dedicated members who religiously attend any and all public programs that even hint of content related to the Fair. And it has given birth to the hope that somehow St. Louis can re-create its coup of 1904 with another great world's fair in 2004. Fascination with the Fair has also given rise to efforts to build a scale model of the grounds and to create a CD-ROM–based visit to the Fair—efforts that have been forestalled only by cost, not by a lack of dedication or enthusiasm on the part of their advocates. Above all, the World's Fair has generated a number of urban myths, which, even if discredited, will never leave St. Louis' urban consciousness.[7] Consumers of local history and of St. Louis' popular culture have turned to the letters and diaries of Fair visitors in search of the sources of urban myths; for descriptions of particular features, events, and Pike rides; and out of nostalgia in an effort to recapture the experience of visiting the Fair.[8]

On a national and international scale, the phenomenon of world's fairs has sparked a new field of historical research. Professional historians, among whom Robert Rydell (*All the World's a Fair*, 1984) is probably the best known, have begun to look at the ideologies and agendas promoted by the turn-of-the-century fair planners and civic leaders—both American and European—who were responsible for mounting a series of ever more spectacular world's fairs, of which the St. Louis Fair was the largest.[9] Their analyses have focused primarily on world's fairs as vehicles for promoting the ideologies of progress and national expansion. This approach has in turn sparked inquiries into how fair visitors reacted to the messages they encountered.[10]

It is here that this publication hopes to make a contribution. The Missouri Historical Society is making a series of original diaries and letters from the 1904 World's Fair—diaries and letters written for private audiences—readily available to historians and students of world's fairs so that they may investigate the visitor experience. The surviving personal records of Fair visitors can reintroduce contemporary audiences to the multidimensional and multisensory aspects of the Fair-going experience. They illustrate that the Fair, by virtue of its magnitude and impermanence, was a landmark event in the lives of Fair visitors. They also provide insight into how the individual Fair visitor experienced the World's Fair intellectually. For students of Rydell's scholarship, however, visitors' diaries and letters can be disappointing: Fair visitors' narratives seldom addressed issues in the terms used by Fair planners to articulate their ideologies and agendas. Thus, exploring this issue requires redefining and broadening the inquiry beyond an analysis of Fair visitors' responses to the Fair planners' presentation of the ideologies of progress and expansion to include an identification and analysis of the subjects and issues as defined by Fair visitors themselves.[11] Such analysis, however, first requires a brief re-examination of the 1904 St. Louis World's Fair and its context.

※

The 1904 Louisiana Purchase Exposition in St. Louis was one of a series of American world's fairs that took place between the Gilded Age and the advent of World War I—fairs which in turn had evolved within a world context. Initiated by the first truly international exposition, London's "Crystal Palace" of 1851, world's fairs were a cultural construct of the modern industrial and expansionist nation-state that offered a forum for a nation to juxtapose its prowess and progress in any and all fields against that of other participating nations before its own increasingly affluent and educated middle class. The fairs were justified on the grounds that they promoted peace by bringing the world together and the edification of the citizenry by their educational content. In practice, these world's fairs were characterized by the same intense competition that governed trade relations and the international quest for overseas empire, while their educational content was structured so as to encourage consensus rather than debate among the middle classes at home.[12]

Over several decades these increasingly massive expositions followed the phenomenon of the rising industrialized and expansionist nation-state, appearing first in England, then in continental Europe, and soon thereafter in the United States. They eventually attracted the interest of the South American nations, Russia, Japan, and even China, as these nations, too, made their bids to join the ranks of modern nations as regular participants in international expositions, if not necessarily as hosts.

With the Centennial Exposition in Philadelphia in 1876, the United States joined the game by staging its first successful international exposition. Then, in 1893, the World's Columbian Exposition in Chicago set the standard for the American world's fairs that were to follow. And follow they did, rapidly upon the heels of one another. Held often in younger American cities and moving generally westward, these fairs celebrated first European and then American expansion and were evidence of the arrival of the United States on the world stage.[13] Like the world's fairs of Europe, the American international expositions were an innovation. Definable as world's fairs by virtue of their international scope and their mass audiences, they were hybrid entities that combined trade fairs with spectacle and popular entertainments to create a utopian and transient reality. Paid for by a combination of private and public funds, each fair was conceived, planned, operated, and governed by a combination of local elites, professional fair planners, and regional, national, and even international dignitaries who together defined for these events an increasingly well articulated ideology of progress and expansion.

By the turn of the century, popular reform movements born of the rapid industrialization and social turbulence of the Gilded Age had coalesced and given rise to "cooperation between previously discrete social groups now united under the banner of 'public interest.'"[14] Cooperating within established political and social frameworks, they instituted a movement of Progressive reform, to which political, social, and business elites eventually subscribed. As was the case with Tory Democracy or governmental socialism in Europe, American Progressivism was a phenomenon whereby conservative leaders embraced reform, thereby defusing popular discontent and threats to social order.[15]

Central to Progressivism were the beliefs that the methodology of science could be applied to social as well as technical problems and that it was indeed the legitimate role of governing elites and even government itself to oversee this process. In the minds of turn-of-the-century thinkers and reformers, technical progress and social progress were linked: both were measurable, both were inherently moral, and progress defined civilization itself. Faith in progress was also bound to the concept of America's Manifest Destiny and ultimately justified American overseas imperialism at the end of the century.[16] Much of Frederick Jackson Turner's frontier thesis had drawn heavily on contemporary scientific thought,[17] for example, as had European theories of Social Darwinism. In the American context, territorial expansion and the degree to which the wilderness was transformed and the frontier "civilized" were deemed to be measures of the nation's progress.

Not only did these ideologies permeate late nineteenth- and early twentieth-century world's fairs, but fair planners consciously promoted them. Wilbur O. Atwater, chief of the Department of Agriculture at the 1893 World's Columbian Exposition in Chicago, asserted, for example, "The exposition should not be merely a show, a fair or a colossal shop, but also and pre-eminently an exposition of the principles which underlie our national and individual welfare, of our material, intellectual and moral status."[18] Thus, as Rydell has concluded, world's fairs offered a "cohesive explanatory blueprint of social experience" to "millions of fairgoers in the wake of . . . industrial depressions and outbursts of class warfare."[19] As such, the American world expositions attempted to be vehicles for education and controlled democratization as well as tools through which social consensus could be built in an increasingly diverse and pluralistic society. The audience—the mass of fair visitors—was thus a necessary participant in a world's fair. As education came to be an ever higher priority within industrialized societies, fair planners consciously assumed the role of educators. And as the world inched toward and entered the twentieth century, science and technology, coupled with renewed prosperity and peace (in the Western world if not elsewhere), seemed to offer limitless possibilities. Among them were an ever-improved standard of living, widespread access to knowledge, and an increasing belief that the masses of people, not just the elite, could participate in and benefit from this progress if they were appropriately educated.

Fair planners used every tool at their disposal to communicate their views and values to their audience. Official publicity, official histories, official photographs, and even the space they selected and the architectural styles they chose were vehicles for communicating their views and values to fair visitors. The latter factors were important in that they defined the environment within which the fair-visiting experience took place. Beginning with the 1893 World's Columbian Exposition, fair planners adopted a neoclassical architectural style, opting for a conservative approach in the face of a turbulent and rapidly changing society. Formal, controlled, and unified, a fair so designed evoked Frederick Law Olmsted's Central Park in New York: a "stable institutional prop for a nation confronting fast social change."[20] For thirty years the neoclassical style continued to dominate. In the American context, neoclassical columns and domes, punctuated by formal gardens and lagoons, evoked the seemingly timeless symbolism of ancient Rome—republican, yet imperial.[21] Extravagant staging was possible only because world's fairs were, by their very nature, temporary. Their transience and impermanence made them ephemeral, while their grandiose scope made them virtual realities. The world's fair was a utopia from which one could escape the realities of daily life, ponder the wonders of the world, and visualize a limitless future.

Like other American world's fairs that took place at the close of the Gilded Age and into the Progressive Era, the 1904 St. Louis World's Fair provided a forum for the articulation of the ideals of progress and national expansion to a massive audience. Officially named the Louisiana Purchase Exposition, or LPE, it commemorated the centennial of America's "largest land deal," the 1803 purchase of the Louisiana Territory.

St. Louis earned the right to host the Fair only after failing in its bid to secure the 1893 World's Columbian Exposition. St. Louis businessman and Democratic Party politician David R. Francis, who as Missouri governor had led the ill-fated fight for the 1893 Fair, proved fabulously successful the second time around. With aggressive efficiency and the avid support of the city's commercial leadership, he secured the local and regional support he needed to make his bid for St. Louis as the site of a centennial celebration of the Louisiana Purchase. Local promoters raised five million dollars by popular subscription, secured a like appropriation from the city, and with minimal difficulty even obtained another five million dollars from the federal government by the end of 1901. Armed with funds, Francis, now in office as President of the Louisiana Purchase Exposition Company, or LPE Co., sold the Fair to the world, securing the promise of participation from all but two American states and from over sixty foreign governments. At home, he and his corporation obtained the use of the western half of St. Louis' largest and most beloved public park—Forest Park—located at the city's central western edge, and then proceeded to lease again as much space to the west and north in St. Louis County. By 1904, when the Fair opened—one year later than initially planned— over fifty million dollars had been spent to create the largest-ever world's fair.[22]

This Fair epitomized the ideals of the Progressive Era. In content, structure, and organization, it was in many ways a larger version of the 1893 Chicago Fair, and its planners borrowed much from Chicago's experience while always endeavoring to outdo its predecessor.[23] But taking place a decade later, following the economic depression of 1893-97 and the Spanish-American War of 1898, the Louisiana Purchase Exposition took American world's fairs to a new level. The agenda of Progressive reform and the ideology of imperialism were arrayed in St. Louis with more sophistication and refinement than at Chicago. In addition, the Fair stimulated Progressive reform in its host city.

For St. Louis, mounting a world's fair was an enormous undertaking. Not only did the Fair company face the monumental task of building a small city in Forest Park and ensuring sufficient national and international participation to make the event an unqualified success, but the city of St. Louis itself needed to prepare to play host. As planning for the Fair began, however, the city was still reeling from the effects of the 1893 depression. In addition, city government was notoriously corrupt, politics were factionalized, public services were wholly inadequate, and the electorate was in no mood to accept yet another do-nothing mayor more interested in boodle than public service. Popular wisdom held that the city was controlled by the so-called "Big Cinch," an elite of bankers, lawyers, merchants, and manufacturers who dominated civic affairs from their sheltered enclaves of private places in the city's fashionable West End while they worked hand-in-hand with a corrupt government to share the graft. Labor unrest was rife, and ethnic and class divisions permeated the city. In 1900, when St. Louis was torn by a violent strike of streetcar workers, the depths of those divisions were exposed. Then in October 1902, a year and a half before the Fair opened, Lincoln Steffen's *McClure's Magazine*, in its first of a series of exposés on urban corruption, gave national exposure to St. Louis' ills when it branded the city one of "the worst governed" in the land.[24]

McClure's muckraking attack on St. Louis came as the city was beginning to address some of its problems and was in fact stimulated by the local publicity accorded investigative efforts. Reform mayor Rolla Wells already had been elected to office in St. Louis in 1900. An advocate of using the methods of business to make government more efficient and effective, Wells was typical of the conservative Progressive reformer.[25] Under his administration, St. Louis Circuit Attorney Joseph W. Folk launched an assault on governmental corruption, while the mayor himself undertook to create a "New St. Louis" in preparation for the Fair. Wells addressed the problems of water purification, street improvement, smoke abatement, and shoddy streetcar and rail service, and even attacked the interests of the so-called "Big Cinch" on occasion.

St. Louis Streetcar Strike. *Photograph by George Stark, 1900. As it prepared for the World's Fair, St. Louis was torn by the violence of the streetcar strike. Workers attempted to halt all traffic by vandalizing the streetcar lines.*

When the Fair opened in 1904, St. Louis' water ran clear, no longer full of sediment; air quality was markedly improved by the reduction of dust due to street paving and the increased use of smoke reduction devices by industry; and the wealthy residents of the city's West End had anted up for the improvement of the streets their property abutted.[26] Though arguably superficial, these improvements were readily visible. On the fairgrounds, labor problems were kept to a relative minimum by virtue of an agreement between the Louisiana Purchase Exposition Company and the St. Louis Building Trades Council,[27] while the Fair-planning elite concentrated on creating an idyllic utopia in Forest Park. David R. Francis governed this process with ruthless efficiency. Having been frequently attacked in the St. Louis press as a member of the "Big Cinch," he became the hero of the day, earning even the adulation of his biggest critic, William Marion Reedy, publisher of the muckraking *Mirror*.[28] Thus St. Louis entered the Progressive Age in large measure due to the impending World's Fair.

The Louisiana Purchase Exposition opened in St. Louis on April 30, 1904, the 101st anniversary of the Louisiana Purchase. As a celebration of American territorial expansion, first across the continent and then overseas, it promoted the virtues of American civilization, culture, and values so as to suggest their superiority over those of the world. As host, the City of St. Louis promoted herself as the great capital of the American West. The exhibits, their arrangement and content, and the controlled space in which the Fair was staged were all calculated to

Opening Day Ceremonies. *Photograph, April 30, 1904. Louisiana Purchase Exposition Company President David R. Francis affirmed the principles and values embodied in the 1904 World's Fair in his opening day address at the base of the Louisiana Monument.*

communicate these fundamental presumptions to Fair visitors. In addition, a nationwide press campaign, a series of "official histories," "official photographs," and even an official periodical, the *World's Fair Bulletin*, promoted the Fair and the Fair planners' values and views to the widest possible audience.[29] Ever cognizant of the standard set by Chicago in 1893, Fair officials boosted the event as truly comprehensive. It was more than a world's fair, they asserted, it was a "universal exposition."[30] In his opening-day address, LPE president David R. Francis affirmed this concept: "So thoroughly does [the Fair] represent the world's civilization, that if all man's other works were by some unspeakable catastrophe blotted out, the records here established by the assembled nations would afford all necessary standards for the rebuilding of our entire civilization."[31]

Francis' grandiose presentiments aside, the scope of the exhibits at the LPE was indeed massive, so massive that they demanded sensible organization and arrangement. That organization was established by LPE director of exhibits Frederick J. V. Skiff, a widely acclaimed authority on expositions. Skiff created a system of scientific classification—a veritable taxonomy of the works of man—that consisted of 16 exhibit departments, divided into 144 groups and 807 classes.[32] To derive full value from an exposition, Skiff argued, a visitor "must have the objects of his study so grouped and presented that he may apply himself directly to the examination of them without having to mentally assemble them, himself, from different parts of the Exposition."[33] For Skiff, however, classification was more than a framework for analysis: he believed it gave structure and purpose to people's lives and thereby helped create "a properly balanced citizen capable of progress."[34]

Skiff's exhibit classification system set parameters for the display of objects in relation to one another in order to demonstrate a unilinear progress and to facilitate comparison. For example, the classification schema provided for the exhibit of historical locomotives, which was arranged to illustrate their development from the first steam engine through the most modern, most powerful, and largest engine to date—a machine that was aptly named *The Spirit of the Twentieth Century*.[35] In addition, the classification system provided for the exhibition of "process" as well. Group 21 in the Department of Liberal Arts, "Musical Instruments," for example, included a classification for the display of materials and processes for the manufacture of instruments.[36] Thus the St. Louis World's Fair built upon a phenomenon characteristic of the American expositions, the use of tableaux display techniques aimed at informing the visitor regardless of his level of knowledge or expertise.[37] At the LPE this was taken to a new height. Many exhibits contained actual working factories, including one for the manufacture of light bulbs in the Department of Manufactures, while the Department of Mines and Metallurgy boasted a working anthracite coal mine. Even the power plants of the Exposition were working exhibits, each classified appropriately and each open to the public.[38] To facilitate comparison between societies and cultures, the exhibits of individual nations within a particular department were then physically segregated. Thus, the accomplishments of the nations of the world and of the races of man were laid out "for the inspection of the world—for the study of its experts, by which they may make comparisons and deductions and develop plans for future improvements and progress."[39]

Indeed, the architects of exhibits at the LPE, as at other world's fairs, believed that the past was the guide to the future, and that the point of the exhibits was to demonstrate that civilization "was advancing in some known direction." The past, or history, enabled both society's "experts" and the individual Fair visitor to extrapolate that direction from observations of the progression of society, or any particular aspect thereof, from its origins to the present.[40]

Clearly, the Fair planners and officials in the Division of Exhibits intended that the LPE do much more than display the wares of individual manufacturers or nations for each other's edification. They were also seeking to educate a mass audience. As it was for society at large, education was an increasingly important theme in world's fairs as they evolved. At the LPE, Fair planners embraced the view that was articulated at the 1900 Paris Exposition, that "education was the source of all progress."[41] They then took it further by establishing a centrally appointed Palace of Education and by placing Education first in the exhibit classification scheme, claiming "a departure in exposition practice from the commercial and manufacturing."[42] As world's fairs evolved, the exhibitions expanded beyond the display of industrial products and works of art. By 1904, at the St. Louis Fair, the exhibit classification system endeavored to be so comprehensive that ideas themselves were exhibited. Thus "Education," "Social Economy," and "Anthropology" were exhibited alongside "Manufactures," "Machinery," and "Art."

The classification system even included a Department of Physical Culture that sponsored athletic competitions, among them the 1904 Olympics, and a Department of International Congresses, under whose aegis a number of national and international conferences convened to discuss topics ranging from jurisprudence to international peace.[43] It was in the areas of the seemingly unexhibitable that the ideologies of progress and national expansion were most overtly showcased and where an idyllic and utopian future was set forth as attainable.

In that the Fair planners' concept of progress, like that of society at large during the Progressive Era, presupposed that the methods of science could be applied in any field, categories such as Education and Social Economy were areas where scientific techniques could be used to improve man's social condition. In the Department of Education, for example, methods for the education of the disabled were demonstrated in model classrooms, while in the Department of Social Economy, exhibits focused on ways in which the state as well as private charitable institutions could improve social conditions in areas such as the regulation of industry and labor or in civic improvement.[44] One of the more remarkable exhibits was a Model Street. "The street itself, 1,200 feet long, with a center roadway forty-two feet wide and grass lawns on either side between roadway and sidewalks, was in paving, parking and entire equipment a Model Street indeed, worked out according to the most approved methods of the most advanced cities, and showing the finest examples of curbing and of paving made with asphalt. . . ."[45] Housed on the Model Street were model civic institutions of the type that America in the Progressive Age was beginning to support or improve, including a playground and a hospital, which served as the Exposition's day care center and infirmary. With its broad avenue and neat and tidy appearance, the Model Street was a superb illustration of the "City Beautiful" ideal that was just gaining its adherents at the turn of the century.[46]

In the Department of Anthropology, where turn-of-the-century man's study of man was exhibited, concepts of progress blended with theories of race to create a scientific rationalization for national expansion, imperialism, and the subjugation of conquered peoples. The centerpiece of the Department of Anthropology was an outdoor ethnological exhibit that consisted of three groups of tribal peoples imported from outside of North America (Ainus from Japan, Pygmies from Africa, and Patagonians from Argentina) and representatives of at least fourteen Native American peoples from within the United States. As described in one of the official histories of the Fair, this exhibit showed "actual race types or varieties of mankind, living as at home in primitive huts or teepees. These living groups occupied dwellings erected by themselves chiefly from materials brought from their native lands for the purpose. They engaged in the accustomed occupations, prepared and ate their accustomed food, so far as possible, and wore their usual apparel."[47] The American Indian exhibit was accompanied by a suttler's trading post, where the Native Americans could secure foodstuffs and supplies, and by the United States Indian School exhibit, which illustrated reservation-based education.

This exhibition of people in their natural habitats offered an opportunity for the scientific study of various peoples about whom little was known, while educating the Fair-visiting public about the science of anthropology, its applications, and its implications for the future progress of man as man, not just as producer. Based on the work of Lewis Henry Morgan (1818-1881), the science of anthropology had

defined four stages of human progress: barbarism, savagery, civilization, and enlightenment (*Ancient Society*, 1877). Each of these terms had very specific meanings within the discipline. Anthropologist Franz Boas, whose humanistic inclusiveness prompted him to see in anthropology a science for the study of the community of man as a whole, warned of the dangers of "an exaggerated valuation of the standpoint of our own period, which we are only too liable to consider the ultimate goal of human evolution, thus depriving ourselves of the benefits to be gained from the teachings of other cultures."[48]

Others, however, fell into the trap that Boas warned about, thus causing the ethnological exhibits to validate pre-existing popular prejudices. This is most evident in the official histories and the *World's Fair Bulletin* articles that promoted the ethnological exhibits. They betray that the exhibiters and interpreters of the young science of anthropology at the LPE not only adhered to the widespread popular belief in the inherent morality of progress, but also held that progress was evidenced by technical accomplishment. Peoples and races that lacked evidence of significant technical advancement, at least as measured against the West, were deemed to be not only less civilized, but inferior. Popularizations of the new science of anthropology also included the view, for example, that the "broadness of sympathy and thoroughness of honesty are peculiar to civilized men."[49] Similar expressions permeate the language of the top officials in the Division of Exhibits at the LPE. W. J. McGee, Chief of the Department of Anthropology at the Fair, described the various races represented at the LPE in terms that leave no doubt as to his understanding of progress. The peoples at the Fair ranged, he wrote, "from smallest pygmies to the most gigantic peoples, from the darkest blacks to the dominant whites, and from the lowest known culture (the dawn of the Stone Age) to its highest culmination in that Age of Metal, which, as this Exposition shows, is now maturing in the Age of Power."[50] For Director of Exhibits Frederick Skiff, the Fair as a whole then illustrated "the record of the social conditions of mankind, registering not only the culture of the world at this time, but indicating the particular plans along which different races and different peoples may safely proceed, or in fact, have begun to advance towards a still higher

Girls from the United States Indian School in the Children of All Nations Parade. *Stereograph, Keystone View Company, 1905. Indian school children, dressed in Western fashion for this parade, illustrate the values of assimilation. Their elders, by contrast, were on display in traditional dress in the ethnological exhibits.*

development."[51] And this particular plan required education—education of nonwhite subject peoples in a manner deemed appropriate by the West.

The outdoor ethnological exhibits were accompanied by a United States Indian School exhibit, supervised by Samuel M. McCowan, Superintendent of the Chilocco Indian Training School in Oklahoma. With it, the U.S. Government attempted to illustrate the virtues of its policy of assimilating Native Americans through its practices of manual or vocational training of Native American children in the English language at the expense of native languages and traditional crafts. It promoted manual or vocational rather than academic training, because, according to McGee, "experience has shown that among all aboriginal peoples the hand leads the mind."[52] It championed assimilation by juxtaposing reservation education against a baseline symbolized by traditional Native American handicrafts. On one side of the school, "little Indian children were trained in kindergarten work; the older children showed their proficiency in the three R's . . . [and] exhibited skill in civilized handicrafts," while on the other side of an aisle "the elders carried on primitive industries."[53] Thus the visitor to the school was

confronted by the sharpest of contrasts, "between the old and the new, the barbaric and the enlightened," a contrast anchored in the presumption that Native American cultures could not have a modern existence.[54] Fair officials in fact often gave voice to the supposition that the Native American, or more accurately Native American culture, already had effectively died out.[55]

The Department of Anthropology exhibits were not limited to the outdoor ethnological displays. The department also offered archaeological displays; a section on anthropometry, where the various races of man were weighed, measured, and classified; and a Section of History. Headed by St. Louis journalist Florence Hayward, the Section of History attempted only to offer an overview of the history of the Louisiana Territory. It did so, however, within a philosophical context whereby it offered an important link in the perceived unilinear progress of mankind. "The exhibits of the Section of History at the Exposition," the *Official History of the Louisiana Purchase Exposition* explained, "were designed to illustrate important steps in the settlement and development of the Louisiana Territory, from the days of the first explorers through the time of the transfer to the United States, to the achievements of this centennial period."[56] It consisted most significantly of the Missouri Historical Society's exhibit of Indian artifacts, historical documents, original art, and artifacts associated with the Louisiana Territory and its acquisition by the United States. According to W. J. McGee, this exhibit illustrated "the most remarkable example of territorial conquest the world has thus far seen—the transformation of the Louisiana Purchase Territory from a wilderness, trod only by wandering tribes and wild beasts, into a family of rich commonwealths, within the space of a century."[57] Thus the Section of History provided the link between the aboriginal, prehistoric past of the Louisiana Territory, as exemplified by the remnants of the Native American tribes who had once dominated the region, and the modern American states that by 1904 had been carved out of that space. The inclusion of the Section of History in the Department of Anthropology lent scientific credence to the concept of historical progress.

Adjacent to the outdoor ethnological exhibits of the Department of Anthropology lay the

Philippine Exposition. *Edited by A. C. Newell, 1904. The cover of this promotional booklet on the Philippine Exposition juxtaposes the American-trained Filipino soldier against the "savage" Filipino tribesman.*

United States Philippine Exposition. The Philippine Exposition had been proposed by the American administration in the Philippine Islands and funded by Congress in response to domestic controversy over the advisability of the annexation of the islands. The Insular Government in the Philippines, led by William Howard Taft prior to his appointment as Secretary of War in January 1904, hoped to use the exhibit to make a case for a continued American presence in the Philippines and to stimulate American economic investment. Located opposite the outdoor anthropological exhibits across Arrowhead Lake, the Philippine Exposition occupied forty-seven acres of land. A virtual fair within a fair, it contained a series of exhibit buildings that functionally paralleled the great exhibit palaces of the Fair as a whole. It included a reproduction of the walled city of Manila, which housed an exhibit on the military history of the Philippine Islands from the time of the first western contact (Magellan), while separate buildings contained exhibits on commerce, government in the Philippines, education, agriculture, ethnology, fisheries, and forestry. On the periphery of the grounds were the encampments of the Philippine Scouts and Constabulary and several small "villages" that housed Filipino tribal peoples in circumstances that attempted to replicate their native environments.[58]

The Philippine Exposition, in its display of native Filipino peoples, presented virtually the same message as did the Department of Anthropology. The tribal peoples were arranged so as to demonstrate levels of progress or degrees of civilization, from the Negritos, "the lowest type humans in the Islands," to the Christianized Visayan, a "high type of native people."[59] The role of Americans in the Philippines, as portrayed by the Philippine exhibit, was at least in part that of beneficent educator. One measure of Filipino progress under American tutelage was that in the three years since the islands had been turned over to American civil administration, "the English learned by the Filipino people . . . is greater in amount than the Spanish they acquired in the four hundred years of Spanish rule."[60] To promote the concept of America as educator of its alien wards, a model school sat on the grounds of the Philippine Reservation and was attended by the children of all but the Negritos and was even staffed by a Visayan teacher.

The greatest recognition, however, was accorded the Philippine Guard and the Philippine Constabulary, regular army units of Philippine troops officered by Americans. A battalion of each, accompanied by a full orchestra, paraded and drilled daily on the grounds of the LPE, serving as "a fair representation of what can be done with the native when properly handled by competent American officers."[61]

The Philippine Exposition took the logic of the Department of Anthropology and the Section of History a step further.[62] With the acquisition of the Philippine Islands, the United States was beginning to export its civilization overseas and challenge that of Europe, not only militarily, but also culturally. The creators of the Philippine exhibit believed that America was extending its values, its culture, and above all its progress beyond the Louisiana Territory, beyond the North American continent, beyond the Western hemisphere, out into the world at large. The United States, they held, had joined the ranks of the colonial powers, not as a mere exploiter like the Spanish, but as a standard bearer of civilization and progress, as a model for the rest of the world to emulate. And, in fact, this accomplishment was a highly moral one in the eyes of the Fair planners, even if it had been accomplished through war. As Frederick Skiff argued, "ambition, competition, strife and friction are essential to progress. Without these nations would sleep and men would die."[63]

The themes of progress and expansion, so well exemplified by the anthropological and Philippine exhibits, permeated the entire Fair. British historian John M. McKenzie has written, "Imperialism was more than a set of economic, political, and military phenomena. It was a habit of mind. . . ."[64] As such it was a pervasive subtext of the entire Louisiana Purchase Exposition. This is no better illustrated than on the exterior grounds of the Fair itself.

Taking its cue from the Chicago World's Fair, the LPE's Commission of Architects, under the chairmanship of LPE Director of Works and St. Louis architect Isaac S. Taylor, deemed "that a classic and academic style be used in the main group of Buildings following closely the purer types" and be built to a "uniform module and scale."[65] Then, to ensure consistency throughout the grounds, the commission was empowered to rule on "all matters of design, sculpture and color treatment," even those "affecting the question of design in such works as State Buildings, private structures, etc."[66] This was accomplished within a space of 1,272 acres in the western half of St. Louis' Forest Park and on adjacent land to the west and north, a space much larger than that occupied by the Chicago Fair in Jackson Park. When completed, the so-called "Main Picture" at the LPE bore an uncanny resemblance to the "White City" of Chicago. For in St. Louis, as in Chicago, the space allotted for the fairgrounds was transformed from a wilderness to a utopia of massive neoclassical exhibit palaces decorated with allegorical sculpture, separated by broad avenues and symmetrical lagoons, and appointed by formal gardens and statuary. State and national pavilions, specialized buildings and exhibits, the entertainment strip (known as "the Pike" at the St. Louis Fair), and the Fair's infrastructure filled in the remaining portions of the grounds. The Main Picture was, of course, the focal point. The only significant difference, however, was that in Forest Park, as opposed to Jackson Park, the natural topographical feature of "Art Hill" suggested that the Main Picture be laid out in a fan shape rather than at right angles, with the main boulevards radiating outward from the locus of Festival Hall atop Art Hill, while water cascaded down the hill itself, feeding a network of lagoons. The eight most ornately decorated of the twelve great exhibit palaces fanned out at the base of Art Hill and the Cascades. Between them stood the Plazas of Orleans, St. Louis, and St. Anthony; George Kessler's beautifully designed Machinery Gardens and Sunken Gardens; and a network of lagoons that could be traversed by a series of bridges, each bearing the name of an explorer or statesman associated with the Louisiana Territory.

The sculpture of the fairgrounds was carefully conceived to impart the history of the Louisiana Territory as understood by the Fair planners. Chief of Sculpture Karl Bitter devised a scheme both allegorical and historical that in style and content was designed "to create a picture of surpassing beauty and to express in the most noble form which human mind and skill can devise the joy of the American people at the triumphant progress of the principles of liberty westward across the continent of America."[67] As described in *The American Monthly Review of Reviews*, the free-standing grounds statuary symbolized "the history of the Louisiana Territory, representing the four successive occupants of its

soil: First, the wild animals; second, the Indians; third, the discoverers and pioneers, the hunters, trappers, and explorers; and fourth, the advanced races, French, Spanish, and American, that have built up its present status of civilization."[68] Thus the concept of the unilinear progress of civilization as exemplified by American expansion into the Louisiana Territory was illustrated throughout the grounds of the Fair. On the neoclassical exhibit palaces, allegorical sculpture, purely classical in style and in subject, represented themes of progress in the mechanical, industrial, visual, liberal, and educational arts. On the U.S. Government Building, the one structure in the Main Picture that was not designed by a member of the LPE Company's Commission of Architects, the building sculpture was similar, "typifying the progress of the nation, and at the same time giving the ornamental ideas uniformity. . . ."[69]

The most remarkable feature of this architectural and artistic schema was that it was conservative. The adoption of this form in Chicago in 1893 as the one appropriate for American world's fairs has been commonly cited as the reason for an abiding conservatism and the predominance of the beaux-arts style in American architecture, especially public architecture, in the twentieth century.[70] Neoclassical architecture and sculpture—the idiom of the "American Renaissance"—was appropriate for American world's fairs at the turn of the century because it had the "perfect historical pedigree." It reinforced the concept of unilinear progress, traceable as it was from Greece and Rome, via the Enlightenment, the Age of Reason, and the French Revolution, to the American Revolution, and finally, at the Louisiana Purchase Exposition, to the Louisiana Purchase itself. At the LPE, the architecture and sculpture of the Main Picture was a metaphor for the values of American society. The great exhibit palaces, with their uniformity of style and dimension, allowed little room for deviation, though there was ample opportunity for creativity within well-circumscribed guidelines; the symbolic nature of the building decorations permitted a republican interpretation of their classical forms, thus differentiating them from parallels employed by the European monarchies, and the historical statuary on the grounds communicated the peculiar American combination of values of the pioneer spirit, republicanism (or democracy), progress, and Manifest Destiny.[71] In its use of the vast space at its disposal—more than that of the 1893 Chicago Fair, the 1898 Omaha Fair, and the 1900 Paris Fair combined—the LPE was a metaphor for the Louisiana Purchase Territory. To use the words of Frederick Jackson Turner: "perhaps most fundamental of all in its effect is the emphasis which the Louisiana Purchase gave to the conception of space in American ideals. The immensity of the area thus opened to exploitation had continually stirred the Americans' imagination, fired their energy and determination, strengthened their ability to handle vast designs, and made them measure their achievements by the scale of the prairies and the Rocky Mountains."[72]

The landscaping also complemented this vision. Just as Frederick Law Olmsted had laid out a utopian city in Chicago, George Kessler, best known for his design of the Kansas City parks and boulevard system, laid out the LPE grounds. The decision to take advantage of the natural topography of Forest Park and to forego the initially planned grid-like design in favor of a fan-shaped plan almost certainly owes its origins to Kessler.[73] In addition, he was most probably responsible for allowing the state pavilions to reside along gracefully curved roads among untouched trees in a region south of the more formal Main Picture. Such an arrangement, Kessler wrote, "gave to each [state] building a fine setting; the forest serving as a splendid background for the whole and the entire picture suggesting the possibility at least of a beautiful City in reality." In the Main Picture, by contrast, "Opportunity was . . . given for planting the large [silver] maples that lined the principal roads in the main part of the grounds and which, aside from furnishing welcome shade, served to frame the buildings and show them in pleasing relief against green foliage." With Kessler, therefore, the LPE fairgrounds became a microcosm of "The City Beautiful," at once formal, yet not rigidly so. It was urban, yet pastoral; functional, while offering opportunity for repose. It signaled the legitimacy of governmental involvement in the managing of urban space in the service of providing for the health and the moral well-being of the citizenry.[74] Thus the fairgrounds themselves were a manifestation of the principles being promoted in the exhibits of the Fair's Department of Social Economy.

Kessler's design of the World's Fair grounds, like the Fair's conservative and structured architecture and sculpture, helped to shape the visitor experience. Just as the tableaux display technique inside the exhibit halls was a vehicle for communicating with the Fair visitor, the landscape, architecture, and sculpture of the Fair communicated the ideals of professionalism, coherence, and structural, political, and social unity.

The music, pageantry, and the popular culture of the Fair served a similar purpose. World's fairs, from their very inception with London's Crystal Palace, had asserted that their raison d'être was, in part, to improve the tastes of the middle classes. Thus they had promoted art as well as industry. Indeed, the LPE promoted art in all its forms with a well-developed Department of Art and a separate Bureau of Music. Simultaneously, though, the sideshow, or Midway Plaisance, or Pike, persistently attracted the attention of fair visitors to a greater degree than did the fine arts. In Philadelphia in 1876, Fair planners had tried to ban sideshows from the grounds. Chicago Fair planners, learning from this experience, had permitted the establishment of the Midway Plaisance as an integral part of the event and had tried to control its content and thus legitimize it as educational. That Fair's exhibits official had even tried to present the Midway's troupes of exotic, non-Western entertainers and its sideshow "native villages" as "anthropological" exhibits. This enabled the Fair planners to capitalize on the drawing power of the sideshow without compromising the "educational" mission of the Fair.[75]

At the St. Louis World's Fair, this process continued. On the one hand, the Pike was established just north of the Fair's Main Picture, in close proximity to the main gate. From a financial point of view, "this enhanced its value. . . ."[76] But, on the other hand, efforts were made to minimize the tastelessness and sensationalism of the sideshow atmosphere so that the Pike would not undermine the Fair's overall educational mission. United States Commissioner of Indian Affairs William A. Jones, for example, adamantly opposed the display of American Indians in "Wild West shows" as had occurred at Chicago and tried vigorously to keep "tribal villages" off of the Pike, where violence and warfare might be promoted at the expense of proper anthropological display. Ultimately, the

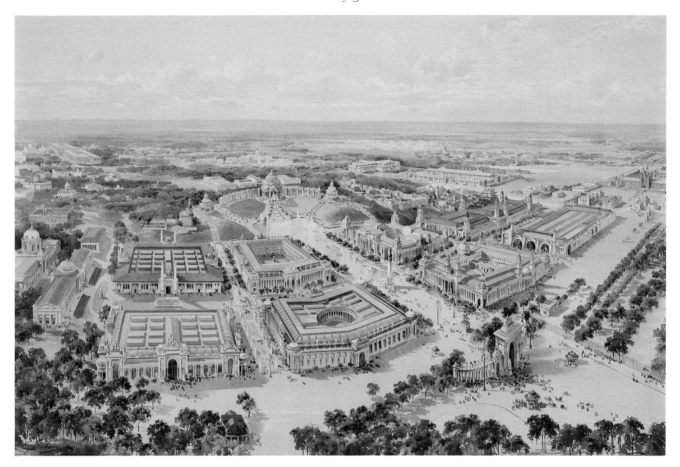

World's Fair, St. Louis, 1904. *Color lithograph, drawn by C. Graham, Gray Lithograph Co., 1903. This somewhat inaccurate rendering of the fairgrounds illustrates how the Commission of Architects took advantage of the natural topography of Forest Park in its development of the fan-shaped layout of the "Main Picture."*

demands of commerce won out, however, as a "Cliff Dwellers" concession displaying southwest Indians in the role of the prehistoric Anasazi and an Alaskan concession displaying Eskimos did eventually materialize. These, as well as Cummins' Indian Congress, were accepted only after their promoters agreed to limit the displays to crafts, customs, and ceremonies, and to refrain from staging shows that memorialized violence.[77] Thus, when compared to Chicago's Midway Plaisance, the LPE's Pike saw little in the way of the display of tribal peoples.

The demands of commerce did still permit the overall marketing of the exotic, however. A multitude of commercial "villages," both on the Pike and off of it, purported to re-create faraway lands and introduce visitors to alien cultures— both Western and non-Western. The Tyrolean Alps promoted an idyllic vision of Bavaria, while the Jerusalem Concession Company re-created the walled city of Jerusalem and populated it

with one thousand native residents. Even violence was memorialized, though not in a way that made use of American Indians. In an amphitheater somewhat removed from the Pike, the veterans of the South African battles of Colenso and Paardenberg re-created the Boer War, while the U.S. Naval Exhibition re-created the Spanish-American War's Battle of Santiago (Cuba) in miniature. The LPE Company, having tempered the "tastelessness" of the lucrative Pike concessions only somewhat, legitimized them by labeling them as "educational." Thomas R. MacMechen of the World's Fair Press Bureau asserted that the "Pike seeks to elevate the dominion of entertainment." In a lengthy article detailing the Pike concessions, he peppered his prose with terms like "educational," "scientific," "artistic," and "authentic," while colorfully promoting the excitement and thrills the visitor might find in the Fair's entertainment district.[78]

In the realm of the fine arts, the LPE made accommodations to public taste as well. While many forms of popular music (ragtime, banjo music, mandolin club music, etc.) were not admitted to the concert halls, parade grounds, or even the bandstands, the LPE Bureau of Music "early adopted the idea of having the musical features based upon the idea of suiting the tastes of the majority of the public, without being trivial."[79] Drawing on Chicago's experience, the Bureau of Music chose to promote concert bands, military marching bands, and organ music over symphony orchestras, choral music, and opera. The bureau spent almost 60 percent of its $450,000 budget to bring concert bands to St. Louis, while only 28 percent funded orchestral music.[80] In its forms, greater attention was paid to the popular march or waltz over more sophisticated though less popular ones.

Music, the colorful personalities of the Pike, and even the tribal peoples brought to the Fair by the Department of Anthropology and by the Philippine Exposition were all important to one other significant aspect of the LPE, that of pageantry. Parades of varying sizes and significance were daily occurrences at the LPE. Some consisted of little more than the dress parade of a state militia unit in front of a state pavilion, while others were full-blown spectacles, complete with speeches and processions including everyone from mounted U.S. Cavalry units to the tribal peoples of the Philippine Exposition. Many took place on "special days," days set aside for celebration by and in honor of specific national, local, ethnic, or sectarian groups. These special day celebrations and their accompanying pageantry were suggestive of late nineteenth-century civic holiday celebrations in the way that they used an assortment of activities to amuse and educate the Fair-visiting audience. The typical Progressive Era civic holiday celebrations that historian David Glassberg has described generally consisted of "a central . . . theme stated in an oration and reinforced visually through decorations, aurally through music, and behaviorally through giant processions of diverse local groups marching together to symbolize their dedication to common ideals."[81] World's Fair special day celebrations were identical in structure and thus played a role similar to that of civic celebrations at large by giving definition to the values of progress and expansion before a mass audience.

The Louisiana Purchase Exposition played to an audience of over twelve million paid visitors, half of whom were from the St. Louis region.[82] Although accounting for multiple visitation would reduce this total, the St. Louis World's Fair clearly attracted enormous interest. For the individual St. Louis–area resident, it offered an opportunity that would never be repeated. As Fair visitor Sam P. Hyde observed, "Coming generations may want to see a world's fair and be able to pay for it but they come high and there will certainly not be another in our day."[83] The Fair provided an occasion to see, hear, and experience things that an individual might never encounter again. Edward V. P. Schneiderhahn alluded to this when he made note of attending a concert of the Berlin Band at the Fair: "Our taste will be better than our opportunities hereafter."[84] The diaries, letters, and memoirs that follow in this volume all buttress this assessment. Written for the most personal of reasons and intended for the most private of audiences, narratives such as these constitute a rich resource for an investigation of the significance of the 1904 St. Louis World's Fair for the individual Fair visitor.

Several criteria have governed the selection of the four Fair visitors' accounts that are published in this volume. All were written by people from the St. Louis area who made multiple visits to the Fair, but who played no role other than that of visitor. All of the texts were written close to the event and were written only for the self, or at most, for family and intimates. All are literate and substantive in content, and lengthy enough to provide insight into the temperament and character of the authors. Finally, though this is fortuitous and due exclusively to the limited number of good examples from which to choose, the four texts were written by people from different stations in life and each took a different form. Two of the writers lived in St. Louis, one in Belleville, Illinois, and one in Cadet, Missouri. Three of them were men, one a woman. All were white. One was an attorney, one a bookkeeper, one a carpenter, and one the wife of a farmer. The texts themselves took the varied forms of diaries, letters, essays, and illustrated photo-memoir.

The Crowd on Opening Day. *Photograph, April 30, 1904. The 1904 World's Fair played to an audience of over twelve million paid visitors.*

Deliberately excluded are journalistic accounts, contemporary histories, and subsequent recollections. Contemporary newspaper and journalistic accounts, while written close to the event, were too often influenced by hidden agendas and motives. Local reporting, for example, was inevitably shaped in part by the stake that the local press had in the St. Louis community, causing reporting and promotion to often become one and the same. In addition, contemporary press accounts were colored by the journalists' need to attract and hold large audiences. Thus their accounts often tended toward the sensational and even the voyeuristic. Finally, much of the press reporting on the Fair, particularly in popular magazines, appeared in large measure due to the aggressive and tireless efforts of the LPE Company's Bureau of Press and Publicity to publicize the Fair and its goals and purposes as widely as possible. Consequently, much of the popular reporting on the Fair tells more about the agendas of the Fair planners than about the impact of the Fair on the individual visitor. The contemporary histories and publications such as the *World's Fair Bulletin* and the *Official Guide*, as the official organs of the Fair company, are even more suspect.[85]

Recollections of the St. Louis World's Fair that were recorded subsequently, including oral histories, are likewise excluded, though for different reasons. Intervening years taint memory, causing the "recollection" to be more useful as an indicator of how community memory of the Fair has evolved than as a record of the Fair visitor's experience. Memory is tied to structures of power—in this case the LPE Company itself and the "official" record it left. It is also "heavily influenced by positions and interpretations stated in public."[86] Finally, memory is continually undergoing a process of construction and reconstruction. Once it is removed temporally from its origin, it loses much of its validity.

This leaves for analysis only the unpublished accounts of individual Fair visitors who wrote close to the event and only for themselves, their families, or their friends. Even these accounts have their limitations. If indeed memory is constructed rather than replicated, a narrative written close to an event and never intended to be read by another is still already edited, already a construct. The limitations of one's own language skill and the limitations of time, plus the fact that memory begins to fade within hours, keep even private diaries from being completely accurate. Furthermore, the motivation to write or otherwise record an experience is variable. Few Fair visitors wrote descriptions of their visits. Of those, few communicate more than litanies of "what I saw today." And of those that do offer significant insight into the writer's experience, few have survived. Worse, those that have are idiosyncratic. Thus there are four narratives presented here, insufficient in and of themselves to offer an adequate sample from which methodologically sound generalizations can be made.

The first narrative, actually consisting of two texts, was composed by St. Louis attorney Edward V. P. Schneiderhahn. Schneiderhahn was the son of a German-American sculptor of religious art, Maximilian Schneiderhahn. One of at least eleven children, Schneiderhahn was raised in a deeply Catholic household: one of his brothers and three sisters ultimately took religious vows. Throughout his own life, Schneiderhahn remained a deeply religious Catholic, never missing confession or mass and never failing to record same in his daily diaries. He was well educated in St. Louis' parochial schools, graduated from St. Louis University in 1894, and subsequently took his law degree at Washington University, also in St. Louis. As of 1904, Schneiderhahn was about thirty years of age, as yet unmarried, and still lived at home with his father, stepmother, and younger siblings. Professionally, he was engaged in the private practice of law, sharing office space with an older practitioner, and had a promising career ahead of him. His extensive civic activities included his membership in the German-American Catholic Central Union, a national federation of German-Catholic associations that was just embarking on a period of conservative social activism.[87] Schneiderhahn's own activism included supporting orphanages and lobbying state government against the liberalizing of divorce laws. Later in life, Schneiderhahn went on to serve as a St. Louis alderman and as one of the first members of the St. Louis City Plan Commission. He became legal advisor to John Cardinal Glennon and his successor, the then-Archbishop Joseph E. Ritter, service for which Pope Pius XII made him a Knight of St. Gregory in 1943. His abiding conservatism surfaced when he led the campaign in St. Louis for movie censorship in the 1910s. He died in St. Louis in 1948.[88]

Schneiderhahn first took up his pen in 1890 at the age of fifteen and, despite an increasingly busy career, sustained his diary until 1913, filling seven volumes. He wrote, he claimed, because "it is a good training, if for nothing else than to develop character and the habit of observation."[89] Not surprisingly, his daily entries for 1904 are peppered with references to his multiple visits to the World's Fair. After the close of the Fair, he then wrote a twenty-six page World's Fair memoir. Because Schneiderhahn wrote as an exercise in self-discipline rather than to create a record of his personal life, his diaries tell little about him biographically. He virtually never named names, mentioning friends by initial only, and he never discussed business or his clients except in the abstract. His writing was introspective, the record of a man seeking moral self-improvement. On occasion, though, he could be a superb descriptive writer, and when something offended his sensibilities, he could craft some very pointed prose. The 1904 World's Fair provided him with ample opportunity to provide posterity with both.

The second text was written by Edmund Philibert. Like Schneiderhahn, Philibert was also a St. Louisan, young, Catholic, and unmarried. Although his lineage can be traced back to Jean Baptiste Ortes, one of St. Louis' earliest settlers and land owners, Philibert was not from a family of financial means. The son of a tinsmith, Henry Ortes Philibert, and his wife, Sarah Jane Fitzwilliam, Edmund was himself a carpenter. Approximately thirty years of age in 1904, he lived with his mother and at least one sister, Angela, at 4206A Lexington in north St. Louis. Never marrying, Philibert continued to reside with his unmarried sister in either St. Louis or St. Louis County at least until 1917, when he disappears from the St. Louis directories. Throughout his adult life, he worked in carpentry or related fields.[90]

Philibert, unlike Schneiderhahn, was not a writer. His penmanship is that of a schoolboy, and his writing is characterized by misspellings (corrected in the version printed in this volume), idiosyncratic punctuation, and run-on sentences, all suggestive of a limited formal education. A skilled tradesman, and one whose woodwork was reportedly extraordinary, he was also an adept observer.[91] During 1904, he made twenty-eight visits to the 1904 St. Louis World's Fair and dutifully recorded each one of them, often in exceptional detail. Appended to this record is an accounting of every penny he spent.

The third text consists of a handful of letters written by Florence McCallion, Edmund Philibert's sister, to her husband, Frank, in Cadet, Missouri. Little is known of her, as only a handful of her letters have survived. Close in age to Edmund, she went to work as a clerk with the *St. Louis Republic* in 1900, where her sister Angie was already employed. In that same year, Florence's correspondence with Frank J. McCallion, a farmer who lived in Cadet and an old Philibert family friend, began. By 1903, Florence had left her job and married Frank. During the summer and fall of 1904, she spent an extended period in St. Louis with her family, recovering from an unnamed "malady" and attending the World's Fair at every opportunity, usually in the company of her brother Edmund or other family members.[92]

For much of her St. Louis stay, Florence's husband remained in Cadet attending to his farm. A series of very affectionate letters addressed to him have survived and include descriptions of Florence's Fair visits. Among them is one letter describing a visit made in the company of her brother Edmund, a letter that can be contrasted with Edmund's own account of that same day. Also included is a letter describing a visit to the grounds after the Fair's close. Both Florence's penmanship and grammar reveal her to have been rather better educated than her brother, a situation not uncommon in tradesmen's households, where a son might leave school early to enter an apprenticeship or otherwise seek employment.

The fourth and final text was written by Sam P. Hyde of Belleville, Illinois. Written in 1909—five years after the Fair—this volume is much more than a simple text. Penned in calligraphy, it is beautifully illustrated by Hyde's original sketches and contemporary snapshots. Although it was not composed as close to the event as were the other narratives included in this volume, Hyde's "Recollections of the Fair," as an illustrated photo memoir, is unique in its manner of presentation and does offer contemporary visuals.

Born in the rural midwest around 1850, Samuel P. Hyde resided in outstate Missouri for most of his life until he and his wife, Ida, and their family moved to Belleville in the mid-1890s. Throughout his adult life, Hyde worked as a bookkeeper, first in Missouri, and then for twenty-two years in Belleville for Hucks Hardware Store, before

retiring in 1916. A Protestant, he was an elder in the First Presbyterian Church in Belleville and treasurer of the Laymen's Missionary Society. Though a bookkeeper by trade, he was an artist by inclination and a collector of art objects, war relics, and coins.[93]

Hyde initially began to prepare his recollections of the Fair "simply [for] the preservation of some views taken by myself and friends." But, he continued, "my effort to present them in attractive form has led me into reminiscences of some personal experiences."[94] That "attractive form" consists of calligraphy and original two-color illustrations and sketches, which annotate his photographs or stand in lieu of them where his reminiscences took him into areas for which he lacked photographic documentation. Though colorfully written, his prose is replete with misspellings and unconventional punctuation, reflecting his bookkeeper's training and artistic inclination. The narrative's organization, topical rather than chronological, is characteristic of after-the-fact memoirs. This, combined with the five-year delay between the Fair and the assembly of the memoir, makes Hyde's document more of a reconstruction than the other narratives included in this volume.

Since world's fairs played to such enormous audiences, any study that departs from Robert Rydell's investigation of the ideologies and agendas promoted by the turn-of-the-century fair planners inevitably leads to some speculation as to how fair visitors reacted to the lessons set forth at each fair. It is that question that has, at least in part, stimulated this effort to explore the St. Louis World's Fair visitors' diaries, letters, and memoirs. Such sources, due to their private nature and temporal proximity to the event, are likely to be the most honest renderings of the Fair-visiting experience, and hence potentially the most valuable resource for an investigation into how individual Fair visitors responded to the Fair planners' ideologies of progress and expansion. It is with these sources that one might attempt to answer a number of questions that are framed by today's understanding of the Fair. How did the Fair visitors learn the lessons of the Fair? How did they respond to the exhibition of tribal peoples from all over the world? What did they think about the Philippine exhibits and about their promotion of American imperialism? Were they impressed by the concepts of ethnic and racial hierarchy that the Fair planners so shamelessly promoted? Did they see how the ideologies of progress and expansion permeated all aspects of the Fair's educational message?

Unfortunately, researchers who have dug into this to date have found little that is conclusive. One writer who investigated just this question in his Reed College senior thesis fell into the trap of selectively quoting the few isolated references that these very same Fair visitors made, thus enabling him to conclude only that there is insufficient evidence to draw definitive conclusions.[95] He did observe, however, that there was ample evidence that the Fair visitors found the techniques of display effective. Certainly a reading of Schneiderhahn's diary and memoir and Philibert's diary, in particular, bears out this conclusion. Both men made multiple comments from which one can infer that they observed and learned from both the relational nature of the displays and from the exhibit of processes. When it came to evaluating the visitor response to concepts of race theory and the justifications for American expansion that underlay many of the Fair's exhibits, however, this young scholar was able to say very little. He

Igorot Child, Philippine Exposition. *Photograph, Mrs. W. G. Staley Album, 1904. Observation was often akin to voyeurism as Fair visitors gaped at tribal peoples on display in the ethnological exhibits and in the Philippine Exposition.*

ultimately turned to contemporary press accounts as a barometer of public opinion and concluded that though there was little thoughtful commentary, there was some evidence of voyeurism.

The presentation of people as objects was certainly an invitation to voyeurism, despite the efforts of the St. Louis Fair planners to place such displays within a carefully constructed interpretive context. Local publicity accorded controversies over matters such as the relative nakedness of many of the Filipino tribesmen and the procurement of dogs for the Igorots' regular dog feasts fed this voyeurism. Not surprisingly, evidence of it surfaces in the narratives that follow. In a tone that communicated a sense of having done something slightly naughty, Florence McCallion related to her husband, for example: "What do you think, we went to see the Igorots. They look like bronze statues."[96] Sam Hyde made a similar passing reference when he explained that although the Igorots held no interest for him, "they seemed to have a tremendous attraction for the ladies."[97] As a group, these Fair visitors generally did not question the legitimacy of the ethnological exhibits or speculate about what the display represented. McCallion's description of the Igorots as "bronze statues" and Edmund Philibert's comment that the Patagonians "were very lazy looking" suggest a readiness to accept the exhibits at face value and a tendency to see the tribal peoples more as objects than as fully human.[98]

Schneiderhahn, whose diary and memoir contain no references to the ethnological exhibits, focused his attention on the Philippine Constabulary and the Philippine Scouts—native Filipino military units under American command. Both units performed regular parade drills at the Fair, and each sported its own band. A popular feature, the Filipino bands also attracted the interest of Sam Hyde and Edmund Philibert, both of whom made special trips to hear one or the other of the bands or watch their parade drills. Only Schneiderhahn looked beyond displays and parade drills to draw the conclusion desired by the planners of the Philippine Exposition, that it "proved the high civilization already attained."[99] This basically constitutes the extent of this group of Fair visitors' commentaries on the ethnological exhibits.

With such limited material, it is impossible to conclude how the ethnological exhibits as a whole or the Philippine exhibits in particular shaped the opinions of the Fair visitors. One is either forced to conclude, as did the Reed College senior thesis writer, that there is insufficient material to draw a conclusion, or one must refocus the inquiry. This refocus requires pulling back from a search for descriptions of the ethnological exhibits or the Philippine Exposition to an analysis of the diaries, letters, and memoirs from the Fair as a whole. It also necessitates an investigation into the absence of commentary.

That there are precious few references to the ethnological exhibits is in and of itself significant, especially when one also notes a similar absence of overt commentary on the phenomenon of imperialism or Western expansion, race theory, or Social Darwinism. The only commentary on the significance of the Philippine Exposition as a whole was Schneiderhahn's, alluded to above. Similarly, the only reference to American territorial expansion was in a description of the Louisiana Purchase that appeared in Schneiderhahn's recapitulation of "the occasion to which indirectly [the Fair] owed its birth," in which he observed that "the whole wilderness has been changed."[100] This relative absence of commentary emerges as significant when one considers that individuals comment on that which they find remarkable—either in a positive or negative sense. Thus Schneiderhahn, for example, made several references to how much he disliked the "naked statuary" at the Fair, and the immodest gowns shown in some of the costume exhibits, while the carpenter Edmund Philibert described woodwork and other kinds of craftsmanship in great detail. The apparently remarkable absence of commentary on the race theories that underlay many aspects of the Fair suggests that the Fair visitors did not find them extraordinary. Or, perhaps, they simply just did not think in such terms. Neither anthropological concepts of a hierarchy of race nor the presentation of American territorial expansion as a progressive and moral imperative challenged the Fair visitors' notions of how the world was or should be. These issues attract attention today because late twentieth-century American society has come to value diversity as well as assimilation, has learned that technology can be employed for less than moral ends, and generally sees civilization and progress as ambiguous concepts.

The absence of commentary on such issues in these 1904 narratives tells us that these Fair visitors, at least, saw little or nothing in the educational message of the Fair planners that upset their understanding of the world. These Fair visitors were not drawn to the ethnological exhibits any more than they were to other special features of the Fair. They took in the ethnological exhibits in due course and commented upon them accordingly.

This then leads us to refocus the inquiry into an examination of how the Fair visitors looked at the Fair as a whole. These four writers, despite their varying backgrounds and methods of writing and despite the fact that their texts offer an insufficient sample from which to make generalizations, do permit a few general conclusions about how individual Fair visitors experienced the 1904 St. Louis World's Fair. Looking at the narratives as a whole, there is ample evidence to be extracted indicating that they understood civilization in terms similar to those the Fair planners articulated. There is a subtext to these narratives that reveals a basic faith in the concept of progress and in its inherent morality.

This subtext surfaces in a variety of ways. It is, not surprisingly, most obvious in Edward Schneiderhahn's narratives. In terms of his education and his conservative, social-reformist orientation, he of all the writers in this publication shared the greatest common ground with those who articulated the ideologies of the turn-of-the-century fairs. The subsequent development of his career strengthens this conclusion. Schneiderhahn's interest in civic reform, for example, is revealed in his description of one of the German rooms in the Palace of Varied Industries. Noting how the ballot box stood in the center of the German Council Chamber, he asked, "Would it not aid in repressing corruption in part at least to have a ballot box in our municipal council chambers?"[101]

In addition, in Schneiderhahn's case, but also with the more plebian Edmund Philibert, there are multiple examples of a fascination with what technology had to offer, even though neither was technically trained. Both men were engaged by the Westinghouse steam turbines for example. Schneiderhahn wrote that after studying the Westinghouse exhibit, he now understood "the reason of its greater efficiency and enormous speed when compared with other steam engines. . . . The steam turbine engine will work a revolution in steam engines."[102] Philibert, a superb observer despite his apparent lack of formal education, offered a detailed description of the Westinghouse steam turbine. "With the interior exposed," he wrote, "it looked like a big axle with any amount of small steel projections on it, there were corresponding projections on the inside of the covering, and it seemed as though there would be less than one half inch space between the two sets of teeth when closed, one set stationery, the other revolving at a terrific speed."[103] On other occasions, Philibert offered similar detail about technical matters, whether describing the functioning of a bolometer or a radiophone.[104]

Fair visitors were also captivated by the militia displays and parades, and cited the regimentation of these presentations as particularly attractive. Schneiderhahn admired the parade of St. Louis Car Company employees in uniform on Transportation Day.[105] Philibert commented similarly when he described the drill of the Philippine Scouts. "It was a very nice sight," he wrote. "They paraded and went through the manual of arms and then had a Calisthenic drill which looked very nice as their hands encased in white gloves all moved together keeping time to the music of the band."[106] Sam Hyde offered a more general comment that associated progress with military prowess: "Every civilized nation had its sailors, its soldiers and its military band."[107]

The interest that sophisticated technology and military-style regimentation held for these Fair visitors, none of whom were militiamen or technicians, must be understood in context. Formal parades and drills were a common form of civic display at the turn of the century, one which reinforced American civic values of progress, republicanism, strength, and order.[108] The formal marching of uniformed industrial laborers coming on the heels of a period of violent labor unrest, both in St. Louis and across the nation, was a symbol of the reordering of society, while daily militia parades were emblematic of republicanism and national strength, both physical and moral. The performances of the Philippine Scouts and Constabulary were evidence of the progressive virtues of American expansion. From the Fair visitors' open admiration of these symbols, one can infer a general acceptance of that for which they stood. Likewise, the fascination with steam turbines and other technical wonders just as the wide scale electrical lighting of private homes was becoming a real possibility suggests that the Fair

St. Louis Car Company's "Co. H." *Halftone, St. Louis Car Co. at the Universal Exposition, St. Louis, U.S.A., 1904. Uniformed St. Louis Car Company employees marched in formation at the Transportation Day Parade. This group, "composed of stalwart young mechanics from the various departments," was organized like a military company just for this occasion.*

visitors were genuinely entranced with the promise technology and science held for their daily lives.

There is also a subtext to these narratives that suggests that their authors understood the concepts of civilization and the hierarchy of the races of man in much the same way as did the Fair planners. This can be illustrated by an examination not just of their passing comments on the ethnological exhibits, but also of their assessments of the different nationalities present at the Fair as a whole. As Sam Hyde wrote, it seemed "the gods took their places to look down . . . on the passing throng from every nation under heaven. Savage and civilized, Polock, Siberian, Scandinavian and Hottentot."[109] This articulation of the dichotomy between "savage and civilized" surfaces throughout these World's Fair narratives in a variety of ways. For example, it is evident in a tendency to ascribe peculiar characteristics to people of different nationalities, in the casual use of derogatory ethnic epithets, and in the Fair visitors' puzzlement over how to categorize the Japanese.

All of these Fair visitors gave expression to ethnic stereotypes to one degree or another. Schneiderhahn repeatedly ascribed "national characteristics" to different peoples and used them to explain historical developments. Most commonly, his comments were applied to European ethnic groups. The Germans he described as "habituated to thoroughness" and as "stolid, thrifty and conservative."[110] The French he found prone to the licentious. Recounting the Pike parade on opening day he observed, "The women advertising 'Paris' were of course the most shameless."[111] The French, in his mind, were also "quick and prone to change," which, he asserted, explained why there was "so much elation" that the French Third Republic "has lasted from '70 to this day."[112] Regarding Americans, Schneiderhahn applauded "Yankee ingenuity," which he contended was, as usual, "shown in all those matters which involve application of devices and methods to solve commercial difficulties."[113]

Although Schneiderhahn seldom had similar observations to make about other non-European nationalities, he did frequently comment on their exhibits. Persian rugs, "despite the fact that their prices were forbidding, . . . all looked shabby," he wrote.[114] The Chinese exhibit "impressed . . . as topsy-turvydom," consisting primarily of "space occupiers that centre the thought mainly on the time that it took to make these things."[115] Yet, in observing the handwork of Europeans, Schneiderhahn found much to admire. The Austrian glassware exhibit, for example, he characterized as being of "indescribable richness and daintiness."[116] In general Schneiderhahn approved of Western handicrafts as evidence of industriousness and creativity, but seemed to see only confirmation of backwardness in non-Western handwork, suggesting a predisposition toward an admiration of what the West had to offer and a presumption that the East had little of interest.

Sam Hyde betrayed similar prejudices. His prejudices, however, were manifested in a casual use of derogatory ethnic language. While such language was generally the accepted language of the time, his use of it was consistently applied only to nonwhite and non-European peoples. In addition, he applied it even when he found much to admire in a non-Western society. For example, despite the fact that he was quite taken by many aspects of the Japanese exhibits, Hyde persisted in using the term "Jap." Furthermore, he described the Japanese as "a nation of homely men," although he found the Japanese women attractive.[117]

Philibert described different ethnic groups and nationalities in a very matter-of-fact manner, generally without judgment, except when he labeled the Patagonians "lazy looking." He seems to have enjoyed African American, Arab, and Asian entertainers on the Pike as much as he enjoyed white entertainers. On one occasion he confessed to being impressed by several Chinese children who sang in English as well as Chinese: "one sang Yankee Doodle and told his age, he was right cute looking."[118] He was also as complimentary of the artifacts produced by Asian civilizations as he was of those created by Europeans, and seemed to have a genuine interest in them. Like Hyde, though, Philibert made general use of ethnic slang that would not be acceptable today. He possessed the interest of an artisan in the exhibits and artifacts he viewed, and was inclined to admire skill wherever it appeared. However, in his observation of peoples on display, he seems to have been a noncritical observer who accepted both exhibits and entertainments as they were presented, thus suggesting that the presentation of non-Western societies at the Fair did not challenge his world view.

Ethnic stereotyping and the general use of pejorative ethnic slang in these World's Fair narratives was generally reflexive and thoughtless; it was the accepted language of the time. Schneiderhahn, Hyde, and Philibert were simply products of a society that saw racial and ethnic issues in certain terms, and like others around them, they used those categories and terms. When it came to describing the Japanese, however, a different pattern emerges.

As a non-Western civilization that had embraced western technology and was using that technology to defeat the Russians militarily just as the Fair was taking place, the Japanese did not fit the hierarchy of the races of man that the Fair planners promoted. The Japanese exhibits, which demonstrated Japan's facility with Western technology while showcasing traditional Japanese art forms, placed this unexplained and remarkable anomaly in full view. Japanese participation at the 1904 World's Fair attracted the attention of the Fair planners, the publicists and press, and the Fair visitors alike.

This phenomenon was the subject of a recent seminar paper that focuses on the Japanese Osaka Fair of 1903 and Japanese participation at the St. Louis Fair in 1904.[119] Examining the writings of Fair planners, publicists, and journalists, the author observed the difficulties that the American Progressive elite faced in fitting the Japanese into their schema. Certainly, more than one publicist commented on this matter, noting, for example, that Japanese military success against Russia had elevated Japan in Western eyes.[120] The anthropologists at the Fair found their world view even more confounded by the intellectual problem presented by the seemingly Caucasoid Ainu of Japan who were on display in the ethnological exhibits. Anthropologist Frederick Starr, analyzing the Ainu, observed, "here we find a white race that has . . . proved inferior in life's battle to the more active, energetic, progressive, yellow people, with which it has come in contact." This was a great puzzle for him. "Who are the Ainu? Where did they come from? What is their past?" he asked.[121]

Among the visitors whose narratives follow, the Japanese and their exhibits attracted more commentary than did the exhibits and peoples of any other nation represented at the Fair. All offered observations on some aspect of the Japanese presence at the Fair. Florence McCallion, for example, was charmed by the Japanese culture. The novelty of taking "green Japan tea made by the Japanese, and served by Japanese girls in native costume" at the Japanese Garden comes through in her description of that experience. She also, apparently, did not really know what to make of the Japanese as an ethnic group, given her evident surprise that "some of the girls were as white as we are."[122] Her brother Edmund Philibert, who was with her at the Japanese Pavilion, accepted the Japanese at face value. He was, however, impressed by the Japanese, as he commented positively on their exhibits across the board, equally enjoying the traditional Japanese arts as represented in the Japanese Garden or the Varied Industries Building and the technical as exemplified by the Japanese transportation models in the Transportation Building.[123]

Japanese Exhibit, Palace of Transportation. *Photograph, 1904. Including a relief map of Japan on the floor, pictorial representations on the walls, and Japanese-style draperies and decorations, this exhibit of shipping and rail transportation in Japan embodied the union of technology and traditional art forms characteristic of the Japanese participation at the 1904 World's Fair.*

Schneiderhahn reacted much like Philibert, applauding both the traditional Japanese arts and Japan's increasing use of Western technology. But, given that Schneiderhahn, unlike Philibert, generally exhibited a dislike of traditional Eastern art forms, this approval of Japanese traditional arts constituted a departure from the norm for him. It seems that Schneiderhahn may have been more open to Japanese art forms than he was to other non-Western arts primarily due to Japan's increasing adoption of not only Western technology, but also Western practices and procedures. In viewing the same transportation exhibit that Philibert had observed, Schneiderhahn commented: "It is curious to note how the Japanese have copied the art of illustrating dry commercial statistics by pictorial representations. The Japanese section of the Transportation Building is full of such illustrations. They certainly intend to apply everything they see that they feel themselves capable of applying. And if they are not yet able to apply, they will learn until they can apply whatever they see. That is the impression the Japanese make."[124] Clearly, Schneiderhahn approvingly saw the Japanese as imitative of Western technology and methods. Imitativeness, combined with the virtues of patience and determination, made the Japanese, in his view "a rapidly progressing people."[125] This perspective suggests an acceptance on Schneiderhahn's part of the concept promoted at the World's Fair that the path of progress for non-Western societies required emulation of the accomplishments of the West.[126]

Sam P. Hyde, whose memoir contains lengthy passages describing various aspects of the Japanese exhibits and Japanese people, alone of these four Fair visitors suggested that the Japanese were the equal of the West, despite their distinctive history. "Their displays," he wrote, "were of especial interest from the fact that unlike the other civilized nations, their civilization was about on a par with our own though it had developed on different lines and entirely independent of us."[127] This view, however, ran contrary to the unilinear notions of progress that informed the Fair planners' classification system and the anthropologists' portrayal of non-Western people. Victorious in war against a Western power—Russia—Japan had joined the ranks of modern nations on its own terms. This accomplishment was a troublesome riddle, for

Japanese achievements in technical and military areas raised the possibility that there might be other "paths of progress" or other definitions of "civilization" that the Fair planners and the anthropologists had not considered.

The conclusion to be drawn from this exercise is that these Fair visitors, whose diaries, letters, and memoirs we have, generally understood the world as did the Fair planners. Their absence of commentary on what they see as unremarkable—the status of subject peoples in the Philippines, the hierarchical notion of the races of man—combined with their commentary on the remarkable—the dilemma of how to understand the Japanese, a dilemma shared by the Fair planners and publicists—suggests a shared world view. This group of St. Louis–area white lower-middle-class and middle-class Fair visitors did not fundamentally disagree with or question the world view of the Fair planners. Only when they were provoked into assimilating something that did not fit, as with the Japanese, is there wide discrepancy in the views they articulated.

This does not mean that Fair visitors were mindless in their acceptance of what they saw. The variable interpretations accorded the Japanese is a case in point. There are others as well; each offered occasional critical commentary, even if only to suggest that a particular item or feature of the Fair failed to impress. In some cases critical commentary was linked to personal belief or a perceived moral failure. Such criticism surfaced in Schneiderhahn's diary when he was offended by the "unworthy" content of modern art as represented by the impressionistic and realistic schools. "The highest mission of art is to elevate," he countered. "Any less conception does not rise to the truth."[128] In other cases, Schneiderhahn was critical because he saw no benefit in pursuing a given course. Although, for example, "a German high-speed locomotive was very interesting," Schneiderhahn doubted "whether such high speed, 80 miles per hour, will have much commercial utility."[129]

Intangible quality of life issues also stimulated criticism. Schneiderhahn disliked automobiles, for example. "A whole city of these puffing, mad, and stinking ugly things would not look very well in your judgment," he wrote.[130] Both Schneiderhahn and Hyde were skeptical of the wisdom of altering Forest Park so that the World's Fair could be staged. "It was a pity . . . to see giant monarchs of the forest fall before the woodman's ax to make room for the exhibit palaces," Schneiderhahn wrote. "Standing on one of the hills, in the preexposition period, one could see a whole plain that had been swept bare of patriarchs of the forest such as few cities could boast to possess."[131] Hyde also felt that it was "a sad sight to see the beauties of nature marred, and forest trees that had been fifty years in growing, cut down in an hour." Writing well after the Fair closed, he had had opportunity to observe the price of the World's Fair. He continued: "The very idea of restoring the park was a farce on its face though stipulated in a heavy bond, restored but how?"[132] Eventually Forest Park was returned to the City of St. Louis. Rather than being restored, it was transformed—from a virgin forest into a sculpted urban park of controlled spaces. This was one form of progress that Hyde and Schneiderhahn, at least, had doubts about. It seems that these two men might have liked to keep the wilderness.

Lost in the exploration of questions such as these, however, is the fact that the experience of visiting a world's fair was more than an excursion into the realm of turn-of-the-century concepts of progress and expansion. "A World's fair is its own excuse," wrote George R. Leighton in *Harper's Magazine*. "It is a brief and transitory paradise, born to delight mankind and die." It is "a combination of beauty and bombast, and is the expression of a complex idea involving trade, the arts, national, local, and individual prestige, uplift, and the universal hankering for a holiday." Writing in 1960, Leighton was exploring the history of American world's fairs just as New York was preparing to open its own World's Fair of that year.[133] Although the world's fair phenomenon evolved within a demonstrable historical context and clearly was a vehicle for the communication of certain ideologies to Fair visitors, from the visitors' point of view, Leighton's assessment of the importance of world's fairs is probably closer to reality than is Rydell's, which serves the historian's perspective.

The bulk of the Fair visitors' narratives that follow tell of their encounter with "a brief and transitory paradise." They validate the assertion that the Louisiana Purchase Exposition was part spectacle—a massive virtual reality. They demonstrate the significance of the Fair in their lives and illustrate how the Fair engendered its own immediate nostalgia. They also reintroduce the contemporary reader to the multidimensional and multisensory nature of the Fair-visiting experience.

Popular memory of the Fair in St. Louis is to a large extent based on the photographic images left by the official Fair photographers. Formalistic, structured, and controlled, they are captioned by brief interpretive texts written from the perspective of the Fair planners. Thus the collective memory is formed largely by a single sense—the visual—and then is limited to the 8 x 10 photo or at best the projected image. The Fair visitors' experiences, by contrast, were multidimensional and multisensory.

The physical setting of the Fair prompted multiple attempts at commentary. "The picture is grand. The scale immense. The distances enormous," wrote Edward V. P. Schneiderhahn on opening day, revealing how the first feature of the Fair to strike a visitor was its enormity.[134] The Fair was truly massive in scope. Occupying 1,272 acres, it required rail travel for Fair visitors to get around, and multiple visits if one was to see more than a glimpse of what the Fair had to offer. The Main Picture alone was of an unsurpassed magnitude. Filling a good third of the fairgrounds, it offered one spectacular vista after another as the visitor moved from one vantage point to the next. And indeed, simply enjoying the environment was a favorite pastime at the Fair. Describing the buildings at night, Sam P. Hyde recalled how he spent "many an hour . . . watching these lights as one who hates to be awakened from a pleasant dream."[135] Edmund Philibert developed a pattern of Fair-visiting whereby he regularly enjoyed his bag lunch in front of fairgrounds railway station No. 2, from which he had an unobstructed view toward the west wing of the Terrace of States. He also regularly stopped off to view the Cascades when they were in operation, and after the exhibit palaces closed, he almost invariably took a turn up and down the Pike.[136]

The distances and scope of the Fair meant that it could not possibly be seen in a single visit. Edmund Philibert, with his careful record of his twenty-eight visits, gives us a sense of the physical aspect of visiting the Fair, as each daily account provides not only a summary of what he saw and which buildings he visited, but also a description of the route he took. It was not uncommon for this man of modest means to take several rides on the Intramural, the fairgrounds railway, to get

The Zenith of Beauty. *Stereograph, Keystone View Company, 1904. The view from Art Hill across the Cascades was one of many at the World's Fair that Fair visitors experienced multidimensionally.*

around—at a cost of ten cents per ride. His description of his July 30th visit to the Fair gives a sense of the ground he typically covered:

> . . . we went to the Sunken Garden and rested, then started for the intramural, . . . we boarded a car at station No. 15 and rode to No. 3 . . . [we] walked to the Ferris Wheel and back, and rode to Station No. 12 where we climbed the hill to the Colonnade of States. Viewed the illumination of the Cascades and grand basin and descended steps on west side crossed Jefferson and DeSoto bridges and walked along Plaza St. Louis to the Pike. After walking up and down a little we took the intramural at Station No. 1 and rode to No. 14 where we left the grounds and took a Taylor ave. car for home. . . . [137]

As might be surmised from Philibert's account, distance and scope not only overwhelmed one visually, but exacted a physical toll from the Fair visitor as well. Florence McCallion, in questionable health, explained in her letters home to her husband that she, too, rode the Intramural at the Fair. "If the buildings are very far apart," she complained, "you know it is too much of a walk for me."[138] Distance and scope could also be

psychologically taxing. As the end of the Fair approached, Schneiderhahn wrote: "It is unthinkable what may all be seen. The mind reels at the mass of various and wonderful exhibits." On the next evening, after visiting the Fair again, he wrote of "a sort of nervous tension" that apparently stemmed from trying to see as much of the Fair as possible before it closed while at the same time meeting his professional obligations and maintaining his diary.[139]

The Fair thus assaulted all senses. "There is so much going on," Schneiderhahn noted, "concerts and meetings etc. that this is truly a world's meeting."[140] The daily special events, parades, and musical performances, plus the noise and activity of the Pike, provided an enormous physical stimulus. The daily band concerts and the occasional parade or military drill attracted the attention of all four writers and invited description. On the Pike, where noise was de rigueur, the push of crowds and assault on the senses could be overpowering, as Sam Hyde related in his description of Thanksgiving night on the Pike:

> Trouble had begun early on the Pike. A thousand pedestrians thronged the great thoroughfare beneath ten thousand electric lights whilst the din of cowbells, whistles, megaphones, the infernal yelling of the

barkers mingled with the boom of cannon in the sham battle shows, and every body making all the noise they could with every conceivable device that would produce discord upon general principals rendered a pandemonium that I don't expect to hear again this side of Hades.[141]

Schneiderhahn, in describing closing day, found the noise and the press of the crowds oppressive. He preferred a quieter setting: "The two trips up the Pike," he wrote, "were made amidst the universal din and with much merriment. But the party's trip in the quieter parts of the World's Fair picture permitted much more real enjoyment. For the crowd on the Pike was getting unruly."[142]

Human interaction, not only on the Pike or among the crowds, was a central aspect of the Fair-visiting experience. For Edward Schneiderhahn, companionship enhanced his experience. He complained on one occasion, "It is unsatisfactory to be alone at the Fair but no one would go with you."[143] Sam Hyde, by contrast, preferred solitude on the fairgrounds. He particularly enjoyed his Thanksgiving Day visit, he recalled, "because I was alone and free to follow up any adventure and take my time where I most enjoyed the sights. The fact is I was handicapped when ever I had company. Nothing knocks all the sentiment and enterprise out of a man like an eternal 'O come on.'"[144] Edmund Philibert also seemed to enjoy solitude; he often visited the fairgrounds alone. When he did so with family, he frequently separated from them and went off alone for a period of time.[145] Florence McCallion, a woman visiting relatives, was always in someone's company. For her, though, the absence of her husband on the occasion of several of her Fair visits was clearly a factor that helped define her experience.[146] The type of activity in which the individual engaged also seems in part to have been determined by whether one was alone or had company. Taking in the Pike entertainments, for example, was invariably a social activity, while serious study of an exhibit called for solitude. Of course if something in an exhibit captured one's attention, one could always make a point of showing it to companions at a later date. Edmund Philibert's diary is full of references to such experiences.[147] Schneiderhahn made a second trip into the Temple of Mirth, a funhouse concession on the Pike, in order to share his amusement with friends.[148]

The weather also had an impact on the Fair visitors. Florence McCallion, more limited in her opportunities to go to the fairgrounds, wrote of the disappointment of having an outing to the Fair ruined by rain.[149] Schneiderhahn reported that rain was an uncommonly frequent occurrence during the summer of 1904, while Sam Hyde pleasantly recalled how rain on the Fourth of July led him and his friend Ben to spend an unplanned hour watching as "maids and matrons young, old, and so so trying to save their skirts [from the mud] presented a display of hosiery worthy of the great Fair."[150] As the year wore on and winter approached, the cold began to drive Fair visitors inside. Edmund Philibert frequently took refuge in the Department of Machinery power house or at other sites housing the Fair's power plant.[151] On another occasion he remarked on how peculiar it was that the Filipino tribesmen seemed comfortable in their loincloths despite the frigid weather.[152]

Then there was the matter of expense. None of the four diarists, memoirists, and letter writers whose narratives follow were people of significant financial means. Going to the Fair was a costly matter, with admission set at fifty cents for adults. The expense did not stop at the admission gate. Every Pike concession, lemonade booth, ride on the Intramural, and many special events, not to mention the streetcar ride to and from the fairgrounds, increased the tariff. Sam Hyde, Edmund Philibert, and Florence McCallion all commented on the cost. When Philibert visited the Pike for the first time, he complained about his visit to the Tyrolean Alps. "The mountain and village scene were fine," he wrote, "but I was disappointed as I expected to see the passion play have a railroad trip through the Alps, etc. for one admission price but when inside I found that each of these were extra."[153] Writing in 1909, Hyde still recalled the expense, and commented on exactly the same phenomenon as did Philibert. In addition, he remembered the high prices attached to many of the souvenirs and other products for sale in vendors' booths. "We would like to have purchased some of the beautiful things we saw," Hyde wrote, "but the prices on every thing were simply fabulous. It looked as if the rule was to estimate a fair price for an article, multiply it by two, add fifty per cent for tariff, another fifty percent for freight, twenty five more upon general principals and ten and two fives for Francis."[154] The costs of visiting the Fair could mount up rapidly.

The detailed accounting kept by Edmund Philibert, who dutifully recorded every penny he spent, shows that he spent an average of $1.95 for each of his Fair visits.[155] When one considers that the rate paid a working union carpenter was only $0.55 per hour,[156] making frequent trips to the Fair must have consumed a very significant portion of Philibert's disposable income. Preoccupation with cost surfaces throughout Philibert's narrative and clearly influenced how he was able to enjoy the Fair.

The letters, diaries, and memoirs of the Fair also reveal an awareness of the Fair's temporary nature. While today's nostalgia about the Fair is often manifested in urban myths and the souvenir collecting mania, the immediate nostalgia experienced by the Fair visitors was revealed in how and why they wrote, how they visited the Fair, and their repeated expressions of resigned regret that the Fair was escaping from them even as they experienced it.

Three of the writers whose narratives follow were motivated by the Fair to write when they normally would not have. In December 1904, after the Fair closed, Schneiderhahn suspended his daily diary entries to devote a month's writing to recapturing his Fair experience. "It did not seem right," he wrote, "to pass that subject with the few disconnected and scant memoranda you had been able to make."[157] Philibert, apparently, never kept a diary, except during 1904. That diary, unlike Schneiderhahn's record of his daily life, consisted exclusively of his Fair narrative. Interestingly, his early entries are short and rather superficial. But with each visit, he became increasingly descriptive—as if he were growing obsessed with capturing something he knew would be fleeting. Sam Hyde, according to the first page of his photo memoir, had not intended to write at all, but found himself compelled to as he sat down to assemble his photo album.[158] Florence McCallion, judging from the expressions of affection that characterize her letters to her husband, would certainly have written to him during their separation regardless. The tone of her writing, however, reveals a conscious desire not just to communicate with her husband but also to share her Fair-visiting experiences on an intimate level. She wrote: "I did wish that you were with me yesterday. I had such a lovely time at the Fair.

Sunday Visitors at the Fairgrounds. *Photograph, c. 1902. Even before the buildings began to rise, St. Louisans were engaged by the 1904 World's Fair. A pre-Fair outing to the grounds was a common experience.*

There was only one thing that marred my pleasure, and, that was your absence. I thought about you all day and evening. I wish you could come up and stay at least a month and go to the Fair every day."[159] These four Fair visitors knew that this event would be a central one in their lives. Writing was a way to capture and share the experience, if only with their future selves.

As the Fair progressed, so too did the frequency of their visits. In a one-line entry dated November 11-25, Schneiderhahn wrote simply, "Worked hard and put in every spare minute at the Fair."[160] He then proceeded to attend the Fair on five of its last six days. On each day of those visits he found the time to write an uncharacteristically lengthy diary entry. Similarly, nine of Edmund Philibert's twenty-eight Fair visits took place during the last month of the Fair. Each of these last visits grew increasingly frenzied, as he ran madly from one building to the next, attempting to see everything while he still could. Ever concerned about his finances, he loosened his purse in November and spent significant sums going on Pike rides and attending shows that he had shied away from earlier.[161]

The Fair did not just capture the imagination of the Fair visitors on opening day, or when its impending closure made frequent visitation urgent. St. Louis–area Fair visitors began visiting the Fair from the day construction first began on it in Forest Park. In his memoir, Schneiderhahn recalled how he would visit the grounds on Sundays during the pre-Exposition years and enjoy "a quiet stroll among the buildings which became prettier every month."[162] Sam Hyde also recalled frequent pre-Exposition visits in his post-Fair memoir. He wrote:

> Our first visit was just after the surveyors had finished their preliminary work and the hills and valleys bristled with their stakes. . . . We went again when the hills and valleys were disappearing before the dredge and scraper and the face of the landscape was changing every day. And again when the sights of the vast buildings had been marked and long trains of cars were unloading lumber and iron and sewer pipe and rock and sand and cinders. And we were there when the skeletons of the buildings began to rise from the broad acres that had been leveled by the hand of man.

> We went in the winter when the molding of the statuary and decorations in staff was going on in enclosed buildings and finished sections of the work set out to dry. . . . We saw the palaces rise in grandeur and beauty like visions of the night. . . . We went as long as we could go in free and when they closed the gate we paid the fare and went for we knew it was once for all and the chance of a lifetime.[163]

After the Fair as well, when demolition was underway, area Fair visitors returned to survey the site. Edmund Philibert and Florence McCallion were among them. They enjoyed a glass of lemonade for "old times sake," and Florence noted that at certain places "we could almost imagine we were at the Fair."[164]

The World's Fair was a utopian world that took possession of the minds of these St. Louis fairgoers. They scrambled to get their fill of it while they could—ever cognizant of its temporary nature. Schneiderhahn's description of closing night gives the best sense of this and illustrates the evolving nostalgia the Fair itself was creating:

> With Alf and Julia went to Fair. Last time. . . . After attending the closing day exercises . . . , passed rapidly through the Manufacturers, Liberal Arts, Government, Mines and Education Buildings, not to see anything, but for the purpose of casting a last look on scenes that had become familiar and dear and from which we must part forever. . . . We went out into the Main Picture to view the Cascades and the beautiful Festival Hall for the last time resplendent in all their indescribable glory. . . . At promptly twelve o'clock President Francis turned the switch that controlled the power and the light. The flood of light grew fainter and fainter and of a sudden all was darkness. The Cascades were silent. The scene was dead. The World's Fair no more. . . . Our company passed out of the gate, not entirely silent, for we remarked the want of joviality, but we were altogether grave and very much subdued in spirit. For it was indeed a solemn occasion. It is a hard task to become reconciled to the end of the Worlds Fair.[165]

Even Philibert, whose text is largely limited to description, gave voice to similar feelings at the end of the Fair. Writing on November 30, the day before the Fair's closing, he reported overhearing some girls "laughing and joking and having a gay time, but nevertheless it seemed to me they were sorry, that the ending of the Fair was so near."[166] Attending alone on closing day he did not stay to see the lights turned off. He described his final view of the Fair in this way:

> I walked through the Sunken Garden and along the Government Terrace and over the Plateau of States. . . . I walked up to the Grand Basin and sat watching the Cascades awhile, then I ascended to the Terrace of States and as this was my last opportunity I spent some time in viewing the Cascades and illumination in all directions, then descending the east steps I walked along by the Grand Basin and Plaza of St. Louis taking a farewell look at everything as I went, and it made me feel a little sad to think that it would soon be all over forever, for I had spent many pleasant days there. . . .[167]

For each of the four Fair visitors, there is substantial testimony indicating that the Louisiana Purchase Exposition was an important event in their lives. The multiplicity of visits, the impulse to create a record of the experience, and the nostalgia of the closing night are only three evidentiary factors. Additional proof lies in the inevitable closing line offered by Philibert, Schneiderhahn, and Hyde—a line that is remarkable in its similarity. Philibert comforted himself with the words: "Everything must come to an end sometime."[168] Schneiderhahn cited Thomas Grey's *Elegy Written in a Country Churchyard*, when he reported that closing night reminded him of the poet's saying: "'The Boasts of heraldry, the pomp of power and all that beauty all that wealth ever gave, await alike the inevitable hour, the paths of glory lead but to the grave.'"[169] Sam Hyde cited *Macbeth*. Almost as if he could not believe the Fair had ever taken place, he quoted: "'Were such thing here as we do speak about, or have we eaten of the insane root that takes the reason prisoner?'"[170] Florence McCallion, who failed to leave a last letter from the Fair, revealed her nostalgia for the Fair in her May 1905 letter to her husband, which described the "ruin and desolation" of the fairgrounds after the Fair's closure. "Edmund and I were both wishing the Fair was going on," she wrote.[171]

❧

The 1904 St. Louis World's Fair was thus a central experience in the lives of these four St. Louis area residents. It held their attention for months or even years, it prompted them to write and to seek other ways of capturing the moment, it created its own nostalgia, and it created and re-created memories for subsequent consumption. It was also a central event in the life of the City of St. Louis. Certainly this group of Fair visitors' excitement was enhanced by their residency in or proximity to the host city.

As detailed above, the Louisiana Purchase Exposition was one of a series of American world's fairs that took place at the end of the nineteenth and start of the twentieth century, when America was just beginning to assert herself as a major world power. The St. Louis World's Fair took place as the world was beginning to shrink, but before it shrank to the point that access to firsthand knowledge and experience of other nations and other peoples was readily available to the average person. It took place just as science and technology were beginning to offer major enhancements to daily life, but before each home had electricity. It took place just as government was assuming an active role in improving the quality of urban life, but before public park systems and public playgrounds were the norm. It took place in an age when the future seemed limitless, when a widely held belief in a unilinear progress could define the future and ensure advancement "towards a still higher development." The 1904 St. Louis World's Fair offered a vision of a future utopia to over twelve million Fair visitors. The Fair itself was a metaphor for this anticipated utopia—controlled and ordered, governed by a well-articulated consensus, and imbued with enormous opportunity for creativity within a defined framework. With mass communications and ease of travel in the future, the World's Fair was a unique opportunity for the individual to see and experience that which might never be seen or experienced again.

Still, it is impossible to state that Fair visitors learned the "lessons of the Fair" or that the records left by Fair visitors are evidence of the success of the Fair planners' promotion of the ideologies of progress and expansion. That causal link cannot be established from the sources evaluated here. What is clear is that the Fair visitors—at least those considered here—were products of the same forces and the same society that gave rise to the St. Louis World's Fair. Their views and their reactions to the Fair generally indicate an identification with the world view that underlay and informed the intellectual structures, the exhibits, the architecture, the use of space, and the entertainments they encountered at the World's Fair.

Within the context of America in the Progressive Era, the St. Louis World's Fair was an opportunity not only for the promotion of the ideologies of progress and national expansion, but also for the defusion of threats to political and social stability in America. But while the conservative, reformist elite worked to co-opt and use popular reform impulses to defuse popular dissent, the massive size, spectacle, and pageantry of the Fair may have played a role in co-opting the individual Fair visitor's attention. The Fair numbed the visitor. Even Edward V. P. Schneiderhahn, an exceptionally critical diarist and Fair visitor who sought out opportunities to broaden his knowledge at the St. Louis Fair, complained of this: "In fact sometimes, or rather often you came to the Fair with the purpose to see something—in the buildings—but would stop so long on the outside contemplating (the right word) the architectural beauties of the buildings that there would be little if any time left for inspection of exhibits." In many regards the Fair was an enormous pageant, both as a whole, and in its presentation of daily events. Both the whole and its individual parts were replete with all the hallmarks that historian David Glassberg has identified as characteristic of local civic holiday celebrations. As George Leighton noted, world's fairs satisfied a "hankering for a holiday," but on a grand scale. "Historical consciousness," Glassberg wrote, "is . . . shaped by public historical imagery that prompts individuals to associate their personal experience and particular traditions with larger, public historical themes."[172] The Fair as pageant accomplished much the same.

The Fair as spectacle had a similar effect. The exhibits closed at 6:00 P.M., but the grounds remained open until 11:00. For five hours Fair visitors partook of the vistas, the concerts, and the entertainments and rides on the Pike. If the accounts of these Fair visitors is an indication, many did not arrive on the fairgrounds until mid-afternoon, especially during the week, when work schedules and other obligations demanded their attention. Schneiderhahn and Philibert in particular, though they made multiple visits to the Fair, often arrived only in the mid-afternoon. Thus much of their time was not passed examining exhibits. It was spent enjoying one or another aspect of the spectacle. Despite the best efforts of the Fair planners to stress the educational content of the Fair and to offer ample opportunity to improve the taste of the middle classes, Fair visitors spent much of their time simply taking in the entertainment. While the Fair visitors occasionally enjoyed a gondola ride on the lagoon or attended a concert in the evening, most frequently they toured the Pike. Philibert's best descriptive passages refer to Pike entertainments or rides. Likewise, both Florence McCallion and Sam Hyde devoted disproportionate parts of their narratives to describing the Pike and its entertainments. McCallion, for example, recounted her amazement at the realism of the Boer War re-creation: "The horses would fall down as if shot," she wrote, "and lie down a long time perfectly motionless just like they were dead."[173] Sam Hyde, long after the Fair, still marveled at the Pike's temptations, confessing his belief that "if the pike had been a mile longer it would have led to hell."[174] His description of the Pike's forbidden fruits recalls Florence McCallion's sense of naughtiness when she went to see the Igorots. Only Schneiderhahn appears to have eschewed the Pike to any degree, but even he enjoyed its tamer entertainments and made the obligatory trek up and down it on closing night. In the end, spectacle was what ultimately held the attention of the Fair visitors, whether it was Florence McCallion's enjoyment of the Boer War or Edward Schneiderhahn's pleasure in taking in the "unforgettably beautiful" and "indescribably grand" scenes that the 1904 World's Fair had to offer for seven short months in St. Louis' Forest Park.

1. Edward V. P. Schneiderhahn World's Fair Memoir, following his daily diary entry for December 1, 1904, in the Schneiderhahn Diaries, vol. 6, pp. 67-92, Missouri Historical Society Archives, St. Louis (hereafter: Schneiderhahn Memoir).

2. Schneiderhahn characteristically referred to himself in the second person.

3. For three theses that have been written at St. Louis–area universities or by St. Louis students studying elsewhere, see: Clara Rose Mutschnick, "St. Louis Prepares for a World's Fair," Master's thesis, St. Louis University, 1945; Martin Rudolph Brueggemann, "St. Louis' 1904 World's Fair: A 'Thick' Exposition," Bachelor of Arts thesis, Reed College, 1987; Hiroko Takada, "Image of a Modern Nation: Meiji Japan and the Expositions, 1903-1904," Senior Seminar Paper, school unkown, 1992. Articles have appeared most commonly, though not exclusively, in the publications of the Missouri Historical Society in St. Louis and the State Historical Society of Missouri in Columbia: Henry S. Iglauer, "The Demolition of the Louisiana Purchase Exposition of 1904," *Missouri Historical Society Bulletin* 22 (July 1966), pp. 457-67 (hereafter: MHSB); Ted C. Hinckley, "When the Boer War Came to St. Louis," *Missouri Historical Review* 61 (April 1967), pp. 285-302 (hereafter: MHR); James J. Horgan, "Aeronautics at the World's Fair of 1904," MHSB 24 (April 1968), pp. 214-40; Stephen J. Raiche, "The World's Fair and the New St. Louis," MHR 67 (October 1972), pp. 98-121; Frank O'Brien, "Meet Me in St. Louis," *Washington University Magazine* 44 (Spring 1974), pp. 7-13; Stuart Seely Sprague, "Meet Me in St. Louis on the Ten-Million-Dollar Pike," MHSB 32 (October 1975), pp. 26-31; Eugene F. Provenzo, Jr., "Education and the Louisiana Purchase Exposition," MHSB 32 (January 1976), pp. 99-109; Irene E. Cortinovis, "China at the St. Louis World's Fair," MHR 72 (October 1977), pp. 59-66; Jane Anne Liebenguth, "Music at the Louisiana Purchase Exposition," MHSB 36 (October 1979), pp. 27-34; Russell M. Magnaghi, "America Views Her Indians at the 1904 World's Fair in St. Louis," *Gateway Heritage* 4 (Winter 1983-1984), pp. 21-29 (hereafter: GH); Karen M. Keefer, "Dirty Water and Clean Toilets: Medical Aspects of the 1904 Louisiana Purchase Exposition," GH 9 (Summer 1988), pp. 32-37; Robert A. Trennert, "A Resurrection of Native Arts and Crafts: The St. Louis World's Fair, 1904," MHR 87 (April 1993), pp. 274-92; Sharra A. Vostral, "Imperialism on Display: The Philippine Exhibition at the 1904 World's Fair," GH 13 (Spring 1993), pp. 18-31. Of variable quality, these articles constitute the lion's share of the extant historical publications on the St. Louis World's Fair, as there is no monographic study of the topic. The best study of the Fair within the context of St. Louis history is James Neal Primm, *Lion of the Valley: St. Louis, Missouri*, 2d ed., (Boulder, Colo.: Pruett Publishing Co., 1990), chapter 9, pp. 345-418.

4. Results of survey conducted by Katharine T. Corbett, Director of Interpretation at the Missouri Historical Society, in 1994, in preparation for the Missouri Historical Society's exhibit *Meet Me at the Fair: Memory, History, and the 1904 World's Fair*, scheduled to open June 1996 (hereafter: Corbett, World's Fair Survey).

5. This was the title that a local popularizer of the St. Louis World's Fair chose for her own book. See: Dorothy Daniels Birk, *The World Came to St. Louis: A Visit to the 1904 World's Fair* (St. Louis: The Bethany Press, 1979). For a similar approach, see: Margaret Johanson Witherspoon, *Remembering the St. Louis World's Fair* (St. Louis: Comfort Printing Co., 1973), and "St. Louis Celebrates: The World's Fair of 1904," MHSB 11 (October 1954), pp. 54-72.

6. See, for example: Robert L. Hendershot, *The 1904 St. Louis World's Fair: The Louisiana Purchase Exposition Mementos and Memorabilia* (Iola, Wisc: Kurt R. Krueger Publishing, 1904) and Carl S. Ebert, *A Story of St. Louis World's Fair Spoons* (n.p., 1982?).

7. Some of these myths include the belief that the ice cream cone, iced tea, the hot dog, and even the hamburger were all invented at the 1904 World's Fair. In addition, it is widely held that the axle of the great Ferris Wheel lies buried under a golf course in Forest Park, and that a St. Louis neighborhood takes its popular name—Dogtown—from the presence of the dog-eating Igorots of the Philippines at the World's Fair. When asked what they associate with the 1904 World's Fair, St. Louisans overwhelmingly mention the ice cream cone. See: Corbett, World's Fair Survey, 1994. On the importance and persistence of myth in history, even in the face of knowledge to the contrary, see: Michael Frisch, "American History and the Structures of Collective Memory: A Modest Exercise in Empirical Iconography," *Journal of American History* 75 (March 1989), pp. 1130-55 (hereafter: JAH).

8. Sprague, in "Meet Me in St. Louis on the Ten-Million-Dollar Pike," for example, made use of World's Fair diaries "to take advantage of first-hand accounts, and to try to recapture the immediacy of an actual visit to the Pike" (p. 26, note).

9. Robert W. Rydell, *All the World's a Fair: Visions of Empire at American International Expositions, 1876-1916* (Chicago: University of Chicago Press, 1984) and *World of Fairs: The Century-of-Progress Expositions* (Chicago: University of Chicago Press, 1993). For a history of world's fairs from the international perspective, see: Paul Greenhalgh, *Ephemeral Vistas: The Expositions Universelles, Great Exhibitions and World's Fairs, 1851-1939*, Studies in Imperialism Series, John M. MacKenzie, gen. ed. (Manchester, U.K.: Manchester University Press, 1988). For an analysis of one aspect of the St. Louis World's Fair from a perspective influenced directly by Rydell's work, see: Vostral, "Imperialism on Display." The scholarly literature on world's fairs is growing rapidly. See: Richard D. Mandell, *Paris 1900: The Great World's Fair* (Toronto: University of Toronto Press, 1967); Reid Badger, *The Great American Fair: The World's Columbian Exposition and American Culture* (Chicago: N. Hall, 1979); Burton Benedict, *The Anthropology of World's Fairs: San Francisco's Panama Pacific International Exposition of 1915* (Berkeley, Calif.: Scolar Press, 1983); James B. Gilbert, *Perfect Cities: Chicago's Utopia of 1893* (Chicago: University of Chicago Press, 1991); Robert Muccigrosso, *Celebrating the New World: Chicago's Columbian Exposition of 1893* (Chicago: Ivan R. Dee, 1993); Neil Harris, et al., *Grand Illusions: Chicago's World's Fair of 1893* (Chicago: Chicago Historical Society, 1993); and the relevant chapters of Neil Harris, *Cultural Excursions: Marketing Appetites and Cultural Tastes in Modern America* (Chicago: University of Chicago Press, 1990) and David Nasaw, *Going Out: The Rise and Fall of Public Amusements* (New York: Basic Books, 1993). Most of these works are compatible with Rydell's scholarship if not influenced by it. Even those works that predate Rydell's 1984 *All the World's a Fair* see world's fairs as cultural phenomena that communicated the values of their age to a broad audience. Only Muccigrosso overtly challenges Rydell by arguing that interpretations such as his present a distorted view of the past by projecting current values and standards backwards.

10. Virtually all of these scholarly studies of world's fairs discuss and cite at least the most widely publicized visitor accounts as evidence of the fairs' impact. The most adventurous foray into the question of visitor reaction, though, was undertaken by an undergraduate student at Reed College. See: Brueggemann, "St. Louis' 1904 World's Fair."

11. The concept of reader-response criticism, borrowed from the world of literary criticism, might offer a framework for addressing some of these issues, although that will not be attempted in this publication. As Jane Tompkins defined it, "reader-response critics would argue that a poem cannot be understood apart from its results." Likewise, perhaps, one could then argue, the 1904 World's Fair cannot be understood apart from its impact on the individual visitor. For a good survey of reader-response criticism, see: Jane P. Tompkins, "An Introduction to Reader-Response Criticism," in Jane P. Tompkins, ed., *Reader-Response Criticism: From Formalism to Post-Structuralism* (Baltimore: Johns Hopkins University Press, 1980), pp. ix-xxvi (quote on p. ix). For Lawrence W. Levine's adaptation of reader-response criticism to the impact of mass consumer culture on audiences, see his article "The Folklore of Industrial Society: Popular Culture and Its Audiences," *American Historical Review* 97 (December 1992), pp. 1369-99 (hereafter:

AHR). For a critique of Levine's efforts, see: T. J. Jackson Lears, "Making Fun of Popular Culture," *AHR* 97 (December 1992), pp. 1417-26.

12. Greenhalgh, *Ephemeral Vistas*, especially pp. 12-24.

13. Between 1893 and 1916, world's fairs took place in Chicago (1893), Atlanta (1895), Nashville (1897), Omaha (1898), Buffalo (1901), St. Louis (1904), Portland (1905), Seattle (1909), San Francisco (1915), and San Diego (1916). Rydell, *All the World's a Fair*, passim.

14. David P. Thelen, "Social Tensions and the Origins of Progressivism," *JAH* 54 (September 1969), p. 341.

15. Kenneth McNaught, "American Progressives and the Great Society," *JAH* 53 (December 1966), pp. 504-20. Although McNaught's argument focuses on what he sees as the defeat of socialism in America by Progressivism, or Whig democracy, as he calls it, his framework has an application here. It reinforces the conclusion that the Progressives co-opted much of the program of dissenting groups in American society, thereby rendering them incapable of presenting a significant threat to the established order.

16. See: Walter L. Williams, "United States Indian Policy and the Debate over Philippine Annexation: Implications for the Origins of American Imperialism," *JAH* 66 (March 1980), pp. 810-31, whose main argument is that American Indian policy was the precedent for overseas imperialism, especially in the Philippines, both in terms of the right to subjugate and the need to guide and educate.

17. William Coleman, "Science and Symbol in the Turner Frontier Hypothesis," *AHR* 62 (October 1966), pp. 22-49.

18. Quoted in Rydell, *All the World's a Fair*, p. 7.

19. Ibid., p. 2.

20. Geoffrey Blodgett, "Frederick Law Olmsted: Landscape Architecture as Conservative Reform," *JAH* 62 (March 1976), p. 872. Olmsted, among his many other accomplishments, was also the landscape architect for the 1893 Chicago World's Fair.

21. On neoclassical fair architecture in general, see: Greenhalgh, *Ephemeral Vistas*, pp. 128-29; on the architecture of the Chicago World's Fair, see: Wim de Wit, "Building an Illusion: The Design of the World's Columbia Exposition," in Harris, et al., *Grand Illusions*, pp.41-98; on the symbolism and persistence of neoclassical architecture as a conservative form in the years following the 1893 Chicago World's Fair, see: Geoffrey Blodgett, "Cass Gilbert, Architect: Conservative at Bay," *JAH* 72 (December 1985), pp. 615-36. Robert Muccigrosso, who has tended to challenge Rydell's interpretation of world's fairs, also notes the "imperial" aspect of the neoclassical architecture, although he makes the distinction between "imperial" and "imperialistic." Muccigrosso, *Celebrating the New World*, p. 185.

22. Primm, *Lion of the Valley*, pp. 395-99; Mutschnick, "St. Louis Prepares for a World's Fair," passim. In addition, there are four major "official histories," all of which recount basically the same story but from a self-congratulatory perspective. See: Mark Bennitt, ed., *History of the Louisiana Purchase Exposition* (St. Louis: Universal Exposition Publishing Company, 1905); John Wesley Hanson, *The Official History of the Fair, St. Louis, 1904* (St. Louis, 1904); David R. Francis, *The Universal Exposition of 1904*, 2 vols., (St. Louis: Louisiana Purchase Exposition Company, 1913); and J. W. Buel, ed., *Louisiana and the Fair: An Exposition of the World, Its People, and Their Achievements* (St. Louis: World's Progress Publishing Company, 1904-1905). For the official records, see: Louisiana Purchase Exposition Company Records, Missouri Historical Society Archives, St. Louis (hereafter: LPE Co. Records).

23. This is evidenced in part by the presence of a number of reports and other documentary materials from the Chicago Fair in the records of the Louisiana Purchase Exposition Company, and by the fact that a number of Fair planners, especially in the area of exhibits, had worked at the Chicago Fair before being asked to join the LPE Company. See, for example, the Reports of the Divisions of Works and of Concessions from the World's Columbian Exposition, 1893, and the transcript of a conversation

between LPE concession chief Norris Gregg and Paul Blackmere, December 1902, LPE Co. Records, Box 2/Series II/Folder 2, and Box 13/Series V/Subseries I/Folder 2, respectively.

24. Primm, *Lion of the Valley*, pp. 345-93; Alexander Scot McConachie, "The 'Big Cinch': A Business Elite in the Life of a City, St. Louis, 1895-1915" Ph.D. diss., Washington University, 1976; Dina M. Young, "The St. Louis Streetcar Strike of 1900: Pivotal Politics at the Century's Dawn," *GH* 12 (Summer 1991), pp. 4-17; Steven L. Piott, "Modernization and the Anti-Monopoly Issue: The St. Louis Transit Strike of 1900," *MHSB* 35 (October 1978), pp. 3-16. Lincoln Steffens' exposé on St. Louis corruption appeared in two installments: Claude H. Wetmore and Lincoln Steffens, "Tweed Days in St. Louis: Joseph W. Folk's Single-handed Exposure of Corruption, High and Low," *McClure's Magazine* (October 1902), pp. 577-86, and Lincoln Steffens, "The Shamelessness of St. Louis: Something New in the History of American Municipal Democracy," *McClure's Magazine* (March 1903), pp. 546-60. These two essays comprise two of the eight chapters of Steffens' *Shame of the Cities*, published in New York in 1904.

25. Primm, *Lion of the Valley*, pp. 388-89. The archetype of the Progressive politician as one who embraces the methods of business in government was developed by Robert H. Wiebe and Samuel P. Hays. For a discussion of the concept within the context of the history and historiography of Progressivism, see: Richard L. McCormick, "The Discovery that Business Corrupts Politics: A Reappraisal of the Origins of Progressivism," *AHR* 86 (April 1991), pp. 247-74.

26. Primm, *Lion of the Valley*, pp. 383-93; Raiche, "The World's Fair and the New St. Louis"; Keefer, "Dirty Water and Clean Toilets," pp. 34-35. On St. Louis civic reform and the "City Beautiful" movement in St. Louis after the Fair as well as before, see: Edward C. Rafferty, "Orderly City, Orderly Lives: The City Beautiful Movement in St. Louis," *GH* 11 (Spring 1991), pp. 40-62. Wells' reform agenda was typical of that of Progressives in general. See: McCormick, "The Discovery that Business Corrupts Politics," and Stanley K. Schultz and Clay McShane, "To Engineer the Metropolis: Sewers, Sanitation, and City Planning in Late-Nineteenth-Century America," *JAH* 65 (September 1978), pp. 389-411.

27. Minutes, Committee on Grounds and Buildings, January 2, 1902, LPE Co. Records, Box 2/Series II/Subseries I/Folder 2. The Central Trades and Labor Union, a socialist body, was excluded from this agreement, as preference was accorded the Building Trades Council, a much more conservative organization.

28. George R. Leighton, "The Year St. Louis Enchanted the World," *Harper's Magazine* (August 1960), p. 46. For more on Reedy, see: John T. Flanagan, "Reedy of the *Mirror*," *MHR* 43 (January 1949), pp. 128-44, and Raiche, "The World's Fair and the New St. Louis," pp. 102-5. Pre-Fair publicity, engineered by the LPE Company's Department of Press and Publicity, attempted to counter St. Louis' reputation and promote St. Louis as a well-governed and clean city with a laudable track record. Such boosterism was inevitably accompanied by a shameless adulation of David R. Francis. See, for example: T. R. MacMechen, "The City of St. Louis, The Best Governed Municipality in the United States," *World's Fair Bulletin*, March 1904, pp. 12-16 (hereafter: *WFB*) and Edmund S. Hoch, "A Fifty-Million-Dollar Exposition," *National Magazine* 18 (May 1903), pp. 165-81.

29. See, for example: Frederick M. Crunden, "The Louisiana Purchase Exposition," *The American Monthly Review of Reviews* 27 (May 1903), pp. 547-56 (hereafter: *AMRR*); David R. Francis, "The Greatest World's Fair," *Everybody's Magazine* 10 (April 1904), pp. 437-51; and Hoch, "A Fifty-Million-Dollar Exposition." Several periodicals devoted entire issues to the World's Fair. Among them were: *National Magazine* 20 (July 1904) and *The World's Work*, August 1904 (hereafter: *WW*). *The World's Fair Bulletin*, published by the Louisiana Purchase Exposition Company, first appeared in print in November 1899 and continued publishing monthly through the end of the Fair in December 1904. The two

almost contemporaneously published official histories are: Bennitt, ed., *History of the LPE*, and Hanson, *Official History of the Fair*. Both were published by the LPE Company, as were numerous souvenir editions of official photographs, such as *The Forest City* (St. Louis, 1904), which appeared as a weekly serial from April 14 through November 3, 1904. For a discussion of how the official photography of a world's fair could be used to create a popular image, see: James Gilbert, "Fixing the Image: Photography at the World's Columbia Exposition," in Harris, et al., *Grand Illusions*, pp. 100-132.

30. See, for example, the title of David R. Francis' own two-volume history of the Fair, *The Universal Exposition of 1904*. The various exposition catalogs likewise used the phrase in their titles. See, for example: *Official Catalogue of Exhibitors, Universal Exposition, St. Louis, U.S.A. 1904: Department N, Anthropology*, rev. ed. (St. Louis: The Official Catalogue Company Inc., 1904), and *Official Catalogue Philippine Exhibits, Universal Exposition, St. Louis, U.S.A. 1904* (St. Louis: The Official Catalogue Company Inc., 1904).

31. David R. Francis' opening address, April 30, 1904, printed in "The Opening Ceremonies of the Louisiana Purchase Exposition, St. Louis, U.S.A., April 30th 1904," *WFB*, June 1904, p. 10.

32. *World's Fair, St. Louis: Official Classification of Exhibit Departments* (St. Louis, 1902?).

33. Frederick J. V. Skiff, "The Universal Exposition, An Encyclopedia of Society," *WFB*, December 1903, pp. 2-3.

34. Quoted in Rydell, *All the World's a Fair*, p. 159. Skiff had formerly served as director of the Colorado exhibit at the Chicago World's Fair and director of the United States exhibit at the Paris Exposition in 1900.

35. See: Isaac F. Marcosson, "Transportation as a Measure of Progress," *WW*, August 1904, pp. 5095-109.

36. *Official Classification*, p. 8.

37. Greenhalgh, *Ephemeral Vistas*, p. 21.

38. *Official Guide to the Louisiana Purchase Exposition* (St. Louis: The Official Guide Co., 1904), pp. 78-80.

39. Skiff, "The Universal Exposition," p. 2.

40. Greenhalgh, *Ephemeral Vistas*, p. 23.

41. Howard J. Rogers, "Educational Exhibit," *WFB*, December 1903, p. 4.

42. Francis, *The Universal Exposition of 1904*, vol. 1, p. 318; Provenzo, "Education and The Louisiana Purchase Exposition," passim; Greenhalgh, *Ephemeral Vistas*, pp. 18-22.

43. The establishment of Departments of Education, Social Economy, and Anthropology is one feature that distinguishes the St. Louis World's Fair from Chicago's; there were no Departments of Education or Social Economy at the Columbian Exposition, and the field of anthropology was covered in the less mature Department of Ethnology. Likewise, the Chicago Fair did not include a Department of Physical Culture, though international congresses were a notable feature of the Chicago Fair. See: Rossiter Johnson, ed., *A History of the World's Columbian Exposition* (New York: D. Appleton & Co., 1897), vol. 2, "Departments."

44. For contemporary accounts of the purposes of these two exhibit departments, see: Howard J. Rogers, "Social Economy," *WFB*, February 1904, pp. 10-13, and "Educational Exhibit," pp. 4-6. See also: "The Model Street: An Object Lesson in Municipal Government at the World's Fair, St. Louis, U.S.A.," *WFB*, August 1904, pp. 16-18.

45. Bennitt, ed., *History of the LPE*, p. 554.

46. On the City Beautiful movement, see: William H. Wilson, *The City Beautiful Movement* (Baltimore: Johns Hopkins University Press, 1989).

47. Bennitt, ed., *History of the LPE*, pp. 673-74. For other contemporary accounts of the anthropological exhibits, see: W. J. McGee "Anthropology," *WFB*, February 1904; Hanson, *Official History of the Fair*, pp. 265-78; *Official Guide*, pp. 92-93; and *Official Catalogue of Exhibitors, Anthropology*, passim. The best historical accounts are: Magnaghi, "America Views Her Indians," and Trennert, "A Resurrection of Native Arts and Crafts" (on the

Native American exhibits), Phillips Verner Bradford and Harvey Blume, *Ota Benga: The Pygmy in the Zoo* (New York: St. Martin's Press, 1992), and Rydell, *All the World's a Fair*, chapter 6.

48. Franz Boas, "The History of Anthropology," in Howard J. Rogers, ed., *Congress of Arts and Science: Universal Exposition, St. Louis, 1904* (Boston: Houghton, Mifflin and Company, 1906), vol. 5, p. 482.

49. Michael A. Lane, "New Dawns of Knowledge: III—Man, Individual and Race," *National Magazine* 20 (July 1904), p. 416.

50. McGee, "Anthropology," p. 4. See also: W. J. McGee's address to the International Congress of Arts and Science at the LPE: W. J. McGee, "Anthropology and Its Larger Problems," in Rogers, ed., *Congress of Arts and Science*, vol. 5, pp. 449-67.

51. Address of Frederick J. V. Skiff on opening day, April 30, 1904, in "The Opening Ceremonies of the LPE," p.12.

52. W. J. McGee, "Introduction," in *Official Catalogue of Exhibitors, Anthropology*, p. 9.

53. Bennitt, ed., *History of the LPE*, p. 678. See also: McGee "Anthropology," p. 6.

54. McGee, "Anthropology," p. 6.

55. Frederick E. Hoxie, "Exploring a Cultural Borderland: Native American Journeys of Discovery in the Early Twentieth Century," *JAH* 79 (December 1992), pp. 969-95. Describing the Native American ethnologic exhibits, McGee wrote: "The several [Indian] groups will typify aboriginal life; and both special students and general visitors will find in them an index to the inner life of the Red Race whose rise and passing form the opening epic of American history." In describing the Pygmies of Africa, W. J. McGee made a similar statement, calling them the true aborigines of Africa and asserting that they were dying out. His argument implied that they were in fact being winnowed out in a Darwinian fashion, having proved themselves unfit and thus unable to survive in the modern industrial age. McGee, "Anthropology," p. 5. In the case of Native Americans, the great irony of the Anthropological exhibits at the LPE is that by providing a forum for the display of Native American arts and crafts, the Fair stimulated a major boost in their popularity and may thus have helped encourage the survival of the same Native American cultures it denigrated. See: Trennert, "A Resurrection of Native Arts and Crafts."

56. Bennitt, ed., *History of the LPE*, p. 683.

57. McGee, "Introduction," in *Official Catalogue of Exhibitors, Anthropology*, pp. 9-10.

58. For contemporary accounts of the Philippine Exposition, see: William N. Swarthout, "A Descriptive Story of the Philippine Exhibit, World's Fair, St. Louis, U.S.A.," *WFB*, June 1904, pp. 48-58; Hanson, *Official History of the Fair*, pp. 295-328; Bennitt, ed., *History of the LPE*, pp. 463-81; *Official Guide to the LPE*, pp. 122-23; A. C. Newell, ed. and comp., *Philippine Exposition, World's Fair, Saint Louis* (n.p., 1904?), passim; and *Official Catalogue Philippine Exhibits*, passim. The best historical accounts are to be found in Vostral, "Imperialism on Display," and Rydell, *All the World's a Fair*, chapter 6.

59. Illustration accompanying Swarthout, "A Descriptive Story of the Philippine Exhibit," p. 53.

60. Ibid., p. 50.

61. Ibid., p. 56.

62. See: Williams, "United States Indian Policy," passim.

63. Address of Frederick J. V. Skiff, in "The Opening Ceremonies of the Louisiana Purchase Exposition," p. 10.

64. John M. MacKenzie, "Forward," in Greenhalgh, *Ephemeral Vistas*, p. ix.

65. Minutes, Commission of Architects, July 10, 1901, LPE Co. Records, Box 2/Series II/Subseries II/Folder 1.

66. Report of the Division of Works, 1905, pp. 10-11, ibid., Box 2/Series II/Folder 1.

67. Karl Theodore Bitter, "Sculpture for the St. Louis World's Fair," *Brush and Pencil* 13 (December 1903), pp. 167-68.

68. Crunden, "The Louisiana Purchase Exposition," p. 550.

69. James F. Early, "The Sculpture of the United States Government Building," *WFB*, January 1904, p. 40.

70. Neil Harris, "Memory and the White City," and Wim de Wit, "Building an Illusion," in Harris, et al., *Grand Illusions*, pp. 15-17 and p. 58; Blodgett, "Cass Gilbert," pp. 615-36.

71. Greenhalgh, *Ephemeral Vistas*, pp. 127-29.

72. Frederick J. Turner, "The Significance of the Louisiana Purchase," *AMRR* 27 (May 1903), p. 584.

73. George Kessler was engaged by the LPE Company as Chief of Landscape Architecture on July 1, 1901. The fan-shape design was first offered as an option over the initially proposed grid-like plan on July 29, 1901, and was adopted the next day. The minutes of the LPE Commission of Architects do not, however, attribute the proposal to any one member. Minutes, Commission of Architects, July 29 and July 30, 1901, LPE Co. Records, Box 2/Series II/Subseries II/Folder 1.

74. George Kessler's role in the planning of the LPE has yet to be studied. For the most part he is known for his design of the Kansas City Park system and for his impact on the fledgling profession of urban planning, to which he devoted his energies in the years following the LPE. In St. Louis, he is known for his redesign of Forest Park following the Fair. Virtually no published account of the LPE, however, even so much as mentions his name in connection with the layout of the fairgrounds. Only Edward Rafferty's study of Kessler in St. Louis recognizes the importance of Kessler at the LPE and the significance of the LPE as civic "reformers' attempt to represent the ideal of beauty in city design" in St. Louis. See: Rafferty, "Orderly City, Orderly Lives," pp. 40-62, quotation from p. 45, and Edward C. Rafferty, "George Edward Kessler," *GH* 11 (Spring 1991), pp. 63-65; on Kessler in Kansas City, see: Wilson, *The City Beautiful Movement*, pp. 99-125. Also, George E. Kessler Papers, Missouri Historical Society Archives, St. Louis (hereafter: Kessler Papers). Historians have attempted to link the development of the City Beautiful movement to the 1893 Chicago Fair. William Wilson and others, however, are now seeing world's fair landscaping as a product of the same impulses that fed the City Beautiful movement and have ceased trying to establish a causal link. See, for example: Wilson, *The City Beautiful Movement*, and Muccigrosso, *Celebrating the New World*.

75. Greenhalgh, *Ephemeral Vistas*, pp. 41-46; Nasaw, *Going Out*, pp. 62-79.

76. Report of the Division of Works, 1905, p. 5, LPE Co. Records, Box 2/Series II/Folder 1.

77. Trennert, "A Resurrection of Native Arts and Crafts," pp. 282ff.

78. Thomas R. MacMechen, "The True and Complete Story of the Pike and Its Attractions," *WFB*, April 1904, pp. 4-34.

79. "Musical Attractions at the Exposition," *WFB*, February 1904, p. 36.

80. Bennitt, ed., *History of the LPE*, p. 704; Report of the Bureau of Music, 1905, LPE Co. Records, Box 9/Series III/Subseries XVI/Folder 1. For a survey of the music at the LPE, see: Liebenguth, "Music at the Louisiana Purchase Exposition," pp. 27-34.

81. David Glassberg, "History and the Public: Legacies of the Progressive Era," *JAH* 73 (March 1987), p. 959.

82. Both David R. Francis and Rolla Wells claimed that the LPE attracted twenty million rather than twelve million visitors. James Neal Primm argues that they fudged their figures, however, to make them comparable to Chicago's numbers by counting concession and pavilion workers when they entered and left the grounds. Primm, *Lion of the Valley*, p. 415. The published "Official Report of Admissions from April 30th to December 1st, 1904," *WFB*, December 1904, p. 44, indicates that there were 12.8 million paid admissions. In addition, there were 6.9 million unpaid admissions, for a total of 19.7 million visitors. According to the report, free admissions consisted almost exclusively of employees, exhibiters, concessionaires, and children, who were admitted free one day per week in the summer and in November.

83. Sam P. Hyde, Photograph Album and World's Fair Memoir, "Recollections of the Fair," 1909, photocopy in Journals and Diaries Collection, Missouri Historical Society Archives, St. Louis. Original in Missouri Historical Society Photographs and Prints Collection (hereafter: Hyde Memoir).

84. Schneiderhahn Diaries, vol. 6, November 26, 1904, Missouri Historical Society Archives, St. Louis (hereafter: Schneiderhahn Diary).

85. On the activities of the LPE Bureau of Press and Publicity, see the Bureau's Report, in LPE Co. Records, Box 11/Series IV/Subseries II/Folder 1.

86. This was the conclusion drawn as a result of John Bodnar's pioneering oral history study of the people who had worked for the Studebaker Corporation in South Bend, Indiana. See: John Bodnar, "Power and Memory in Oral History: Workers and Managers at Studebaker," *JAH* 75 (March 1989), pp. 1201-21, quotation from p. 1202. Of equal importance is Michael Frisch's discovery of the persistence of the apocryphal in memory. See: Frisch, "American History and the Structures of Collective Memory," pp. 1130-55. Similarly significant is David Thelen's conclusion that memory is constructed and not reproduced, and that the process of construction takes place not in isolation but within "the contexts of community, broader politics, and social dynamics." David Thelen, "Memory and American History," *JAH* 75 (March 1989), pp. 1117-29, quotation from p. 1119. See also: Harris, "Memory and the White City," for a study of how the public memory of the Chicago World's Fair has evolved. No such comparable study yet exists for the St. Louis Fair, although the Missouri Historical Society's exhibit *Meet Me at the Fair: Memory, History, and the 1904 World's Fair* does explore this issue.

87. On the Catholic Central Union, see: Philip Gleason, "An Immigrant Group's Interest in Progressive Reform: The Case of the German-American Catholic," *AHR* 73 (December 1967), pp. 367-79, and Claire Marie Bachhuber, "The German-Catholic Elite: Contributions of a Catholic Intellectual and Cultural Elite of German-American Background in Early Twentieth-Century Saint Louis," Ph.D. diss., St. Louis University, 1984, pp. 71-84, 132-35.

88. Biographical data on Schneiderhahn can be found in: Maximilian Schneiderhahn obituary, November 25, 1923, Missouri Historical Society Vertical Files; "Among Our New Acquisitions," *MHSB* 18 (October 1961), p. 71; Attachment to Frederick H. Kreismann letter to George E. Kessler, June 1, 1911, Kessler Papers, Box 3; *Memorial Volume of the Diamond Jubilee of St. Louis University, 1829-1904* (St. Louis: Press of Little & Becker Printing Co., 1904?), p. 307; and Julie A. Willett, "'The Prudes, the Public, and the Motion Pictures: The Movie Censorship Campaign in St. Louis, 1913-1917," *GH* 15 (Spring 1995), pp. 42-55.

89. Schneiderhahn Diary, December 22, 1904.

90. See: Ortes-Barada Family Tree, by J. L. Cunningham, 1979, and the letters of the Philibert siblings, notably Angie, Florence, and Edmund, 1894-1904, in Philibert Family Papers, Missouri Historical Society Archives, St. Louis (hereafter: Philibert Papers). See also: St. Louis City and County Directories, 1866-1920.

91. Philibert's sister Angie, describing an inlaid chessboard tabletop that Edmund had made, wrote to her sister Florence, "he is such a genius." Letter of Angie Philibert to Florence, August 22, 1897, Philibert Papers.

92. Ortes-Barada Family Tree and letters of Frank and Florence McCallion, May 27, 1900, to October 6, 1904, Philibert Papers; St. Louis City Directories.

93. 1880 Missouri Census, E.D. 268, sheet 2, line 32; 1900 Illinois Soundex, E.D. 81, sheet 11, line 46; 1910 Illinois Census, E.D. 82, sheet 1, line 74; *Belleville Advocate*, May 18, 1898, and January 29, 1904; *Belleville Daily Advocate*, February 22, 1910, and June 19, 1913; Belleville, Illinois, City Directory, 1896.

94. Hyde Memoir.

95. Brueggemann, "St. Louis' 1904 World's Fair."

96. Florence McCallion to Frank, September 24, 1904, Philibert Papers.

97. Hyde Memoir.
98. McCallion to Frank, September 24, 1904, and Edmund Philibert World's Fair Diary, November 26, 1904, Philibert Papers. Edmund Philibert's Diary will hereafter be cited simply as "Philibert Diary."
99. Schneiderhahn Memoir.
100. Ibid.
101. Ibid.
102. Schneiderhahn Diary, September 20, 1904.
103. Philibert Diary, October 29, 1904.
104. Ibid., September 28 and October 29, 1904.
105. Schneiderhahn Diary, July 1, 1904.
106. Philibert Diary, September 3, 1904.
107. Hyde Memoir.
108. Glassberg, "History and the Public."
109. Hyde Memoir.
110. Schneiderhahn Memoir.
111. Schneiderhahn Diary, April 30, 1904.
112. Ibid., December 1, 1904.
113. Schneiderhahn Memoir.
114. Ibid.
115. Ibid.
116. Ibid.
117. Hyde Memoir.
118. Philibert Diary, September 3, 1904.
119. Takada, "Image of a Modern Nation."
120. See the section headed "How Japan Has Already Won What She Fights For," in: "The March of Events—An Editorial Interpretation," *WW*, August 1904, pp. 5207-8.
121. Frederick Starr, *The Ainu Group at the Saint Louis Exposition* (Chicago: Open Court Publishing Company, 1904), p. 110.
122. McCallion to Frank, July 24, 1904, Philibert Papers.
123. Philibert Diary, passim.
124. Schneiderhahn Memoir.
125. Ibid.
126. Admiration of Japanese "imitativeness" was a common element in the American view of the Japanese in the late nineteenth and early twentieth centuries. See: the introductory comments of Robert A. Rosenstone, "Learning from Those 'Imitative' Japanese: Another Side of the American Experience in the Mikado's Empire" *AHR* 85 (June 1980), p. 572. "This image is a comfortable one," Rosenstone wrote, "It helped underwrite arguments for Manifest Destiny and justify expansion into the Pacific by confirming the pleasant idea that the United States was in the forefront of civilized nations, helping to bring the benefits of Western life to those who were unenlightened but anxious to receive the word."
127. Hyde Memoir.
128. Schneiderhahn Diary, November 26, 1904.
129. Schneiderhahn Memoir.
130. Ibid.
131. Ibid.
132. Hyde Memoir.
133. George R. Leighton, "World's Fairs: From Little Egypt to Robert Moses," *Harper's Magazine* (July 1960), pp. 27, 32.

134. Schneiderhahn Diary, April 30, 1904.
135. Hyde Memoir.
136. Philibert Diary, passim.
137. Ibid., July 30, 1904.
138. McCallion to Frank, July 24, 1904, Philibert Papers.
139. Schneiderhahn Diary, November 29 and 30, 1904.
140. Ibid., May 19, 1904.
141. Hyde Memoir.
142. Schneiderhahn Diary, December 1, 1904.
143. Ibid., September 20, 1904.
144. Hyde Memoir.
145. Philibert Diary, passim.
146. McCallion's World's Fair letters, passim, Philibert Papers.
147. Philibert Diary, passim.
148. Schneiderhahn Diary, November 26, 1904.
149. McCallion to Frank, September 24, 1904, Philibert Papers.
150. Hyde Memoir.
151. Philibert Diary, November 12, 1904.
152. Ibid., November 30, 1904.
153. Ibid., May 28, 1904.
154. Hyde Memoir. "Francis" is a reference to David R. Francis, President of the LPE Company.
155. Edmund Philibert's World's Fair expenses, April 30-December 1, 1904, Philibert Papers (hereafter: Philibert Expenses). The average per day cost was arrived at by totaling Philibert's recorded costs and dividing the total by twenty-eight, the number of Fair visits he made.
156. This was the rate paid union carpenters who worked for the LPE Company. Report of the Division of Works, 1905, p. 32, LPE Co. Records, Box 2/Series II/Folder 1. There is no evidence in the Philibert Papers that Edmund Philibert was paid at this scale, or that he was even consistently working.
157. Schneiderhahn Memoir.
158. Hyde Memoir.
159. McCallion to Frank, July 24, 1904, Philibert Papers.
160. Schneiderhahn Diary, November 11-25, 1904.
161. Philibert's frenetic efforts to see everything become particularly evident beginning with his visit of November 22. On his visits of November 10, 12, and 19, he spent an uncharacteristically large amount of money on Pike events. Philibert Diary, passim, and Philibert Expenses.
162. Schneiderhahn Memoir.
163. Hyde Memoir.
164. McCallion to Frank, May 7, 1905, Philibert Papers.
165. Schneiderhahn Diary, December 1, 1904.
166. Philibert Diary, November 30, 1904.
167. Ibid., December 1, 1904.
168. Ibid.
169. Schneiderhahn Diary, December 1, 1904.
170. Hyde Memoir.
171. McCallion to Frank, May 7, 1905, Philibert Papers.
172. Glassberg, "History and the Public," p. 958.
173. McCallion to Frank, September 24, 1904, Philibert Papers.
174. Hyde Memoir.

Edward V. P. Schneiderhahn

Edward V. P. Schneiderhahn. *Halftone, from* Zum Andenken an die Neunundvierzigsten Generalversammlung des Deutschen Roemisch-Katholischen Central-Vereins gehalten in St. Louis, Mo., den 11., 12., 13. and 14. September 1904.

The most sophisticated of the Fair visitors whose writings are included in this volume was Edward V. P. Schneiderhahn. The son of a German-American sculptor of religious art, Schneiderhahn was a St. Louis attorney in private practice with a promising career ahead of him. He was deeply Catholic, well educated, and socially quite conservative. An avid diarist, Schneiderhahn wrote because "it is a good training, if for nothing else than to develop character and the habit of observation." Not surprisingly, his 1904 entries are peppered with references to his multiple visits to the Fair, relevant excerpts of which are reproduced here. After the close of the Fair, he composed a twenty-six-page World's Fair memoir, which is reprinted in its entirety. His lyrical descriptions of what he termed "The Fair in General" still evoke a vivid image of the Fair's "Main Picture."

View north, past the Louisiana Monument, toward Festival Hall. *Photograph, 1904. Schneiderhahn found the Fair's nude statuary, such as this figure at the base of the Louisiana Monument, offensive.*

World's Fair Diary

April 30[1]

Worked part of morning. Afterwards with Adolph[2] went to World's Fair. Opening. The picture is grand. The scale immense. The distances enormous. It is a pity that there are so many statues exhibited even on the grounds absolutely naked. In Chicago[3] it was worse but in no place is there any excuse for this. A proper respect for man, if not decency, ought to be sufficient motive to omit such unnecessary exposure. In the Pike parade[4] too there were some women advertising respective shows by a wanton exposure of their persons. What folly and what a shame. The women advertising "Paris"[5] were of course the most shameless. What good woman would find it possible to expose her person in that manner? None? Just think of the full dress of "ladies." Is there any difference? None except in the number of beholders. And if it be answered that the exposure is not made to be gazed on, the answer may well be, what is it made for, as it is impossible to behold the person without beholding the exposure.

Illumination at night was wonderful far surpassing in brilliancy and grandeur the Chicago exposition. We are so accustomed to the use of superlatives that it is difficult to select adequate terms.

In later notes will take more detailed notice of the Fair and of the several buildings and the exhibits.

1. Schneiderhahn Diaries, select entries, April 30-December 1, 1904, vol. 6, pp. 26-66, Missouri Historical Society Archives.
2. One of Schneiderhahn's younger brothers. Obituary of Maximilian Schneiderhahn, November 25, 1923, Missouri Historical Society Vertical Files (hereafter: MHS Vertical Files).
3. A reference to the World's Columbian Exposition held in Chicago in 1893.
4. The Pike, comparable to the Midway at the 1893 Chicago World's Fair, was the site of the Fair's popular entertainments, sideshows, and rides. Characteristically, a number of the Pike attractions featured exotic peoples and purported to re-create faraway places. A parade of the Pike entertainers was part of the opening day festivities. On the Pike, see: MacMechen, "True and Complete Story of the Pike," "The Creators of the Pike," *WFB*, April 1904, pp. 46-51, and Sprague, "Meet Me in St. Louis on the Ten-Million-Dollar Pike." For a description of the Pike Parade, see: "The Pike Parade," *WFB*, May 1904, pp. 68-69.
5. One of the Pike attractions, "Paris and the French Village," was described by MacMechen as "a reflection of the lively life of the center of fashion" and included a vaudeville.

"The Galveston Flood." *Photograph, 1904. One of the Pike entertainments, this concession claimed to re-create the Galveston, Texas, flood of September 8, 1900, that killed five thousand people in the worst tidal wave disaster in the history of the United States.*

May 19

Worked hard in morning. In afternoon met Rev. brother[6] at Fair. It was a most beautiful day. There is so much to admire and see. Stopped in in the transportation building.[7] The American locomotive machinery far superior. But had no time to stop as we desired to see the buildings. Did not get to see them all. Impossible to describe the beauty of some of them. There is so much going on, concerts and meetings etc. that this is truly a world's meeting.

June 15

Quite a number of conferences to-day. Proceeded well with two matters. Busy in conferences for part of afternoon. Afterwards with Rev. Max went to Fair. After getting there a storm came up and it rained heavily for quite a while. Remained the greater time in the Missouri Building which is lavishly decorated and furnished. It is too bad that this is a mere temporary structure.[8] After the rain had ceased to some extent had supper and then went on the Pike. The Galveston Flood is a most realistic and interesting production. The stage is enormous and the storm scene etc. striking and wonderfully natural. Visited Battle Abbey.[9] The cyclorama of

6. Probably a reference to Maximilian Schneiderhahn, Edward's older brother, who took holy orders and as of 1904 served his ministry at St. Rose of Lima's Church in Silver Lake, Mo. See his biographical entry in *Diamond Jubilee of St. Louis University*, p. 307.

7. The Transportation Building was one of the eight great exhibit palaces that—along with the U.S. Government Building, Festival Hall and the Colonnade of States, and the Cascades and lagoons—formed the focal point, or "Main Picture," of the fairgrounds. These buildings were temporary structures made of staff, a plaster and straw mixture, applied to a wooden frame. They were heavily adorned with statuary, also made of staff. Of these buildings, only the U.S. Government Building was steel framed. *Official Guide*, p. 22. On the construction techniques, see: Report of the Division of Works, 1905, pp. 44-50, LPE Co. Records, Box 2/Series II/Folder 1.

8. One of the state pavilions built by state or territorial governments or commissions to showcase and promote the state and to provide a site of official state receptions. Of these buildings, the Missouri Building was the largest. It was designed by the Fair's Director of Works, Isaac S. Taylor, and stood on high ground south of the U.S. Government Building. For descriptions of the various state buildings, see: *Official Guide*, pp. 105-15. See also: Bennitt, ed., *History of the LPE*, p. 422. Like the great exhibit palaces, the state pavilions were also temporary structures, although some of them were soundly enough built to permit their relocation after the Fair. The Missouri Building, however, was destroyed by fire on the evening of November 19, 1904, toward the end of the Fair. See Edmund Philibert's diary entry for November 19, 1904, for a description of this event, pp. 103-4. The World's Fair Pavilion, built after the close of the Fair, stands today on the site of the Missouri Building. Caroline Loughlin and Catherine Anderson, *Forest Park* (Columbia: The Junior League of St. Louis and the University of Missouri Press, 1986), p. 250.

9. A Pike attraction, "Battle Abbey" presented the "battle history of the American Republic in cyclorama." In addition to Gettysburg, its cycloramas portrayed the battles of Yorktown (Revolutionary War), New Orleans (War of 1812), Buena Vista (Mexican War), Manila (Spanish-American War), Manassas (Civil War), and Custer's last stand.

Fireworks at Festival Hall on Closing Night. *Photograph, 1904. 120,000 incandescent lights lit the fairgrounds and outlined the architectural features of the exhibit palaces at night, while fireworks periodically lit up the sky.*

the battle of Gettysburg was especially interesting to you because you had just finished reading an account in Lossing[10] on the subject. The lecture was very instructive and it was easy for you to fix the points. The village, seminary, cemetery, peach orchard etc. Noted the absence from the screen of the mass of dead and wounded that should have been indicated if the cyclorama, as stated, was the close of the third day's battle. For certainly even if all the wounded and dead from the previous days had been removed the third day was also a day of havoc. But for a picture of the battlefield it was certainly most instructive. Mere reading could not supplant it. There were in the museum many interesting relics of war and war times, and some paintings of noted American battles.

Saw Jim Key the educated horse.[11] It must have cost immense labor to train this animal. Can spell, etc. and does some really wonderful things.

Also went into the Temple of Mirth.[12] The illusions with the mirrors are laughable. Thin and long, fat and powerful, short legs and long head etc. keep one continually laughing.

July 4
Independence Day.

Read the Declaration of Independence. It always sends a thrill through you to read the opening sentence "When in the course of human events. . . ." With Julia[13] and Adolph went to Fair. Remained in Government Building[14] and learned much. Must go back to that section which contains raised map of Gettysburg. Rain. Rain. Rain.

The illumination at night of Festival Hall and States Terrace was wonderful. White, green and red electric illumination.

The rain kept many away from the Fair. It was wonderfully quiet at the Fair. Very agreeable to escape the senseless noise.

10. A reference to Benson J. Lossing, *A History of the Civil War, 1861-65, and the Causes that Led up to the Great Conflict* (New York, 1895). Schneiderhahn characteristically referred to himself in the second person throughout his diaries.
11. Jim Key was an Arabian hambeltonian, owned by Albert R. Rogers of New York.
12. Often referred to as the "Foolish House" or "House of Mirth."
13. Edward's sister, later known as Sister Valeria when she joined the Notre Dame Order. Obituary of Maximilian Schneiderhahn, MHS Vertical Files.
14. The U.S. Government Building, located at the east edge of the Main Picture, was the main site of the United States Government exhibits documenting the various executive departments, including State, Treasury, War, Justice, Post Office, Navy, Interior, and Agriculture. See: Bennitt, ed., *History of the LPE*, pp. 321-41, and *Official Guide*, pp. 94-104.

July 14

Attended to some business in Administration Bldg.[15] World's Fair for Central Verein convention matter.[16] Remained at Fair remainder of day. Met the Misses F. in the Government Bldg. and took notes. The weather towards [evening] was very threatening. But remained. On coming home saw that there must have been a severe rain storm downtown.[17] At the Fair it had not rained a drop. After you were home it began to storm again and continued to storm the entire night.

July 30

In morning hard at work. Good progress in one matter. In afternoon at Fair with Julia. At Government Building. A person could spend a whole week in this building alone. The afternoon transportation parade was most interesting. The division of the St. Louis Car Co. was especially interesting on account of the number of employees all neatly uniformed.[18]

Aug 4

Made satisfactory advances in some work in morning. In afternoon worked on some law points.

In evening with Papa[19] at splendid massed band concert at World's Fair.[20]

Aug 12 & 13

Hard work. In the afternoon of 13th at World's Fair at Philippine exhibition. The drill of the Philippine scouts and troops was instructive and a splendid exhibition. The sham battle made an unusual and exciting spectacle. Did not feel well enough to do any serious work.

Sep 12

Saw to it that the members of the Centre party of Germany were invited by the Central Verein Convention. Said members are now in St. Louis as delegates to the Interparliamentary Peace Congress. Had met Herr Dr. Hauptmann one of the delegates and found him a most estimable gentleman. Could not attend the Convention sessions and was sorry for the speeches would have been most interesting to you.[21]

September 15
St. Louis Day at Fair.[22]

In morning went to St. Charles to try case set for to-day. But it was laid over after some delay. An unwelcome incident occurred in the matter before this which might well have been avoided. With Mr. D. went to Fair direct from St. Charles. Not the mass of people at Fair as were in Chicago Fair on Chicago Day. Not to be expected.

---

15. One of the Fair's few permanent structures, the Administration Building today is Brookings Hall, the administration building for Washington University. The University, which built its new campus at the west edge of Forest Park, leased its new buildings and grounds to the Exposition Company in December 1901, deferring its own occupancy of the new campus until January 1905. *Official Guide*, p. 91, and Report of the Division of Works, 1905, p. 4., LPE Co. Records, Box 2/Series II/Folder 1.

16. The Katholische Central-Verein, or Catholic Central Union, was and is a conservative German Catholic association involved in social reform activities. Its annual convention met in St. Louis September 11-14, 1904. Though it did not convene on the fairgrounds, the convention schedule called for September 15 to be a "World's Fair Day" for Central-Verein members. Schneiderhahn served as chairman of the information bureau for the St. Louis convention. See: *Zum Andenken an die Neunundvierzigste Generalversammlung des Deutschen Roemisch-Katholischen Central-Vereins gehalten in St. Louis, Mo., den 11., 12., und 13. September 1904* (St. Louis: n.p., 1904).

17. Schneiderhahn's home, where he lived with his father, stepmother, and younger siblings, was located at 1129 South Seventh, just at the southern edge of downtown St. Louis. *St. Louis City Directory*, 1904.

18. Railroad and Transportation Day was one of the special celebration days of the World's Fair. Devoted to the transportation interests represented at the Fair, festivities included both a water and a land transportation parade. The St. Louis Car Company, a manufacturer of rolling stock, was represented by three thousand of its St. Louis employees, drilling in formation. *Daily Official Program, World's Fair, St. Louis*, July 30, 1904, and *St. Louis Car Co. at the Universal Exposition, St. Louis, U.S.A., 1904* (St. Louis?, 1904?).

19. Edward's father, St. Louis sculptor Maximilian Schneiderhahn, 1844?-1923. Obituary of Maximilian Schneiderhahn, MHS Vertical Files.

20. Massed band concerts were held in Festival Hall in the summer, with William Weil's band, F. Fanciulli's band, and Emil Mollenhauer and Max Zach's Boston Band each playing first under the direction of their individual leaders and then concluding the evening with the three bands playing together. The August 4 concert was the second such performance. *Daily Official Program*, August 4, 1904, p. 2. These concerts were soon discontinued due to the acoustical difficulties in Festival Hall. Bennitt, ed., *History of the LPE*, p. 706.

21. This conference was one of several international congresses staged at the World's Fair. Actually a meeting of the Interparliamentary Union, an international association of legislators founded in 1888, it had met at the Paris Exposition of 1889 and convened at the St. Louis World's Fair from September 12 to 14, 1904. Dr. Hauptmann of the Catholic Center Party in Germany was one of four German parliamentarians attending the Congress. Bennitt, ed., *History of the LPE*, p. 690; Samuel J. Barrows, *Tour of the Interparliamentary Union Tendered by the Government of the United States* (Washington, D.C.: Government Printing Office, 1905), p. 266.

22. One of the more significant special days was St. Louis Day. Its celebrations and ceremonies encompassed the entirety of the fairgrounds. *Daily Official Program*, September 15, 1904.

Philippine Troops on Parade. *Photograph by Jessie Tarbox Beals, 1904. Officered by Americans, the Philippine troops attracted the attention of Fair visitors impressed by their precision drills.*

The Filipino Scouts and Constabulary

The Philippine Scouts, four hundred of whom were encamped on the fairgrounds for the duration of the Fair, were Filipino soldiers under the command of regular American army officers. Consisting of four units of one hundred men each, they were accompanied by a band of forty-one instruments and were encamped on the grounds of the Philippine Exposition. A virtual fair within a fair, the Philippine Exposition was arranged by the American Insular Government of the Philippine Islands as a way of encouraging American popular support for and economic investment in the newly acquired American colony. The drill of the Philippine Scouts was a regular event conducted for the duration of the Fair.

Companies of Filipino soldiers had been first organized to aid in the suppression of the Philippine Insurrection during the Spanish-American War as early as 1899. In 1901, the U.S. Congress formally authorized the formation of Filipino units, and then in 1902 authorized their use in the support of the civil establishment in the Philippines, after which the Scouts formed a part of the Insular Police. The

Philippine Scouts should not be confused with the Philippine Constabulary, which was organized in 1901 by William Howard Taft. When Taft assumed the office of Civil Governor of the Philippine Islands from the American military, he organized the Constabulary as a domestic military force under the command of American officers. Like the Scouts, the Constabulary was represented at the World's Fair by a specially selected battalion of 280 men, 80 of whom formed the Constabulary Band.

The "sham battle" was a one-time event consisting of a simulated night battle in which the Philippine Scouts repulsed an attack. It was staged on the evening of August 13, 1904, as part of the Philippine Day festivities at the Fair; the date marked the sixth anniversary of the capture of Manila by American troops during the Spanish-American War. On the Philippine Scouts, Constabulary, and the "sham battle," see: Bennitt, *History of the LPE*, p. 475; *Official Guide*, pp. 122-23; Newell, ed. and comp., *Philippine Exposition*; Vostral, "Imperialism on Display"; *Official Catalogue Philippine Exhibits*, p. 269-71.

Detailed View of the Westinghouse Exhibit. *Photograph, 1904. These four 3,000 horsepower steam engines were among those that impressed Schneiderhahn in the Palace of Machinery's massive Westinghouse exhibit.*

But certainly more, many more, would have come if they could have had assurance of transportation facilities.[23]

It was a perfect day. The crowds were inspiring. Went through the east half of the Transportation Building. The locomotive exhibit is certainly very instructive. Met Julia, Alf,[24] & Adolph by accident.

Saw the Fire Works which were beautiful.

It was an ideal day. Sorry you have no time for further comment. It was a great day.

Sep 20

At office in morning. Attended to a good many matters. In afternoon at Fair. In Machinery Building. Astounding mechanical contrivances. Enormous engines. Monster Cranes. Attended lecture in Westinghouse exhibit. Learned much. Will go again to lecture and learn the lesson better. Examined a steam turbine engine, the first you have seen. Understand now the reason of its greater efficiency and enormous speed when compared with other steam engines. Have read so much and never could get a very clear understanding. The steam turbine engine will work a revolution in steam engines.

In evening attended fine concert given by French band. It is unsatisfactory to be alone at the Fair but no one would go with you. Must go when you can. And so must go alone.

Oct 6, 7

Hard work. At Fair for German Day celebration [on the] 6th.

Oct 8

Worked in morning. In afternoon and evening at Fair. In evening enjoyed wonderful Wagner concert by the Berlin Band. The Exposition Company is certainly furnishing wonderful music. The Grenadier Band of London, The Garde Republicaine Band, Paris, and the Berlin Band combine to make the musical feature of the Fair an undoubted success. All these three bands are at present at the Exposition. Do not expect to ever have a like opportunity.

Oct 13, 14, 15

Worked hard. On Saturday went to college to confession.

We are having most beautiful weather. The air is balmy and invigorating. Sorry you cannot get away and go to the Fair.

---

23. Transportation was a concern from the very beginning and was one of the reasons why there was some initial skepticism about using Forest Park as a site for the Fair. See: Mutschnick, "St. Louis Prepares for a World's Fair," p. 28. As opening day approached, the Fair company's Committee on Grounds and Buildings expressed concern over the availability of adequate traffic accommodation to the fairgrounds when it lobbied the City of St. Louis to widen and improve Lindell Boulevard and extend it to DeBaliviere, the location of the Fair's Main Entrance. Minutes of the Committee on Grounds and Buildings, October 16, 1902, LPE Co. Records, Box 2/Series II/Subseries I/Folder 3. The *Official Guide*, p. 16, reported that streetcar lines and railroads could transport up to eighty thousand people to the Fair per hour.

24. Alf is presumably Alphonse Schneiderhahn, another of Edward's brothers. Obituary of Maximilian Schneiderhahn, MHS Vertical Files.

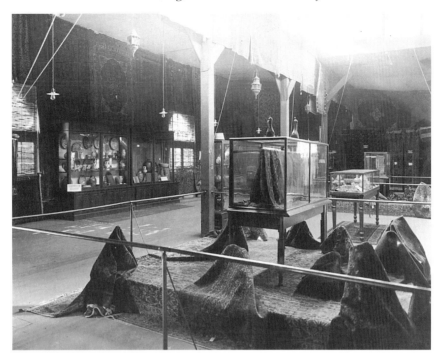

Persian Rug Exhibit, Palace of Varied Industries. *Photograph, 1904. Schneiderhahn found these exotic Eastern hand-crafted rugs unappealing. Simpler rugs were more to his taste.*

Oct 18

Very busy in morning and disposed of three matters. Glad to have them settled satisfactorily.

In afternoon attended diamond jubilee celebration of St. Louis University in Festival Hall World's Fair. There was a distinguished gathering present. President Francis spoke well. But the acoustic properties of the Hall of the poorest. Judge Barclay a splendid chairman. Some Honorary degrees conferred. Doctor of Laws—on Pres. Francis—Justice White and others Master of Arts on Architect Taylor[25]— Chief of Construction—World's Fair—Met Messrs. Gerber and Jennemann[26] at separate times and together we had a pleasant time for some two hours.

In evening at banquet St. Louis University. In point of attendance an immense success. Hope that University will receive some substantial benefit from the impetus given by the Celebration.

Oct 22

Worked hard in morning. With Miss F. went out to Fair and met Alphonse at the Fair. Learned much in varied industries Building.[27] Miniature Swiss carving—wonderful—Persian rugs despite their cost $17,000 for one do not appeal to you—Like the commoner rugs better—Japanese section—wilderness of pottery—clouds of fine needle work. Their every work marvelous. Elephant tusks carved into processions of elephants and other animals. Could not begin to even enumerate the most strange of these works. Thoroughly enjoyed the day. And it is about time to get thoroughly to work. Else the Exposition closes and you have not had the proper benefit.

25. David R. Francis, 1850-1927, President of the Louisiana Purchase Exposition Company; Judge Shepard Barclay, 1847-1925, St. Louis attorney and Missouri Supreme Court Justice; Edward Douglass White, 1845-1921, Associate Justice of the United States Supreme Court from 1894, named chief justice in 1910; Isaac S. Taylor, 1851-1917, St. Louis architect, Chairman of the Commission of Architects that designed the fairgrounds and the building scheme, and Director of Works for the Louisiana Purchase Exposition Company. On the St. Louis University Day Festivities, see: *Daily Official Program*, October 18, 1904, and *Diamond Jubilee of St. Louis University*, p. 218.
26. Most probably Charles Gerber and Theodore Jennemann, both associates of Schneiderhahn's in the German Catholic Central-Verein.
27. One of the eight exhibit palaces in the Main Picture, the Varied Industries Building, along with the Manufactures Building, housed the exhibits of the Department of Manufactures.

German Exhibit, Palace of Fine Arts. *Photograph, 1904. These paintings in the German section in the Palace of Art were of a style that Schneiderhahn found appealing—"classic and perfect."*

Nov 8
Election Day.
Went to Church. Voted. Republican ticket. What have the Democrats to offer but discord. Scratched some unworthy Republicans. . . .

Went to Fair. In Education Building. Learned much in the charity work section.

In evening downtown—election returns. . . .

Nov 11-25 incl.
Worked hard and put in every spare minute at the Fair.

Nov 26
Worked hard in morning. Disposed of some detail work. With Alf went to Fair. Part of the foreign section of Art Gallery.[28] Impressionistic and realistic schools predominant. Pictures that received prizes are mediocre compared to some beautiful pictures that received no mention. The majority of the jury[29] must have been of those schools and obdurate against every other claim. That is so patent that a blind man may see it. The historic paintings in the German section are classic and perfect. They are the best. What far fetched titles some artists use. Some subjects are, from an intellectual standpoint, simply ridiculous, though the criticism might be strongest upon other grounds. It is downright foolish to talk of "art for art's sake."[30] What is the sense of this. Law for law's sake—Government for government's sake—Industry for industry's sake—Crazy—Idiotic—Surprising that men who claim distinction for superior endowments should subscribe to such intellectual "rot." Abandon is not necessary for art. Happily some few "crazy" men cannot destroy the principles of beauty. And the underlying principle is harmony as you

28. The Art Gallery or Palace of Art was the primary permanent Fair structure, necessary in order to house original works of art. The building today is the home of the Saint Louis Art Museum.

29. Works exhibited within any one of the sixteen exhibit departments at the Fair were judged in competition by an international jury. Judging took place during late summer. On the International Jury, see: Bennitt, ed., *History of the LPE*, pp. 743ff.

30. The "art for art's sake" movement in art and literature was primarily a nineteenth-century French phenomenon best reflected in the novels of Gustave Flaubert. For Flaubert and other adherents to the concept of "art for art's sake" (*l'art pour l'art*), in both literature and the visual arts, pure art or aestheticism became their only religion and marked their divorce from a social commitment to the values of their age. As such, "art for art's sake" often signified a contempt for modernity and middle-class liberal values. For them, art in all of its forms served no higher value, nor did it serve political, social, or moral ends. Likewise they believed that art should reflect reality. Unlike those who sought perfection in art (classicists or academy artists), proponents of the impressionistic and realistic schools of the nineteenth century believed that art should recognize the ugly alongside the beautiful and should not attempt to improve upon nature.

Women Repairing Nets, *by Edgard Farazyn. Photograph of painting, 1904. This painting from the Belgian exhibit in the Palace of Art was of a subject and style that Schneiderhahn might have found to be unsuitable, given its "common" theme, broad brush strokes, and softened detail.*

understand it. Whatever is reckless in this regard, whatever tends to create discord in the beholder is not to be commended. What is it for. The highest mission of art is to elevate and the means are innumerable. Any less conception does not rise to the truth and depresses art to a lower level than is its proper right. "Art for art's sake." Indeed! What does that mean? And the men who talk that way do not mean it themselves. For they themselves would at least exclude some things, some representations, some ideas, some conceptions as "unworthy" although the painting might show ever so much *art*. So art is not for art's sake. The range of art is so wide that any artist that selects an "unworthy" object or idea strikes at himself, dims his own fame.

Met Mrs. R. & daughter and son on going from Fair. Took them to House of Mirth on Pike. Enjoyed their hearty laughing.

President's Day[31] at Fair. Beautiful, clear cool day. Great throngs. Much enthusiasm. Attended concert of Berlin Band. Sorry to lose them. Our taste will be better than our opportunities hereafter. The music that we will be apt to hear will not be up to our standard. Went to confession.

Nov 28

Worked hard in morning. In afternoon at World's Fair. Remainder of foreign section of Art Gallery. Some wonderful paintings. It is too bad that the nakedness depicted on some paintings is

so absolute as to deprive one of the opportunity to really enjoy the picture. The appreciation must be intellectual. Absolute nakedness is as revolting in a picture as any unnecessary exposure of the person would be in life. Too bad. There are some gems of landscape in the French and Italian section—But cannot discuss the whole field.

In evening made a call at V.'s. Mrs. V. in bed again—Having a hard siege—

Nov 29

Hard work in morning. In afternoon met Alf at Fair and went through Manufacturers Building. Have not been able to inspect this building's exhibits very well. It is unthinkable what may all be seen. The mind reels at the mass of various and wonderful exhibits.

Nov 30

Worked very hard in morning. In afternoon went to the Fair. Passed through Liberal Arts Building.[32] German section particularly rich. But coming so late in afternoon could hardly see anything.

In evening at office and wrote in diary. Get too impatient now and must use will power to keep at one thing. A sort of nervous tension to try to do too many things at once. It is ridiculous but the pressure is there. How carefully we must watch over ourselves and how impossible it is for us to be perfect. But we should try. Felt happy at the conquest of will over convenience in the matter of going to office. But was not vain over it. Room for great, great improvement.

December 1

With Alf and Julia went to Fair. Last time. Met the Misses R. at the Fair by appointment. Take particular delight in the fact that they are associated with the memories of the last day of the Fair—a day you will never forget. Later in evening met the Messrs. R. by appointment together with their ladies. Mrs. Hy R. and Mr. W. were also of the party and it was a most jolly party. The two trips up the Pike were made amidst the universal din and with much merriment. But the party's trip in the quieter parts of the World's Fair picture permitted much more real enjoyment. For the crowd on the Pike was

31. President's Day was so named as it was the occasion of President Theodore Roosevelt's visit to the World's Fair.
32. One of the great exhibit palaces in the Main Picture, this building housed exhibits that included printing and bookbinding, musical instruments, and the chemical and pharmaceutical arts. See: *Official Classification of Exhibit Departments*, pp. 6-12.

getting unruly. The end of the line we had formed had much trouble with disturbers. The later the hour the rougher the crowd. Had it not been for an overwhelming force of police and guards the mass of people might have deteriorated into a mob. Strange idea. To celebrate the close of the greatest World's Fair ever held by an attempted rioting—in a small way.

With Alf and Julia, after attending the closing day exercises at the Louisiana monument, passed rapidly through the Manufacturers, Liberal Arts, Government Mines and Education Buildings, not to see anything, but for the purpose of casting a last look on scenes that had become familiar and dear and from which we must part forever. After lunch met the Misses R. as stated. Passed through the Varied Industries and Transportation Buildings. Arriving at the Agriculture Building[33] the doors were being locked and nailed (4 PM). The people were carrying the exhibits off bodily. Could not get in. Went to Philippines to see peculiar drill of scouts at 4:30 which the Misses R. had not seen, and which had been the delight of every World's Fair visitor. But the drill was already over, the programme containing an error. Saw much of the various Philippine exhibits. Afterwards attended a performance by Hale's Fire Fighters on the Pike.[34] Very interesting, very instructive and very thrilling—If we would pay more attention to fire prevention it would be better too—

In the evening we were a numerous party. Had some difficulty in meeting at the Alps.[35] Had a ridiculous experience with an excitable French waiter—French blood—fire up in a minute—boil with rage—in a few minutes whistle a popular tune. Why so much doubt whether French governments are stable? Why so much elation that this French Republic[36] has lasted from '70 to this day? Because the French are quick and prone to change.

After a due regard to the prevailing custom of celebrating the close of the World's Fair by passing up the Pike, and making some noise by blowing horns, we went out into the Main picture to view the Cascades and the beautiful Festival Hall for the last time resplendent in all their indescribable glory. The night was wonderfully mild. Shortly before twelve, midnight, the scene was illuminated by beautiful fireworks, but the German House bells tolled a wonderfully solemn farewell. It was most affecting. There were many about you but your thoughts were your own, and you hardly know whether you could give them aptly and accurately. Geo. R. had to leave with his lady before the close on account of great distance. It would be an incomplete statement, if you would fail to report that you felt grateful in a way, that the thoughts of this historic day would always be coupled with thoughts of the excellent company who had been witnesses with you of the event. At promptly twelve o'clock President Francis turned the switch that controlled the power and the light. The flood of light grew fainter and fainter and of a sudden all was darkness. The Cascades were silent. The scene was dead. The World's Fair no more. Passed into history forever. Reminder of the poets saying "The Boasts of heraldry, the pomp of power and all that beauty all that wealth ever gave, await alike the inevitable hour, the paths of glory lead but to the grave."[37]

Our company passed out of the gate, not entirely silent, for we remarked the want of joviality, but we were altogether grave and very much subdued in spirit. For it was indeed a solemn occasion. It is a hard task to become reconciled to the end of the World's Fair. But everything human will have an end. Sic transit gloria mundi.[38] For the Christian however there is nothing so beautiful here that there is not something more beautiful beyond.

---

33. The Agriculture Building was the single largest of the fairgrounds structures. Not as ornately decorated as the eight great exhibit palaces, it was located on the far western side of the fairgrounds, well removed from the Main Picture.

34. One of the Pike concessions, the "Hale's Fire Fighters Exhibition" was operated by George C. Hale, a former Kansas City fire chief who had led a crew in winning first prize in the International Fire Tournament in London in 1893.

35. "The Tyrolean Alps" was a Pike concession that endeavored to reproduce "the classic beauties of the Alpine village scenery of Europe." "German and Tyrolean Alps," *WFB*, April 1904, p. 52.

36. The Third Republic of France, established in 1870 after the overthrow of Napoleon III during the Franco-Prussian War, survived until the invasion and defeat of France by Germany in 1940.

37. Thomas Gray, 1716-71, *Elegy Written in a Country Churchyard*, stanza 9. The passage actually reads: "The boast of heraldry, the pomp of pow'r / And all that beauty, all that wealth e'er gave, / Await alike the inevitable hour: / The paths of glory lead but to the grave."

38. Latin: "So passes away the glory of this world." Thomas á Kempis, c. 1380-1471, *The Imitation of Christ*, part III, chapter vi.

Concert at the Plaza, "The Tyrolean Alps." *Photograph, 1904. Diners, both outdoors and indoors, could enjoy the scenery of an Alpine village in Europe at the "Tyrolean Alps" concession on the Pike. On closing night, Schneiderhahn encountered "an excitable French waiter" at this spot as he waited to meet his party.*

Edward V. P. Schneiderhahn

General View of the Fairgrounds. *Photograph, 1904. This view, looking west along Louisiana Way, pictures the Palace of Education on the left, the corner of the Palace of Manufactures on the right, and the Palace of Varied Industries in the center.*

World's Fair Memoir

The World's Fair

Have felt the necessity of writing a more concentrated article on the World's Fair.[1] It did not seem right to pass that subject with the few disconnected and scant memoranda you had been able to make. And like everything, that, being worthy of special mention, deserves an appropriate introduction, so this article too might be properly commenced by a reference at least to the occasion to which indirectly it owed its birth. It is Sunday to-day. You have leisure. It is snowing out. The room is warm and you like to write something about the Fair. All seems present that might afford the opportunity. Yet do not intend to make an elaborate article, but will write down the present inspiration.

Historic

The World's Fair served to commemorate the acquisition by the United States by purchase from France of the territory known as the Louisiana Territory. Hence the World's Fair Company was officially styled The Louisiana Purchase Exposition Company. This transfer occurred in 1803. A hundred years seems a long time but it is not. You have already lived over 30 years—like nothing—70 years more—or an addition to your age of about twice the time that seems like nothing—would give us the 100 years. The World's Fair is the Centennial of that event. What changes have taken place in that short time? The wilderness has been dotted with a great number of cities—in fact the whole wilderness has been changed. States have been carved out of the acquired territory, many of them containing many millions of inhabitants. In hundreds—in thousands of ways what a surprising what a colossal metamorphosis has been effected in that short time 100 years! And all that vast territory acquired for the small sum of $15,000,000. And it has always appeared strange to you how Jefferson could hesitate about the purchase on "constitutional" grounds;—how he could assert that in making the purchase "the constitution had been stretched until it cracked."[2] This has always seemed to you as the declaration of a man that favored a "narrow" view of the Constitution. The plain truth of the matter is, prescinding for the moment from the Constitution, that every government possesses those powers, which are necessary to its own safety and the safety of the people. A government which does not possess those powers is a government which not alone is fit to be abolished, but one which for the safety of its own people ought to be abolished. And besides the constitutional scruple was extremely far fetched. Jefferson however did go to an extreme in practically closing the purchase and then putting the Congress into the dilemma of either voting the money for a completed transaction or of repudiating their own President. However this is another matter. The Purchase was made and at St. Louis was to be held a World's Fair to celebrate the Centennial of that event.[3] Congress, St. Louis as a corporation and its citizens, Missouri and other States and Foreign Nations voted liberal sums to participate[4] and it was evident long before the gates would be open that the Fair was to be on a scale of almost unthinkable magnificence. A delay occurred by which the celebration was postponed to 1904.[5]

---

1. Schneiderhahn Memoir, in the Schneiderhahn Diaries, vol. 6, pp. 67-92. Schneiderhahn wrote this essay in several sittings between December 11 and 22, 1904, a fact which can be ascertained from small notations at the end of each installment in the original manuscript.
2. Thomas Jefferson, 1743-1826, third president of the United States, 1801-9. The United States purchased the Louisiana Territory during his administration. On Jefferson and the Louisiana Purchase, see: Dumas Malone, *Jefferson the President: First Term, 1801-1805*, vol. 4 of *Jefferson and His Time* (Boston: Little, Brown & Co., 1970), and Alexander DeConde, *This Affair of Louisiana* (New York: Charles Scribner's Sons, 1976).
3. On the history of the movement to bring the Louisiana Purchase Exposition to St. Louis, see: Bennitt, ed., *History of the LPE*, pp. 81-95, and Mutschnick, "St. Louis Prepares for a World's Fair," pp. 5-6.
4. Congress and the City of St. Louis each authorized five million dollars to finance the World's Fair, while another five million was raised by private subscription. State governments, foreign nations, and private exhibitors and concessionaires each funded their own participation. Bennitt, ed., *History of the LPE*, p. 93; Mutschnick, "St. Louis Prepares for a World's Fair," pp. 14-24.
5. On the delay of the Fair, see: Bennitt, ed., *History of the LPE*, pp. 95, 118.

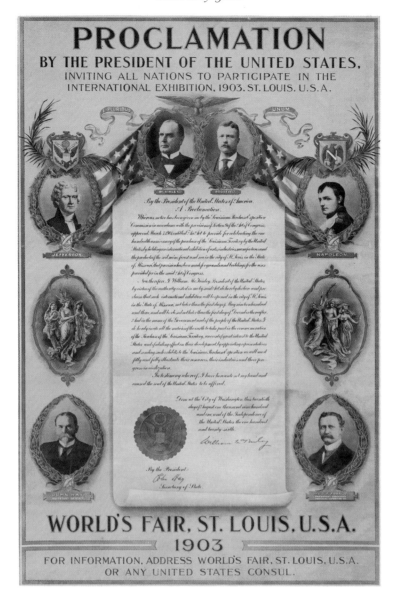

Proclamation by the President of the United States Inviting All Nations to Participate in the International Exhibition, 1903, St. Louis, U.S.A. *Color lithograph, Louisiana Purchase Exposition Company, c. 1901. The Louisiana Purchase Exposition, initially planned for 1903, was postponed for a year.*

Forest Park Site and Preexposition Period

The site selected was the western half of Forest Park.[6] There was a great advantage in this site for picture effects over the site that Chicago had had for its Fair in 1893.[7] The Chicago site was a dead flat. But the Forest Park site was very different. There were prominent hills and while this fact made the construction work more difficult, it enabled at least part of the exposition buildings to be erected so as to take advantage of the elevation and enhance both their own beauty and the beauty of the surroundings. It was a pity however to see giant monarchs of the forest fall before the woodman's ax to make room for the

---

6. Other sites considered included O'Fallon Park, St. Louis Fairgrounds, Prospect Heights and Baden in northern St. Louis, Carondelet Park in south St. Louis, as well as sites on the northwestern and southwestern edges of the city. Loughlin and Anderson, *Forest Park*, pp. 62-66, see especially the map on p. 65; also Mutschnick, "St. Louis Prepares for a World's Fair," pp. 25-29.
7. The 1893 Chicago World's Fair was situated in Jackson Park on Lake Michigan, south of Chicago's downtown.

exhibit palaces. Standing on one of the hills, in the preexposition period, one could see a whole plain that had been swept bare of patriarchs of the forest such as few cities could boast to possess. As time passed it was found that the originally selected grounds had proved inadequate. Large additions were made into the County and almost at the latest moment a tract to the north of the Park was leased which was to become the situs of the attractions that were subsequently and comprehensively grouped under the name "The Pike."[8]

Have gone out to the Fair sometimes on Sundays during the preexposition period, and enjoyed a quiet stroll among the buildings which became prettier every month. It was a pleasure to walk along among the completed exhibit palaces and admire their graceful outline and splendid proportions. Such a ramble always repaid itself splendidly in new courage and energy.

The Fair In General

The picture of the Fair was as a revelation. Its beauty indescribable. Standing in the Place St. Louis and looking south, the eye met the Louisiana monument,[9] an ornamental towering column surmounted by the statue of "Peace" and decorated with tablets and reliefs commemorating the Purchase. Passing the monument and still looking south the eye beheld the grand lagoon and at its further end the beautiful cascades taking their origin out of the main centre of the classic and inspiring and majestic Festival Hall. The Festival Hall was flanked by two gracefully curved rows of colonnades serving as the background for the Louisiana Purchase States[10] statues erected in front on the Terrace of States. Each wing of the colonnades pointed to an architectural gem.

Festival Hall and the Cascades. *Hand-colored photograph, 1904. The focal point of the Main Picture, Festival Hall and the Cascades never ceased to draw the attention of Fair visitors.*

8. This site, known as the Catlin Tract, was not leased by the Fair company until June 1903. LPE Co. press release, statement of D. R. Francis, June 12, 1903, David R. Francis Papers, Missouri Historical Society Archives, St. Louis.
9. The Louisiana Monument, commemorating the Louisiana Purchase, was the site of the of the opening and closing ceremonies. Designed by Karl Bitter, Chief of Sculpture, it was located on the Plaza of St. Louis at the north end of the Grand Basin.
10. There were fourteen colonnades with statuary atop, each representing one of the states or territories carved out of the Louisiana Purchase Territory. They were Louisiana, Arkansas, Missouri, Iowa, North Dakota, South Dakota, Nebraska, Oklahoma, Kansas, Colorado, Wyoming, Montana, Minnesota, and the Indian Territory. As of 1904, present-day Oklahoma was split between the Oklahoma Territory (west) and the Indian Territory (east) and remained so until 1907.

Before the east building was erected a fountain surmounted by a symbolic representation of the "Pacific Ocean" and before the west building was erected a fountain surmounted by a symbolic representation of the "Atlantic Ocean." From these fountains descended smaller cascades inclining to the central and main cascade. Festival Hall, the Colonnades, and end wings and colossal fountains all on the so called Art Hill.[11] The combination was simply overpowering. When the Cascades were in operation and the fountains played one could fancy himself transported to fairy land. But when one would consider in addition the magical view from this eminence of the main picture of the Fair words fail. It cannot be even hinted at by words. Stopped at this central point for hours to drink of the magic inspiration that this wonderful spot offered. The main plan of the Fair had been so arranged that the principal avenues met on Art Hill or at least the view was directed there. Consequently from the Festival Hall and the Wings the view was unobstructed to behold the principal great avenues of the Fair. Wish that you could describe it. But your stock of words dealing with niceties and refinements is unfortunately very limited. And if it were so ample as to include all the words of the English language that might be aptly employed to describe dignity, majestic repose, serene grandeur, classic grace, enchanting beauty the description would fall short of the reality. The beauty of this place was such as to fix the beholder to the spot. It was truly wonderful. The view across the lagoon to the Louisiana monument and the Plaza St. Louis beyond, dotted as the scene was with green trees and all the ornament of art, was simply indescribably grand. But it is impossible for language to express the actual reality. We have become so addicted to the use of superlatives in common speech, that when we are taxed for resources of speech, as in this instance, we are at a loss what to do.

View from Festival Hall north toward the Louisiana Monument. *Photograph, 1904. In this, one of many vistas of the Fair, the Grand Basin is pictured in the foreground, with the Palace of Electricity on the left.*

11. Atop Art Hill and behind Festival Hall was the Palace of Art, now the Saint Louis Art Museum. The landscape feature of Art Hill is still in Forest Park and is still so designated. In place of the original formal Grand Basin at the base of Art Hill, there is now an asymetrical lake.

The U.S. Government Building as seen from the Louisiana Monument. *Photograph, 1904. The Sunken Garden, visible from the Government Building, is flanked by the Palace of Mines and Metallurgy on the right and the Palace of Liberal Arts on the left.*

The multiplicity of beautiful views was astonishing. On account of the manner in which the Fair was laid out, focusing toward Festival Hall, the avenues were not all straight. In consequence the eye sweeping down an avenue, would meet an inspiring view caused by the Exposition palaces that flanked the avenues apparently inclining across the avenue. The view from Machinery gardens[12] east was most beautiful. The Varied Industries Building on the left was graced by rows of classic columns that made this a favorite walk. From the Louisiana monument to the Government Building was a wonderful picture. And the Plaza St. Louis flanked by the Varied Industries and Manufacturers Buildings and studded with trees and gems of art was a joy to the beholder. But you despair of even mentioning all the indescribably beautiful places—and the Sunken Gardens—but enough of general description. It is a pity that it is impossible for language to ever adequately describe feelings. And here at the World's Fair—it was scarcely believable that any beholder could see these unforgettably beautiful scenes without the deepest emotion. It has been your wish, when rooted to some spot by its ravishing beauty, that all would be possessed of the opportunity to behold it. A ramble among the buildings along the avenues or on the plazas was a pleasure. Would never tire of the beauty. In fact sometimes, or rather often came to the Fair with the purpose to see something—in the Buildings—but would stop so long on the outside contemplating (the right word) the architectural beauties of the Buildings that there would be little if any time left for inspection of exhibits. And a gentle stroll down Louisiana way would take one midway between the chief exhibit palaces, past the Louisiana Monument and the Sunken Gardens up to the Government Building. Have no hesitancy in saying that during the World's Fair the avenues of the Fair were the most magnificent walks of the whole globe.

12. Machinery Gardens separated the Palace of Machinery and the Palace of Transportation. It and other landscape features of the Fair were designed and laid out by landscape architect George Kessler. On Kessler's role, see the Introduction to this volume, p. 15.

Government Building

The Government Building stood at the eastern head of Louisiana way on a high terrace. It was a large and graceful and well proportioned Building, and the style of architecture seemed to have been well suited to give the building a combination of attractive and imposing qualities all which were strengthened by the eminence on which the building stood.

The exhibits were wonderfully rich and complete. Certainly in variety of the subjects covered and in the manner of display this was the first building of the entire Fair. Stopped quite a while in the Congressional Library division—but no time to examine the old documents and maps exhibited. The irrigation model taught you much. The work of the Treasury Department was in part exhibited by the Mint Division. This exhibit was always crowded. The Signal division contains many problems you had not time to have solved. The War Department exhibit was very interesting to you specially the ordnance division and the West Point exhibit and their textbooks. It was also curious to note what changes had been brought about in the uniforms in our army since the Spanish war, owing to tropical conditions which American soldiers must now encounter. The Agricultural division contained a vast store of information particularly for farmers. The growth of fungi in trees was exhibited in a way that arrested your attention. The soil experiments were also very interesting, so the roadbuilding models and the reclamation of arid lands by working out the salt etc. The Navy Department had a particularly elaborate display. The large model of United States cruiser provided an opportunity to actually become acquainted with the real conditions on board. The torpedoes with their clock work and self propelling device are certainly a devilish contrivance, one might almost say. The natural history division offered an unending field for speculation. The collection of butterflies was a marvelous harmony of color. The prehistoric animals might frighten any beholder by their size. They looked monstrous— These simple casts looked most forbidding and formidable. The model of a whale served to dispel some ignorance. Jaw bones immense.

The Aerolites[13] were strange messengers indeed. The models of ancient Aztec and Yucatan architecture offer many chances for theorizing about departed peoples. The Post Office exhibit was both instructive and amusing. Unbelievable what persons will put in their mail. The briefs of famous men shown in the exhibit of the Department of Justice might serve as commendable examples of brevity. Nowadays the simplest propositions must be elucidated by 1000 pages, metaphorically speaking. Courts are crowded and are apt to lay too much stress on "cases." So that instead of spending much time on the logic of the situation the inquiry degenerates (generally) into mere case hunting.[14]

It is impossible to cover the vast field of inquiry opened up by a somewhat careful study of the Government exhibits. Spent far more time in the aggregate in this Government Building than in any other Building and learned most from the government Building's exhibits.

Liberal Arts

This was the only Exhibit Palace that had employed color in its exterior adornment. The recess wall, that is the upper portion, had been painted red. The tint was well chosen. The columns of the colonnade surrounding the entire Building received an added beauty from this background. Your architectural knowledge is too limited to enable in language to describe your impressions. This tinting of the background acted as it were as a pleasing rest and change to the eye. Always liked to see this Building.

Of the Interior. Cared little for the China section. Somehow it always impressed you as topsy-turvydom, and could not get your mind down to a patient scrutiny, if general, of twisted dragons, fantastic dogs, full bellied figures and a confused mass of carvings, jim-cracks, and—and space occupiers that centre the thought mainly on the time that it took to make these things. The Austrian section exhibited mainly exquisite glassware of indescribable richness and daintiness. The German section was the principal and most interesting exhibit in this Building. From the Bookmaker's art to the making of

---

13. Meteorites.
14. "Case hunting" is a reference to the search for legal precedent.

organs—canal building—river work—signal lighting—sanitary work—women's finery—all exhibited, displayed and explained with characteristic German thoroughness. Have spent a great deal of time in this section and learned much. Have spent hours in the section devoted to children's books. There was an opportunity to learn the genius of a nation, and in part a chance to ascertain why the Germans become, as a rule, habituated to thoroughness. Some of the children's play books dealt with particular occurrences of the history of Germany in a manner, that retained the idea of child's amusement but added correct instruction. Look at the flippant "stuff" we have here. Wish we would get some notions of the Germans. That life is valuable and no time to be simply wasted. We turn things up side down here. Children are sent to the public schools—Let us begin here— The school plan is: The children must not learn at home. Result: Habit of indolence and ease. Later in life one wonders why the grown up children make so many demands on life and wish to do so little—"Crazy" system—

The French section exhibited some particularly fine state rooms. But some overloaded. The poor man who would have to live in such a palace would have no place on which his eye could rest and repose.

The English section dealt largely with Nile and Palestine explorations. But the charts etc. would have necessitated a long study.

The Building was simply crowded with exhibits which gave the individual business interests ample opportunity to see, and examine and learn from the latest. Yankee ingenuity as usual was shown in all those matters which involve application of devices and methods to solve commercial difficulties. What a variety for instance of devices in the printing and type machine division? And so on down the line. The exhibits showed different tastes in the arrangements of exhibits, some emblematic, involuntarily, of the character of the nation. One might easily spend a month in this Building and when after a month he would be asked "Have you learned all that can be learned in that Building?" Think he would have to say "No."

National Cash Register Company Exhibit. *Photograph, 1904. This exhibit in the Palace of Liberal Arts was one of many assembled by American companies that promoted commercial equipment.*

Manufactures

With regard to the architecture: The dome in the main centre of the south line of the building was a beauty and joy forever. Have stopped and stopped, again and again to contemplate the majestic character of this wonderful architectural gem.

The interior: The Italian section was full of gems of art—but too much naked stuff—The French section contained wonderful gowns. But female modesty is certainly entirely overcome in a woman who would wear some of the extreme décolleté gowns. The exhibit of the Chicago drainage canal kept your attention for hours. The comparison of excavation units of the Chicago drainage canal with the Suez canal was most interesting. The connection of Lake Michigan with the Mississippi river is certainly a foundation for hope of increasing inland river commerce. Our rivers are sadly neglected. We use them only as sewers instead of employing them as highways of commerce. The day must come when such a vast natural capital and advantage will be properly and suitably employed.

The different manufacturers displayed their wares, their methods, and manufactures in prolific abundance. This building was a wilderness of articles of commerce, of dainty fabrics—of a forest of interesting things. But a general gaze is about all that an average visitor could bestow. The number of exhibits was astonishingly large and it was impossible and even silly to attempt to see everything thoroughly.

Varied Industries

The architecture was a fit companion piece to the Manufactures Building across the way. There was nothing overdone (at least it seemed so) about the architecture. All harmonized well.

The German exhibit was beyond question the most complete and both thorough and artistic. Cannot take a fancy to the "new art"[15] jewelry. There is much labor and all that. But it does not suit your taste. Do not like it. The German art rooms are very beautiful and very sombre, very sombre—probably suited to a stolid, thrifty and conservative people. But would prefer a more

Japanese Exhibit in the Palace of Varied Industries. *Photograph, 1904. As opposed to Japan's industrial exhibits, this exhibit featured Japanese decorative arts, many of them traditional.*

---

15. Most likely a reference to *art nouveau*, a late nineteenth-century movement in the decorative arts. The *art nouveau* style was characterized by dense asymmetrical ornamentation and sinuous forms.

cheery room. One of the rooms was a municipal council chamber with the ballot box in the centre. Would it not aid in repressing corruption in part at least to have a ballot box in our municipal council chambers?

The Japanese exhibited an immense number of vases. Beautiful, variegated, and costly. Their handwork is simply marvelous. A most patient and a rapidly progressing people. They certainly are determined to succeed.

Saw some strange contrivances in this Building. A swing where the circular motion is eliminated and a sofa or settee changed or converted into a bed in a moment and a half, one might say.

The Persian rugs made no impression on you. Immense work. But despite the fact that their prices were forbidding they all looked shabby. Preferred the American rugs.

Transportation

Founded on some New York Railroad Station.[16] Enormous arches for entrances. From the very character of the entrances one would expect the building to be devoted to the transportation interests.

Within: Entire trains stood on the tracks. Palatial cars. Dining cars with extraordinary luxury. Mistake of the American public to demand so much luxury. The luxury is then furnished at the expense of safety. Too much money goes into the rolling stock. More money into the roadbed and into safety appliances to prevent accidents would be better. Enormous locomotives were to be seen. Some so large that it would seem that one ought to be justly afraid of them crushing the roadbed over which they travel, and pounding and even cracking the heavy steel rails. Certainly they could only be used on the strongest roads. A German high-speed locomotive was very interesting. Doubt whether such high speed, 80 miles per hour, will have much commercial utility. And one hates to think of the consequences of a disaster at such high speed. A model locomotive turnstile in action, carrying a monster locomotive high in

[the] air, was a spectacle of power and involved much speculation as to how the locomotive got up so high. The museum exhibit of every model of engine from the very beginning of steam propulsion engrossed much of your attention. At first the merest idea—later, and with each new machine, knowledge increases, until we have the complex and powerful machine of to-day.

Was very much interested in the model of the new Washington, D.C., Union Station. The wide plaza that is to be laid out before it heightens the effect wonderfully. Wish that our Union Station had a wide plaza in front of it, instead of a narrow street crowded by a multitude of small stores, some of them not even of genuine business.

"The Spirit of the Twentieth Century." Photograph, 1904. This giant locomotive built by the American Locomotive Co. stood high above the crowds on its railroad turntable in the Palace of Transportation.

---

16. This is incorrect. Although the Palace of Transportation was designed to resemble a "union station" in principal, its design was not based on any one existing structure, but was rather an adaptation of the architectural style prevalent in France at the time of the Louisiana Purchase. Richard Cornfeld, "The Poetic Vision: The Design of the St. Louis World's Fair," *Classical America*, 1973, p. 60.

French Automobile Section, Department of Transportation. *Photograph, 1904. In 1904, when rail and streetcar travel dominated, it was hard to imagine that the automobile was the future of urban transportation.*

The automobile section interested you very little. At present the machines look ugly and cumbrous to you. Their lines must first become beautiful and they stink too much. A whole city of these puffing, mad and stinking ugly things would not look very well in your judgment.

The hearses that were shown prove increase of showiness in this direction—and what does it amount to after all? It is not so much respect for the dead as pride and vanity of the living.

Some of the ancient means of locomotion provided are interesting [features of the] museum division.

Admired a Japanese map of the world. A monster map—handembroidered—From but a short distance it appeared like a large printed map. Thousands passed it with this belief. It was so perfect.

It is curious to note how the Japanese have copied the art of illustrating dry commercial statistics by pictorial representations. The Japanese section of the Transportation Building is full of such illustrations. They certainly intend to apply everything they see that they feel themselves capable of applying. And if they are not yet able to apply, they will learn until they can apply whatever they see. That is the impression the Japanese make.

Machinery

The architecture was complex with a great number of towers. Know too little to give the style a name.[17] The entrances on Machinery Gardens formed a sort of arched walk composed of several dome constructions. It was very beautiful.

Had an opportunity to see some steam turbines. Have read much on this subject but never saw a steam turbine in action until you saw it at the Exposition. The horizontal machine made a tremendous noise. The upright machine 3,000 HP worked as smoothly as a clock. The great additional power, in your judgment, will in course of time revolutionize steam engines. But can the turbine be used where power should be applied in either direction? In your opinion and from what you have heard the turbine is the coming machine.

The lecture in the Westinghouse exhibit as to the making of dynamos[18] proved very instructive.

The power plant of the Exposition[19] impressed by its size. These tremendous machines working so steadily are a picture of reserve force.

What a multitude of different machinery. It is simply astonishing. For every imaginable purpose.

---

17. On the architecture of the World's Fair, see: Cornfeld, "The Poetic Vision," p. 56-66.
18. Generators, especially direct current generators.
19. The power plants, electricity generators, and indeed all of the technical elements necessary to the operations of the fairgrounds were themselves exhibits on public display. See: *Official Guide*, pp. 78-80.

View of the Ferris Wheel from the Cascades. *Photograph, 1904. Looking west from the Cascades, the Palaces of Electricity and Machinery are pictured on the right.*

The working steam engines and humming motors interested you most. Most machines after all are to you little more than machines, so far as understanding their working is concerned. It is curious to note how the exhibitors presented their machines with the signs. The "only" machine for this and that and so forth and the building full of similar machines.

Electricity

Did not like the corners of this building. Structure too massive for "Electricity." The statuary on top of these corner structures not apt as it appeared to you and the exposure entirely too wanton.

The exhibit in which the several processes or steps in making incandescent globes was shown was very interesting. One would not believe that

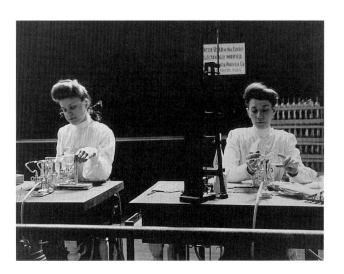

United States Incandescent Lamp Co. Exhibit. *Photograph, 1904. One of the working factories at the World's Fair, this exhibit demonstrated the multiple steps necessary for the manufacture of light bulbs in the Palace of Electricity.*

so many steps were necessary. The different electrical machines and motors were unintelligible to you. The Edison Incandescent Globe Museum exhibit was very interesting. From small beginnings what large things may grow.

There were a number of interesting experiments conducted in the Electricity Building. But as you did not understand them they served simply as a sort of intellectual amusement.

Did not understand how the German chemistry division came to be placed in the Electricity Building.[20]

The applications of electricity to commercial uses in the way of furnishing heat, light and ventilation filled the building.

The English exhibited some minute electrical machines for scientific purposes mainly.

There were some interesting experiments conducted on the outside of the building with high voltage machines, under special precautions, to imitate thunder and lightning. The experiments were so successful that they were a positive annoyance to the bands that gave concerts. A soft passage interrupted by a loud electrical crash—

Education

The rows of Corinthian columns that adorned this building in beautiful harmony, made this one of the most admired of all the Buildings of the Fair.

The public school exhibits were largely a repetition, one of the other. Chiefly dwelled on the Boston and New York City schools' exhibits.

The exhibits of the charity organizations and of the asylums of New York City occupied a great deal of your time, particularly those relating to neglected children. Much remains to be done in St. Louis in this particular regard.

The Harvard astronomical exhibit was very interesting.

The collection of foetus in the Missouri State University exhibit proved very instructive. A

sight of these helpless beings ought to induce everyone to respect human life more sacredly than ever. But what have we to-day. Women refuse to be mothers and parents destroy their own offspring. Frightful. Worse almost than the offerings to Baal. Is it not worse? The one lust— the other religious frenzy or fanaticism. Horrible! Human, intellectual beings conduct themselves worse than beasts. It is a horrible subject to pursue. On the other hand with what gentleness ought not a mother to be cared for that bears an unborn babe? And how careful she ought to be to do nothing to injure the child either morally or physically!

The German medical exhibit was really a chamber of horrors. One ought to be forced to the conviction that it is a terrible presumption to be vain or proud. Some of the diseases are unspeakably revolting. To a serious minded person an inspection of such bold medical facts ought to be salutary. And how little it takes to destroy life?

The German school exhibit was most instructive. The corrections by the teachers of the pupils' work showed characteristic thoroughness. But the German schoolmaster is an honored person—honored to such extent that we Americans do not get an adequate idea. Our teachers on the other hand occupy a different position. A policeman is honored more than a teacher. This would be unthinkable in Germany that a policeman should ever receive more salary than a teacher.

Sorry that the Catholic schools did not exhibit. The exhibitions, such as there were, were not methodized and consequently a comparison was impossible.

Some of the Latin countries exhibited mainly female hand-work.

It was interesting to note the ancient and the modern way of treating the insane.

The Tenement House Law of New York as illustrated in an exhibit proved most interesting.[21] This is practical humanity and ought to be imitated.

---

20. The German chemistry exhibit was actually split between the Palaces of Liberal Arts and Electricity. That portion in the Electricity Building related specifically to the electro-chemical industry. *International Exposition St. Louis 1904: Official Catalogue of the Exhibition of the German Empire* (Berlin: Georg Silke, n.d.), pp. 367ff, 417ff. See also: *World's Fair Souvenir of the Engineer's Club of Saint Louis*, (St. Louis?, 1904), p. 21.

21. This is probably a reference to the exhibit of the New York City Tenement House Department. The exhibit was a grand-prize award winner in the category of working-class housing in the Department of Society Economy (which was housed in the same pavilion as Education). DeLancey M. Ellis, comp., *New York at the Louisiana Purchase Exposition, St. Louis, 1904: Report of the New York State Commission* (Albany, N.Y.: J. B. Lyon Company, 1907), p. 518.

The Cloister of the Palace of Education. *Photograph, 1904. This walkway, between the Corinthian columns of the Palace of Education, was one of many exquisite promenades at the World's Fair.*

Bethlehem Steel Company Exhibit. *Photograph, 1904. This exhibit in the Palace of Mines and Metallurgy featured many of the tools of war.*

Mines & Metallurgy

This was a queer but well proportioned Building adorned by large obelisks and other ornaments to match.

The Building was filled with the various mineralogical specimens gathered from the whole earth. The onyx specimens from Mexico very very beautiful. Liked the Colorado exhibit very much. There was not only order there was an instructive method of arrangement and presentation. The Missouri exhibit was crowded. Did not like the arrangement. The exhibit of granite and stone was unsatisfactory. It did not do justice to the facts. Some of the States exhibited precious gems. From New Mexico or Arizona there were wonderful specimens of petrified wood from the petrified forest.[22] The color combinations were marvelous.

The coal mining exhibits were very instructive. The Bethlehem Iron exhibit was not only interesting but it was curious to note, that the most death-dealing machinery of war is made in the United States in a town that takes its name from the birthplace of the Prince of Peace.

On the whole however the Mines building exhibits a field that offers knowledge only to the mining man. The strange scientific names for mineral specimens that for all the world look alike, are bewildering. The microscope must be the test presumably.

Forestry & Fisheries

A simple but large structure. Strange kinds of wood exhibited. Some of the South American forests ought to offer a wonderful field for investment. But it is to be hoped that when once the lumber man strikes the South American forest that he will not shave off hill and plain and denude the country as he has done in the United States. And we are paying the penalty now. Nobody ever thought of planting anything to take the place of what was cut down. And what would happen when it came to the last tree? The lumber prices are high and getting higher every year. Is it a wonder?

Some of the sections of trees from the Pacific States are veritable monarchs of the forest.[23] They are enormous. What a grand spectacle it must be to see one of these giants from afar? It would appear as a relic of past ages. A monument of the time that is gone forever and a symbol of power and majesty and strength.

The color harmony of the Brazilian exhibit of forest life was very attractive. This was one of the most beautiful exhibits in the Building.

Was very much impressed by the New Jersey mosquito exhibit. Have a wholesome respect for that character. The method employed to exterminate the pest is also very instructive.[24]

---

22. The petrified wood exhibit was from Arizona. Bennitt, ed., *History of the LPE*, p. 445.
23. The reference is to the state of Washington's exhibit of "enormous cross-sections of giant trees." Bennitt, ed., *History of the LPE*, p. 670.
24. This exhibit purported to illustrate "the first scientific investigation ever undertaken by an American State with the object of dealing practically with the mosquito pest." Bennitt, ed., *History of the LPE*, p. 374. The editor has been unable to find an explanation of the "method" mentioned.

San Jose Agriculture Exhibit, Santa Clara County, California. *Photograph, 1904. One of the many county exhibits from the state of California in the Department of Agriculture, the San Jose exhibit featured a structure that was covered in apricots.*

Agricultural Building

This was an enormous structure with no pretension to architecture. Its corridors and aisles summed up, as you are informed, to nine miles in linear distance. The main aisles were regular streets.

The Missouri corn palace (with even its rural pictures made out of corn products) was a splendid method of presenting some facts about Missouri soil.

It would have been impossible to do more than pass a swift glance over all the products of the field. Some of the western states seemed to you to make too much ado about the tallest corn and the biggest potato. The effort to invite additional immigration seemed a little too forced.[25]

The California exhibit was a picture of the land of plenty. Several California Counties had special exhibits and special attractions.

The farm machinery exhibit division was passed—As you understand little or next to nothing about farm machinery.

In the Agriculture Building was mainly impressed by the enormous productivity of American soil. When you aggregate the totals of the several states the figures are simply prodigious. Each state appeared as ambitious to out do all the rest. Agriculture was a field in which it could not be expected that foreign countries should excel in the same measure.

---

25. See, for example: John B. Reed, ed., *Montana, The Treasure State: Its Resources and Attractions for the Homeseeker, Prospector and Investor* (St. Louis: Con. P. Curran Printing Co., 1904).

Indiana Fruit Exhibit. *Photograph, 1904. The display of thousands of plates of fruit in the Palace of Horticulture created an aroma that added an extra dimension to the visitor's experience at the World's Fair.*

Horticulture

Devoted to fruit and flower. The aroma of the apple was at once apparent on entering the Building. And how many different kinds of apples? And the other fruit. The Missouri and California divisions were about the richest, California being the first in place. Truly the land of plenty.

The flowers, at the time you visited the Building, had not been arranged for display.[26]

Fisheries

This was an interesting Building.[27] The work of the United States Fish Commission is surprising. If it is possible to prevent the depopulation (as it were) of the waters, ought there not to be some way, to prevent the cutting down of every tree in the land?

It was curious to note what varieties of fish had become acclimated. It was a pleasure to note whole schools of fish swarm in the waters. Strange appearance of the catfish school.

How easily a fish propels itself? What labor to propel a ship. What a difference in the speed? There is an enormous field of investigation still open here.

The sea horse is certainly a strange creature. The head of a horse and a long tail, with which it fastens itself on limbs etc. make this fish look like a fabled being of the fairy tales—but it is so small.

---

26. Due to the chances for spoilage and the seasonal nature of fruit and flowers, the horticultural exhibits were necessarily rotated. Cut flowers were generally displayed in competitive shows when the flowers were in season. Bennitt, ed., *History of the LPE*, pp. 652-53, and *Official Guide*, p. 89.

27. The Fisheries Building to which Schneiderhahn refers was the building of the United States Commission of Fish and Fisheries, a part of the U.S. Government exhibit at the Fair, located in its own building adjacent to the U.S. Government Building. It should not be confused with the Palace of Forestry, Fish and Game, referred to previously, which housed the general exhibits of those departments. See Bennitt, ed., *History of the LPE*, p. 321.

Egyptian Exhibit. *Photograph, 1904. Displayed in the Anthropology Building on the future campus of Washington University, this exhibit of Egyptian antiquities may have contained some of the oldest artifacts displayed at the 1904 World's Fair.*

Anthropology

The vatican mosaics[28] astonish both by the minuteness of the work and the trueness and perfection of the finish. Some rare specimens from the Vatican library might also be seen.

The Egyptian division was most interesting.[29] The ancient mummy. Little did anyone think, thousands of years ago, that this body would be seen in remote ages in an unknown world at an exposition embracing the globe. The ancient images of the Egyptians prove the labor required to make them. One might learn of many curious beliefs entertained with respect to them, and to the effect of putting them into the tombs or putting them with the dead. The scenes of ancient life were most instructive. What a hard lot did the poor have and what a dangerous position for the rich. And some very foolish persons think the difference now is due to material knowledge instead of to the influence of Christianity.

The ancient Moundbuilders[30] certainly present a great many problems—some probably forever unsolvable. A region for speculation.

Some of the chronicles of the missionaries in the early period of our history are most interesting. The ideas of the extent of the country and of the direction of the rivers as outlined on the early maps seem strange to us. The labor undergone to mark the Indian settlements proves the zeal of these first pioneers on our soil. What are mere commercial adventures in comparison?[31]

---

28. As part of the the Vatican's exhibit in the Department of Anthropology's Section of History, there were forty-nine displays of mosaics designed mostly by Vatican artists in their leisure hours. The remainder of the exhibit consisted of manuscripts from the Vatican Library. Bennitt, ed., *History of the LPE*, p. 685. For a discussion of the anthropological exhibits, see the Introduction to this volume, pp. 10-11.

29. The Egyptian exhibit was in the Section of Archaeology and consisted primarily of objects from a museum in Cairo, transferred to the Fair under the direction of the Egyptian Commissioner. As of 1904, Egypt was under British rule. Bennitt, ed., *History of the LPE*, p. 681.

30. The Mound Builders exhibit was contributed by the state of Ohio and documented the Mound Builders in the Ohio River valley. McGee, "Anthropology," p. 7.

31. The historical exhibit on missionaries, also in the Section of History, consisted of exhibits of original manuscripts documenting the Jesuits in North America. It was mounted by the Saint Mary's College of Montreal, Canada. Bennitt, ed., *History of the LPE*, pp. 684-85.

Art Gallery

The notes under dates of 26 Nov & 28 Nov cover your impression in the main.[32] Delight to see an elevating picture but the effect is greatly diminished to see it side by side with a picture that is intended to prove nothing (accomplish nothing) but that the artist can paint. Art for Art's sake. In every other profession a man is presumed to be able to do what he professes to be able to do, and he is required to prove his worth in a practical way. But why an artist should delight to choose mean topics, morally mean or otherwise unworthy, is almost incomprehensible.

Foreign Buildings

Did not find time for the foreign buildings. Of all the foreign buildings considered the Brazilian Building the most perfect.

Special Events

The British troops that paraded in the summer on the Plaza St. Louis went through a strange ceremony called "Trooping the colors." It was most staid but would be wholly unsuited to the American character. When did British troops drill on United States soil since the War of the Revolution?[33]

Considered the whole Philippine Reservation a special event.[34] It certainly served to disseminate very useful knowledge concerning the Philippine Islands and its peoples. The exhibits, and they were plentiful, proved the high civilization already attained. The musical drill of the Philippine native troops was most interesting.

Music

The French band "Garde Republicaine" you consider to have been the best of all the splendid bands that gave concerts. Then there were the "Berlin Band" of Berlin, the "Grenadiers Band" of London, the "Mexican Band" of Mexico City, The "Marine Band" of Washington, The "Banda Rossa" and Werts Band.[35] It was [the] most wonderful music one had the opportunity to hear. It was delicious. Of an evening to remain for a concert or to go out to the Fair to hear good music. We have heard such good music, we have been spoiled. Our taste is now better than our opportunities.

What beautiful gardening. It was a pleasure to ramble among the walks. The flower ornamentation had been most lavish. The shrubbery was profusely scattered. Everything looked fresh. There was a touch of green that enlivened the whole picture and made it look prettier still. One would hardly tire of the beauty.

But it is not possible to dwell on every feature of the Fair. Have omitted much that struck your fancy and attracted your attention. But in making the above extended notes, extended for your time and purpose, have been guided by the desire to have something to look to as your personal memoranda of the Fair. No pretense

---

32. See Schneiderhahn Diary, pp. 48-49.
33. Schneiderhahn forgets that parts of the War of 1812 between the United States and Great Britain were fought on American ground. The "Trooping the Colors" ceremony took place on the World's Fair grounds on September 22 and 23, 1904, and was conducted by the Essex Fusiliers, *Daily Official Program*, September 22 and 23, 1904.
34. For a discussion of the Philippine Exposition, see the Introduction to this volume, pp 11-13.
35. Appropriately called "concert bands" rather than simply brass bands, some of these bands, like John Philip Sousa's Band, which was also at the Fair, even had stringed instruments. Their repertoire included a much wider range of concert music than simple marches, although marches were featured quite prominently. As to the bands Schneiderhahn mentions: the Garde Republicaine band of Paris was engaged for five weeks beginning in early September; the Philharmonische Blas Orchester from Berlin played for eight weeks at the end of August; the British Grenadier Guards Band was engaged for six weeks beginning at the end of August; the Mexican Government Artillery Band played for six weeks in August and September; the U.S. Marine Band performed at the U.S. Government Building in October; and the Banda Rossa, an American band conducted by Eugenio Sorrentino, played for two weeks at the end of June. Schneiderhahn's reference to Wert's Band is probably intended as a mention of Weil's Band of St. Louis, conducted by William Weil. The official band of the Fair, Weil's band played at least twice daily for the duration of the Fair. There is no mention in the *Daily Official Program* of "Wert's Band." See: Report of the Bureau of Music, LPE Co. Records, Box 9/Series III/Subseries XVI/Folder 1; Bennitt, ed., *History of the LPE*, p. 706; "Official List of Special Days and Events," *WFB*, May 1904, p. 54; *Official Guide*, p. 142; *Daily Official Program*, passim.

Mexican Artillery Band. *Photograph, 1904. Music permeated the 1904 World's Fair. Internationally known concert bands were in residence at the Fair for weeks at a time. Their daily performances gave St. Louis Fair visitors a taste for quality.*

that it should do justice to the subject. But just remember that you have forgotten the Illumination—May there not be other things forgotten?

The pen cannot describe the beauty of the Illumination. Words fail. Magic picture. A flood of light and how harmonious the arrangement? One was lost in wonder. And how the beautiful Grecian columns stood out? And the Festival Hall with its changing illumination of white, red and green. Wonderful! Wonderful. Never expect to see anything so grand again. Too bad that it was a temporary picture.

But so it is with everything of this earth. It passes away. That was your uppermost reflection on the closing day. But cannot help to again express the pleasure to have been with such excellent company at the Fair at the closing day. It is as if the company has been bound together by common participation in an historic event.

Beautiful Fair. Goodbye.

West Pavilion and Floral Garden. *Hand-colored stereograph, Keystone View Company, 1904. The ever-changing, but always meticulously maintained gardens were an important enhancement to the beauty of the buildings.*

Dec 4-21

Have been tremendously busy. Had to steal the time to write the foregoing notes on the Fair. But although the notes are not what you at first had fondly intended them to be they contain your impressions—some of them. Could not defer writing a few notes on the Fair and therefore have taken every minute you could possible spare (more than you could really spare) to write out what you wished to say. It will soon be the close of the year and time for a new resolution to be more methodical in your diary. Will not give up, because it is a good training, if for nothing else than to develop character and a habit of observation.[36]

---

36. This entry was made on December 22, 1904, and can be found in the Schneiderhahn Diaries, vol. 6, p. 93. Schneiderhahn's daily entries, suspended since the closing day of the Fair on December 1, 1904, resumed on December 23.

Palace of Varied Industries at Night. *Color lithograph by Louis Biedermann, in* Supplement to the St. Louis Post-Dispatch, *June 12, 1904.*
This view depicts the Palace of Varied Industries along Louisiana Way as it might have appeared under the nighttime illumination.

Edmund Philibert

In 1904, St. Louisan Edmund Philibert was approximately thirty years old and unmarried. Long in St. Louis, Philibert's family was one of skilled laborers. The son of a tinsmith, Philibert was a carpenter by trade. His diary of twenty-eight visits to the Fair, which follows, reflects an artisan's perspective. Although his narrative is written in an immature school-boy's hand, betraying his limited formal education, Philibert's detailed descriptions reveal a fascination with fine workmanship and a penchant for observation. Following the diary is Philibert's meticulous record of the expenses he incurred during his visits to the Fair.

Louisiana Monument and Palace of Varied Industries. *Photograph by F. J. Koster, 1904. This view looking south across the Grand Basin features the Louisiana Monument on the right, the site of Opening and Closing Day ceremonies, and the Palace of Varied Industries on the left, where Fair visitors could find many of the exhibits of manufactured goods and handwork.*

Plaza in Front of Lindell Entrance. *Stereograph, Keystone View Company, 1904. The Main Entrance to the World's Fair, this entrance at the northeast corner of the fairgrounds was only one of several Fair entrances.*

World's Fair Diary

St. Louis Mo. April 30th 1904[1]

Angie[2] and I made our first visit to the Fair to day: We carried a lunch with us and arrived at the Main Entrance[3] about twelve o'clock. We stood in the Plaza St. Louis in front of the Louisiana Monument where there was speech making until about a quarter to one, but we heard none of the speeches. At a quarter to one the Cascades and fountains started to flow, and the flags on all the buildings were unfurled one after another amidst great cheering by the crowd. We next strolled along Louisiana way to the West end of Transportation Bld'g. where we viewed the parade which was composed of the Pike attractions, headed by the mounted police, we saw Jim Key the educated horse, Esquimaux,[4] Chinese, Japanese, Turks, Indians, Filipinos, Boers,[5] etc. After the parade we sat on the steps in front of

1. Philibert Diary, April 30-December 1, 1904, Philibert Family Papers, Missouri Historical Society Archives.

2. Angie, or Angela A. Philibert, was Edmund's sister. She was employed as a clerk with the *Missouri Republican,* St. Louis' main newspaper, and lived at the same residence as he. See Ortes-Barada family tree, completed by J. L. Cunningham, June 11, 1969, Philibert Papers, and St. Louis City Directory, 1904.

3. The Main Entrance was located at the northeast corner of the fairgrounds near the intersection of Lindell and present-day DeBaliviere. The Jefferson Memorial Building, built with the proceeds from the World's Fair and the home of the Missouri Historical Society's Missouri History Museum, stands today at that location.

4. Esquimaux, or Eskimos, were in residence at the World's Fair on the Pike in the "Esquimaux Village," which purported to re-create a scene from Alaska, complete with Eskimos, sled dogs, and a lake supplying an aquatic theater for canoes. MacMechen, "The Pike and Its Attractions," p. 22, and "Popular Prices of Admission Will Prevail to Shows on the Ten Million Dollar Pike," *WFB,* May 1904, p. 19.

5. South Africans of Dutch descent, the Boers were veterans of the war of 1899-1902 fought between Great Britain and the two Boer Republics (the South African Republic or Transvaal and the Orange Free State) over the future status of South Africa. They were at the Fair participating in re-creations of some of the Boer War battles.

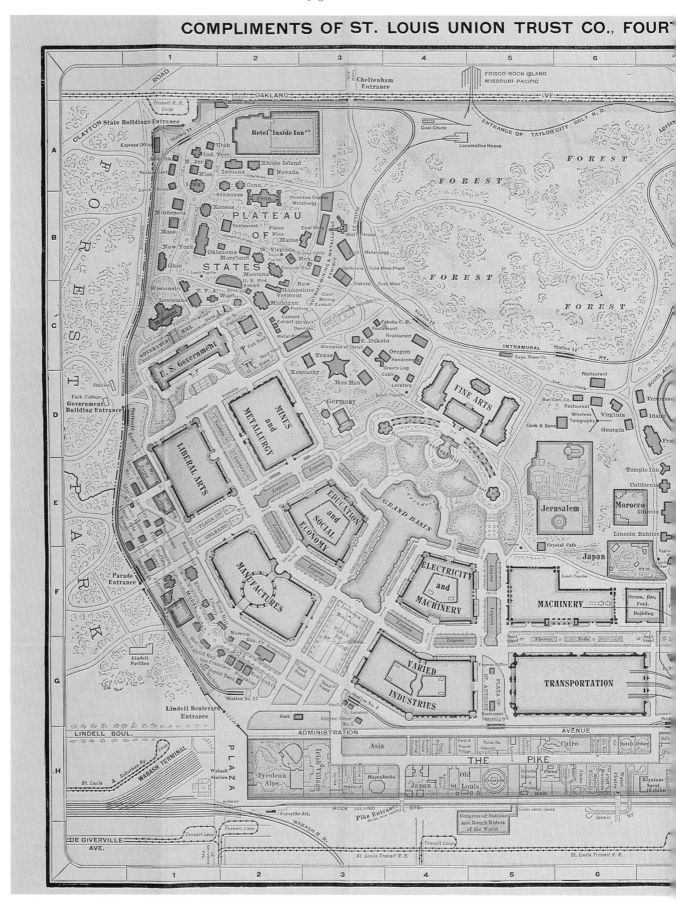

Ground Plan of the Louisiana Purchase Exposition. *Buxton & Skinner Stationery Co., 1904. This map, oriented with the south at the top, was prepared as a souvenir for World's Fair visitors, compliments of St. Louis Union Trust Co.*

D LOCUST STREETS, ST. LOUIS, MO.

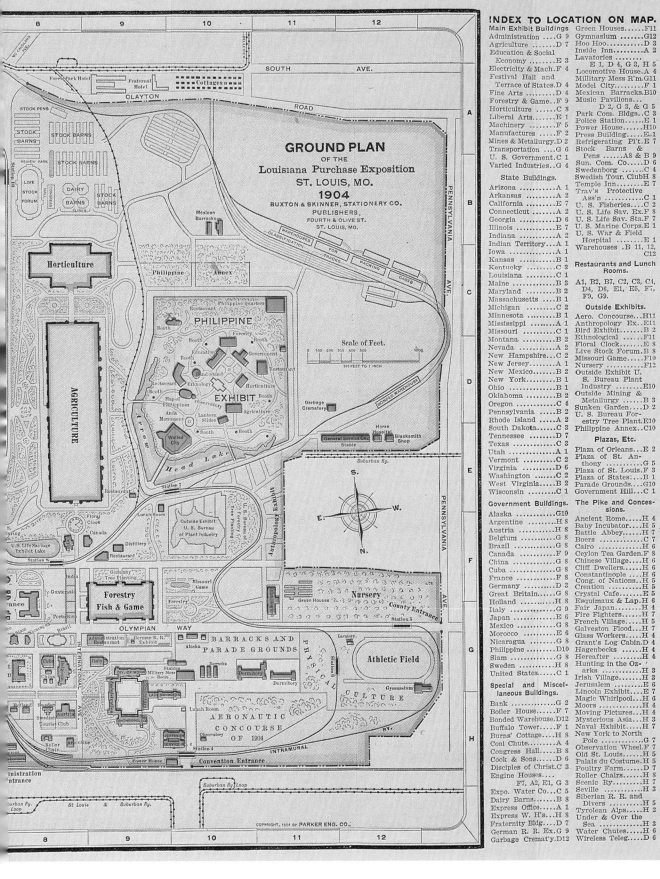

GROUND PLAN
OF THE
Louisiana Purchase Exposition
ST. LOUIS, MO.
1904
BUXTON & SKINNER, STATIONERY CO.
PUBLISHERS,
FOURTH & OLIVE ST.
ST. LOUIS, MO.

Scale of Feet.

815 FEET TO 1 INCH

COPYRIGHT, 1904 BY PARKER ENG. CO.

the unfinished Italian Pavilion[6] and ate our lunch, then we went through the Forestry Bld'g. where we saw live fishes and stuffed animals and birds, and different kinds of wood before and after polishing, also hardwood floors and borders from France, after which we went through Transportation Bld'g. where we saw a model of King Edward's[7] private car, models of the first locomotives, the first locomotive that entered Chicago in the year Oct 1st 1848, a train of Pullman cars, yachts etc. also large locomotives with about seven foot driving wheels. We went through Varied Industries next where Mermod and Jaccard had a cut glass display. It consisted of a punch bowl about two feet in diameter and fourteen inches deep, and two dozen glasses, with fleur-de-lis pattern, all made especially for the Fair. The set was valued at one thousand dollars. In the Liberal Arts Bld'g. we saw models of bridges, canal locks, dams, and a map of New Orleans in 1803 and one in 1903. Then we took the intramural[8] at station No. 16 and rode to No. 1. The car was so crowded we had to stand. After leaving the car we walked up the Plaza St. Louis to the Cascades crossing DeSoto and Jefferson bridges[9] on the way. As we ascended the steps the Cascades showed to better advantage and although a little disappointed at first sight of them in the afternoon, we now both thought they were grand, and stood watching them until the illumination began. As the lights were turned on for the first time the people raised a hearty cheer, for it was a grand sight indeed. We went back to the Plaza St. Louis by the same route by which we had come and left the grounds at the Main Entrance where we had no difficulty in securing a Delmar car.[10] We arrived home about a quarter past nine.

St. Louis Mo. May 21st 1904

I visited the Fair to day for the second time. I entered at the States Entrance[11] about three o'clock and visited the Government Bld'g. where I saw the skeleton of a sulfur bottom whale which was captured at Hermitage Bay South coast of Newfoundland on May 30, 1903. Its length was seventy five feet. The exhibit from the dead letter office contained, watches, umbrellas, lamp chimney, bread, fruit cake, glasses, bricks, etc. The patent office exhibited a machine for reproducing handwriting at a point hundreds of miles away, models of farm machinery in operation. The war department exhibit contained wax figures of officers in full uniform, some mounted on stuffed horses, which looked natural enough to be alive. The navy department had a large model of a warship with wax officers in full uniform, and some real guns mounted on the lower deck. There was also a model of the Capitol, a fine collection of stuffed animals, birds, eggs, fishes, and butterflies. Views of Yosemite valley, moving pictures of clerks, canceling, sorting and delivering mail. When they closed the Bld'g. I took a trip on the intramural and after strolling around for a little while I went home early.

St. Louis Mo. May 28th 1904

I made my third visit to the Fair to day. I met Aunt Lizzie, Mamie,[12] and a young lady from Evansville at the States Entrance about three o'clock. We went through the Government Bld'g. together, and saw work done in the penitentiary by convicts, the weather bureau exhibit and large canon, we also passed through Liberal Arts Bld'g. where we were all weighed, then we walked through the sunken garden to the Missouri Bld'g. where I left the ladies and visited Manufacturers

---

6. Many of the foreign and state pavilions were not complete by opening day and were dedicated and opened throughout May and June and even as late as July. The Italian Pavilion was not opened until June 6. "Italy's Pavilion," *WFB*, July 1904, p. 48.

7. King Edward VII of Great Britain and Ireland, 1841-1910, reigned 1901-10.

8. The Intramural was the fairgrounds railway, a double-track, overhead electric trolley that ran partly on the surface, partly elevated, between two terminals located east and west of the Main Entrance. With a seven-mile right-of-way and seventeen stations, it circumnavigated the fairgrounds except for one point where it ran between the Palace of Agriculture and the Boer War reenactment along University Way (present-day Skinker Boulevard). Promoted as "the modern, up-to-date car for city travel," the Intramural rolling stock was manufactured by the St. Louis Car Company. *Official Guide*, p. 24, and Bennitt, ed., *History of the LPE*, p. 586.

9. There were twelve separate foot bridges crossing the lagoons fed by the Grand Basin. All were named for explorers or statesmen associated with the Louisiana Purchase territory.

10. Reference to the Delmar Avenue streetcar line, which departed the fairgrounds at the Main Entrance at Lindell Boulevard and terminated on Washington Avenue downtown. It was one of several streetcar lines that Philibert traveled from the fairgrounds to his home at 4206A Lexington Avenue in north St. Louis. For a list of streetcar and other transportation lines serving the Fair, see: *Official Guide.*, pp. 13-16.

11. The States Buildings Entrance was located at the southeast corner of the fairgrounds near the Terrace of States, the site of the state pavilions.

12. Aunt Lizzie is probably Elizabeth Philibert Barada, Edmund's aunt. Mamie is most likely Edmund's own sister, listed as "Mimi" on the family tree. Ortes-Barada family tree, Philibert Papers.

U.S. War Department Exhibit. *Photograph, 1904. This exhibit of wax figures in uniform related different messages to two Fair visitors. While Schneiderhahn saw how the conditions of modern warfare necessitated changes in uniforms, Philibert was impressed by the realism of the mannequins.*

Bld'g. where I saw beautiful marble statues in the Italian exhibit, then I went to the Pike for the first time, I visited the Tyrolean Alps, the mountain and village scene were fine, but I was disappointed as I expected to see the passion play have a railroad trip through the Alps, etc. for one admission price but when inside I found that each of these were extra.[13] After walking through the Pike I left for home rather early.

St. Louis Mo. May 30th 1904
  I made my fourth visit to the Fair to day. Visited Machinery and Education Bld'gs.; just flying trips to get a general idea of what they contained: also Electricity Bldg. where I saw the wireless telegraph at work, also telephone girls at work. Made a quick trip through Mines Bldg., and took two rides on the intramural. Visited the Pike and took in Hagenbeck's[14] show, where, like at the Alps I was disappointed, going in expecting to see the whole

Business Street in the "Tyrolean Alps." *Photograph, 1904. While Edmund Philibert enjoyed the views offered in the Pike's "Tyrolean Alps" concession, once inside he was disappointed to discover that partaking of some of the Alps' special features would cost extra.*

13. General admission to the "Tyrolean Alps" was twenty-five cents for adults. As Philibert remarks, special attractions cost extra: twenty-five cents for admission to the Scenic Railway, ten cents for admission to the Magic Grotto, ten cents for admission to the Royal Castle, and twenty-five cents to see the Passion Play (a reserved seat cost an extra ten cents). Children were admitted for fifteen or five cents. "Popular Prices," p. 18.
14. Carl Hagenbeck's Zoological Paradise and Animal Circus was operated by the Carl Hagenbeck Trained Animal Show Company. The show had a scale of amusements. Ten cents was charged for general admission, an additional ten cents was charged for admission to various curiosity shows and for animal rides, and an additional fifty cents was charged for admission to the main show of trained wild animals. "Creator's of the Pike," p. 46, and "Popular Prices," p. 18.

show I found I was expected to pay extra to see the animals perform. The part I saw consisted of all kinds of wild animals, with apparently only a frail fence between them and the spectators. Two long horned animals got in a fight and locked horns, and I was afraid one of them would have its neck broken before they were released. I went home early to day, as it was wet having rained most of the day.

St. Louis Mo. May 31st 1904

I made my fifth visit to day. Spent most of my time in Manufacturers Bld'g. and took a flying trip through Art Palace. Left for home very early, was only in grounds about three hours.

St. Louis Mo. June 18th 1904

I made my sixth visit about this date.[15] Went through Agricultural and Horticultural Bld'gs. also Brazilian, Cuban, Mexican and Belgian Bldgs.

July 9th 1904

I made my seventh visit about this date, I expected to meet Herman, but missed him, I didn't stay long and saw about the same things as usual.

St. Louis Mo. July 16th 1904

I made my eighth visit to Fair to day, met Florence[16] and Angie at Utah Bld'g.[17] From there we went to the U.S. Fisheries and saw Pig, Cow, and Angel fish, a flat fish which looked like a leaf, Pike, Gar, Trout, Salmon, Eel, Turtles, Crabs, Lobsters, and many others, also fish eggs hatching, and small fish about ten or twelve days old, all kinds of appliances for catching, and hatching fish. Then we went to the Government Bld'g. where we saw photographs in natural colours, and pictures which looked as natural as life as though they were genuine bodies instead of flat surfaces. Also saw a working model of the Pneumatic mail tube system which is being installed in St. Louis. The pouches which hold six hundred ordinary letters each can be sent from Union Station to the Post Office in two minutes, and can be sent one after another as fast as they can be dropped into the tube. While looking at this model we met Miss Ackermann[18] and we all stayed together until we left the grounds. When the Government Bld'g. closed we went to the Sunken Garden and ate our lunch,[19] then we walked up to the Cascades by way of the steps leading to the East pavilion, after viewing the Cascades awhile we strolled through the Pike then took a Page ave. car and arrived home about 10:30.

St. Louis Mo. July 23rd 1904

I made my ninth visit to the Fair to day. I met Florence[20] and Angie at the Utah Bld'g. about three o'clock. We took the intramural at No. 14 to No. 9 [and] went through the Horticultural Bld'g. and the Agricultural, in the latter we saw a $1500.00 farm wagon, the trimmings were all nickel plated, and the side of [the] bed inlaid with hardwood, it was made for the Columbian Exposition at Chicago, also a large wagon about 18 ft. high and 40 ft. long, a beautiful inlaid clock about six feet high, made by a convict. In the Horticultural Bld'g. we saw fruit of all descriptions and a potato which was just about the size and looked like a boxing glove, Cactus from Mexico and trees from Japan. We ate our lunch on the East side of the Agricultural Bld'g. and then visited the floral clock, we were just too late to see the hour-glass turn over.[21] Next we went to the Japanese Gardens[22] where Florence and Angie had tea and cakes, I bought a souvenir tea set for Florence, after which we walked over to the Pike and after walking up and down awhile went home about half past seven.

---

15. According to Philibert's list of expenses, this visit took place on June 19, 1904. Cf. p. 117 of this volume.

16. Edmund's sister, Florence McCallion, from Cadet, Mo., was in St. Louis visiting. For accounts of three of her visits to the Fair and one post-Fair visit to the grounds, see pp. 121-27 of this volume. Ortes-Barada family tree, Philibert Family Papers.

17. The Utah Building was one of several Fair buildings that were purchased and transferred to new locations after the Fair. The Utah Building still stands as a private residence in St. Louis' Clayton-Tamm neighborhood ("Dogtown").

18. Possibly Addie Ackermann, in that she, like Angie Philibert, was employed by the *Missouri Republican*. St. Louis City Directory, 1904.

19. Closing time at the Government Building was 6:00 p.m. *Daily Official Program*, July 16, 1904, p. 11.

20. Florence McCallion's own account of this visit to the Fair can be found on pp. 121-22 of this volume.

21. The Floral Clock consisted of a floral face, one hundred feet in diameter, with fifteen-foot high numerals. At the top of the dial was the mechanism. Adjoining it were a five-thousand-pound bell that struck every half hour and an immense hourglass that rotated every hour. *Official Guide*, p. 42. The mechanism today is on exhibit at the Missouri Historical Society, on loan from the 1904 World's Fair Society of St. Louis, Mo.

22. A re-creation of a traditional Japanese Garden, planted with ancient dwarf trees and other plants brought over from Japan and appointed with two Japanese tea houses staffed by Japanese women in traditional dress, the Garden was located just east of the Ferris Wheel. Also on the grounds was the Japanese Pavilion, built in traditional style by Japanese carpenters, and the Japanese Office Pavilion, which served as headquarters for the Japanese Exhibit Association. See Bennitt, ed., *History of the LPE*, pp. 303, 307, 309.

Floral Clock. *Photograph, 1904. The massive Floral Clock, located at the north entrance to the Palace of Agriculture, was a feature of the Department of Horticulture, while its gigantic works were provided by the Fair's Department of Manufactures.*

St. Louis Mo. July 30th 1904

I made my tenth visit to the Fair to day with Mama[23] and Florence. We visited the Missouri Bld'g. first, then Government, and Liberal Arts, then we went to see the parade[24] and Mama met some friends she had not seen for about twenty years. After waiting a long while the parade came, it consisted of mounted police, Jefferson Guards,[25] automobiles, Boer war veterans, Igorottes,[26] Esquimau etc. The St. Louis Car Co. was well represented by its numerous employees.

After the parade we visited the Mines Bld'g. where we saw a model of a coal mine in operation, also gems and precious stones from Tiffany's of New York. Beautiful petrified wood from Arizona, that looked like onyx. Next we went to the Sunken Garden and rested, then started for the intramural, and met Harry and Nellie. After chatting with them awhile we boarded a car at station No. 15 and rode to No. 3 where we saw Miss Ackerman and Hines as we were leaving the car, walked to the Ferris Wheel[27]

23. Jane Fitzwilliam Philibert. Ortes-Barada family tree, Philibert Papers.

24. Railroad and Transportation Day Parade, also described in Edward V. P. Schneiderhahn's diary, p. 44.

25. The Jefferson Guards were the police force of the World's Fair. Organized under the command of regular cavalry officers from the United States Army, the unit was fashioned after the Columbian Guards at the 1893 Chicago World's Fair. Their duty was to patrol and police the fairgrounds and assist regular police as needed. At a strength of 300 men when the Fair opened, the Jefferson Guards ultimately totaled 750. *Official Guide*, p. 148; Hanson, *Official History*, p. 8; Report of the Jefferson Guard, 1905, LPE Co. Records, Box 16d/Series VIII/Folder 4.

26. The Igorots were one of several Filipino tribes brought to the Fair as part of the Philippine Exposition.

27. Known officially as the "Observation Wheel," the Ferris Wheel rose 260 feet above the fairgrounds. MacMechen, "The Pike and Its Attractions," p. 34. For additional information on the Ferris Wheel, see Sam P. Hyde's description of it in his memoir, reprinted on p. 140, also n. 21.

Intramural Station No. 1. *Photograph, 1904. One of seventeen stations that served the fairgrounds railway, this sheltered station doubled as a resting spot for Fair visitors. Edmund Philibert, for example, often enjoyed his brown-bag lunch at Station No. 2.*

and back, and rode to Station No. 12 where we climbed the hill to the Colonnade of States. Viewed the illumination of the Cascades and grand basin and descended steps on west side crossed Jefferson and DeSoto bridges and walked along Plaza St. Louis to the Pike. After walking up and down a little we took the intramural at Station No. 1 and rode to No. 14 where we left the grounds and took a Taylor ave. car for home where we arrived at 11.

St. Louis Mo. Aug. 14th 1904

To day makes my eleventh visit to Fair. I met Florence and Angie at the French Gardens about four o'clock. As I had been through the building before I walked through the gardens while the girls went through the building. I saw trees trained in all kinds of odd shapes some of them bearing fruit. In some parts of France the trees are trained to grow flat against a stone wall, and the sun shining against the wall reflects the light and heat and adds greatly to the trees' growth.[28] Some of the trees were shaped like this

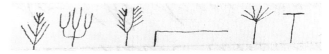

besides some others. Then we went to the Indian

---

28. These strangely shaped trees were called *espaliers* and were fruit trees. Those exhibited in the eight acres of landscaped gardens in front of the French Pavilion were generally between five and fifteen years old. On the French Gardens, see: Bennitt, ed., *History of the LPE*, p. 244. The *espaliers* are described in the *Daily Official Program*, May 13, 1904, p. 15.

reservation,[29] where we saw Chief Geronimo styled The Human tiger, for ten cents he would print his name with a pencil on a slip of paper. Saw the Pygmies[30] who appeared to be naked with the exception of a gunny sack tied around the waist. In the Forestry Bld'g. we saw a beautiful picture called The Wild Swan, painted by Alexander Pope.[31] It represented a Swan hanging on a door and looked so natural that at first I took it for a real Swan and could hardly believe it was a painting. From here we walked to the Administration Entrance[32] and took a Page ave. car, arrived home about half past seven.

St. Louis Mo. August 20th 1904

I made my twelfth Fair visit to day in the company of May and Lucy Byrne and Florence and Angie. We arrived at the grounds about ten o'clock. We visited the Holland Bld'g. first and saw a black walnut wardrobe, one hundred and fifty years old. Next we went to the Austrian Bld'g. where some of the rooms had beautiful paneling and inlaying on the side walls, there was also an exhibit of fine laces, some handkerchiefs costing as much as $150. and $175. each, also a fine art display. We went to the Anthropology Bld'g. next, where we were all weighed;[33] my weight was one hundred and fifty five pounds; height six feet and three eighths of an inch. We saw the Vatican exhibit, which consisted of manuscripts and beautiful mosaics, and a cast of the head and hand of Pope Leo XIII[34] taken the day after his death. In the Missouri Historical Society's exhibit was Daniel Boone's rifle, a Panorama of St. Louis in the year eighteen hundred & forty, portraits of prominent citizens and pioneers, manuscripts, Indian relics, the first church bell used in St. Louis in 1774 and a brass

Statue of *Vulcan*, Alabama Exhibit. *Photograph, 1904. Vulcan, the Roman god of fire, represented the state of Alabama in the Palace of Mines and Metallurgy. Because the Alabama legislature did not vote an appropriation to support an exhibit at the 1904 World's Fair, this statue was paid for by private subscription. Vulcan stands today atop Red Mountain in Homewood, Alabama, from whence it overlooks the city of Birmingham.*

29. The Indian reservation was part of the outdoor ethnological exhibits in the Department of Anthropology, located due north of the Philippine Exposition. Several Native Americans were exhibited there, including the Apache chief Geronimo, who traveled to the Fair from Fort Sill, where he and a number of his band of Chiricahua Apache were still kept prisoner. For a list of the Native American tribal groupings who lived in the outdoor ethnological exhibits, see: *Official Catalogue: Anthropology*, pp. 16-17. Also Trennert, "Resurrection of Native Arts and Crafts."
30. Also part of the outdoor anthropological exhibits, the Pygmies were from the then Belgian Congo (present-day Zaire). The group consisted of four Batwa Pygmies and five representatives of other tribes. On the life and history of one of these men, Ota Benga, see: Phillips Verner Bradford and Harvey Blume, *Ota Benga: The Pygmy in the Zoo* (New York: St. Martin's Press, 1992).
31. One of several animal paintings by artist Alexander Pope, which were exhibited in the Palace of Forestry, Fish and Game. Pope is not to be confused with the eighteenth-century English poet and satirist of the same name. "Interesting Exhibits in the Palaces of Agriculture, Art, Mines and Metallurgy, and Forestry Fish and Game," *WFB*, November 1904, p. 6.
32. The Administration Entrance was at the north edge of the fairgrounds on the west edge of the Pike.
33. One of the features of the anthropological exhibits were anthropometric laboratories for measuring people. Although their apparatus were designed primarily for enabling anthropologists to develop racial classifications according to physical characteristics, average Fair visitors were invited to be measured and have the results compared against existing records. *Daily Official Program*, May 25, 1904, p. 3.
34. Pope Leo XIII, 1810-1903, reigned 1878-1903.

Bird's-eye View of Exposition from Ferris Wheel. *Hand-colored stereograph, Keystone View Company, 1904. The top of the Ferris Wheel provided an unparalleled opportunity to view the fairgrounds from above. Looking toward the east one could see the Festival Hall to the right and the Palace of Electricity to the left, with the reproduction of the Mosque of Omar in the "Jerusalem" concession in the foreground.*

weighing one thousand two hundred pounds. A twenty pound iron shot was floating on it, also at last accounts a penny which I dropped in. A display of $50 000.00 worth of gold dust and nuggets, from Canada, in a small steel safe, also the iron man, Vulcan, from Birmingham Ala. At the close of the Fair, the statue will be removed to a public square in Birmingham.[36] There was a statue of Lot's wife in salt, from Louisiana. Gold and precious stones from Colorado and beautiful petrified wood from Arizona, it was highly polished, and looked prettier than some onyx which I saw later in the same building. May, Lucy and I went through the Government Bld'g. next, while Florence and Angie went to Varied Industries. In our hurried trip we saw a moving picture of the fast mail, went on board the battleship, saw the navy and army officers (Statues) in full uniform, butterflies, fishes etc. We went to the Liberal Arts Bld'g. next as May and Lucy wanted to get a fan there. We saw the map of New Orleans and May showed me about where they lived. We visited the Chinese display where we saw a screen of carved black wood with panels of rich embroidered silk cost twelve hundred dollars, a bridal chamber, a bedstead, furniture of all descriptions inlaid with mother of pearl and some in ivory, all kinds of musical instruments, models of stores, school, weaving, agricultural pursuits, elephants' tusks two and seven feet long carved from top to bottom with figures indicating all of the different pursuits of the Chinese. The largest tusk was seven feet long and valued at sixteen thousand dollars, another one two feet long was five hundred dollars. Coin about eight hundred years old, which looked more like razors than anything else. Next we went to the South East corner of Varied Industries Bld'g. where we were to meet Florence and Angie, we waited a while but saw no sign of them, so went to the St. Louis Monument[37] where we met them after ten or fifteen minutes wait. Then we all took the intramural at Station No. 1 and rode to No. 17. Just as we alighted the rain began to fall so we went under shelter of the station about fifteen minutes then decided to take the Intramural to the nearest point to the Ferris

cannon of the American fur Co. used on Mississippi steamers for salutes. The Egyptian exhibit contained mummies twenty eight hundred years old. In the Brazilian exhibit was a human head with the bones taken out. It was about the size of a large teacup, and had long black hair also a hole in the neck, so it could be placed on the end of a spear and carried as a trophy. We walked over to the Ferris Wheel next, May did not want to go on it at first; she was afraid she would get dizzy, but afterwards she was glad she did go. The view from the top of the wheel was very fine. We made two trips in the afternoon, and in the evening two more to view the illumination which looked fine. The next visit was to the lunch basket. We had a very pleasant lunch on the porch of the Cuban Bld'g. after which we took a ride on the intramural to the Mines Bld'g. where we saw a pot of quicksilver[35] from Texas,

35. Mercury.

36. See: "Colossus of Vulcan," *WFB*, May 1904, p. 15.

37. The St. Louis Monument, titled *The Apotheosis of St. Louis,* was an equestrian statue of Louis IX of France by sculptor Charles Henry Niehaus that stood at the Main Entrance to the Fair. It was later recast in bronze and placed in front of the Saint Louis Art Museum, the building that served as the Palace of Fine Arts during the World's Fair. See: Theodore Finkelston, "The Apotheosis of St. Louis: Politics, Ego and High Ideals in the Making of a Civic Symbol," *GH* 9 (Summer 1988), pp. 2-11.

Wheel. When we reached Station No. 8 the rain had ceased so we took a couple of turns in the Ferris Wheel and enjoyed looking at the illumination after which we walked to the East end of Machinery Bld'g. and took a twenty-five minutes ride on the lagoons in an electric launch. This was one of the most enjoyable events of the day, and at its conclusion we walked to the Administration entrance and took a Page ave. car for home where we arrived about eleven o'clock and found Ed Fitzwilliam[38] awaiting our return.

St. Louis Mo. Aug. 27th 1904

In company of Frank[39] I made my thirteenth visit to day. About half past three we entered at the States entrance and went to the Government bird cage[40] where they were feeding the birds, then we went to the Fisheries Bld'g. passing Washington State Bld'g. on the way, where we saw timbers two feet square by one hundred and ten feet long. Saw about the same as usual in Fisheries Bld'g. Passed the Government Guns and pierced armor,[41] a plate of steel about eight in. thick with projectiles sticking in it and one clean-cut hole about eight inches in diameter where the projectile went clear through, went through Chinese section of Liberal Arts to Manufacturers Bld'g. where we saw them making pocket knives. It is done very quickly and all by hand. Saw them weaving silk handkerchiefs and suspenders, which process was very interesting. Passed through Italian marble Statue display as Frank wished to see it, then started to the DeForest Wireless Telegraph Tower to see the start of the balloon race to Washington.[42] Just as we stepped outside of the Bld'g. we heard a pistol shot, and both balloons started immediately at the report.

The Effect of Coastal Defense Cannon on Face Hardened Plate Steel. *Photograph, 1904. This exhibit outside the U.S. Government Building demonstrated the effect of the American Navy's seacoast defense cannon on the best plate steel available in 1904.*

They ascended slowly and went in a North-Westerly direction. We watched them quite awhile and they were still visible about half an hour after the start. We went through the Education Bld'g. to the Mines Bld'g. where I showed Frank the petrified wood. At six o'clock we met Florence and Angie at the South-east corner of Mines Bld'g. then we all strolled up to the Art Palace passing the Oregon Bld'g. and Grant's log cabin on the way.[43] The Art Palace was closed so we viewed the Cascades awhile then started for the Pike, had lunch at Station No. 2 on the way. We strolled up and down the Pike taking in the free shows that interested us, then took a Delmar car at the Lindell Entrance and arrived home about ten o'clock.

38. Most likely either an uncle or cousin of Edmund's on his mother's side.

39. Most likely Frank McCallion, Edmund's brother-in-law, who joined his wife Florence in St. Louis during the late summer of 1904. See: Frank McCallion to Florence, September 2, 1904, Philibert Papers.

40. The Government bird cage, a free-flight, walk-through structure, was exhibited by the National Zoological Park, operated by the Smithsonian in Washington, D.C. The structure still stands and is part of the St. Louis Zoo. Loughlin and Anderson, *Forest Park*, pp. 95, 265.

41. An outdoor exhibit of the U.S. War Department, the guns were positioned between the U.S. Government Building and the free-flight bird cage.

42. The balloon race, for a purse of five thousand dollars, required that the winner land within two hundred miles of the Washington Monument. Two competitors participated, George Tomlinson of Syracuse, N.Y., and Carl E. Myers of Frankfort, N.Y. Contrary winds made navigation difficult, causing Myers to land northwest of St. Louis near St. Charles, Mo., and Tomlinson to land at Wyoming, Ill. The purse was not awarded. Bennitt, ed., *History of the LPE*, p. 611, and *Daily Official Program*, August 27, 1904, p. 4.

43. Built in 1856 by Civil War general and U.S. president Ulysses S. Grant in southwest St. Louis County, the log structure, called "Hardscrabble," was occupied by the Grants only until 1860. In 1890 a real estate firm moved the structure to the Old Orchard district of Webster Groves, Missouri. In 1904 it was removed to the fairgrounds and erected near the east pavilion of the Palace of Fine Arts. After the Fair it was purchased by Adolphus Busch of Anheuser-Busch and rebuilt near the original site on Busch family land named "Grant's Farm." The structure still stands on that site today and is open to the public as part of a tour of Grant's Farm offered by Anheuser-Busch, Inc. Bennitt, ed., *History of the LPE*, p. 153, and *Historic Buildings in St. Louis County* (Clayton, Mo.: St. Louis County Historic Buildings Commission, et al., 1983), p. 13.

Missouri State Building. *Color lithograph, American Colortype Co.,* Supplement to the St. Louis Globe-Democrat, *April 3, 1904.*

St. Louis Mo. Sept. 3rd 1904

I made my fourteenth visit to day. About four o'clock I met Florence, Lucy and May at the Louisiana Bld'g. which is an exact reproduction of the Cabildo with a plot of ground in front which is a fac-simile of Jackson Square New Orleans.[44] We examined the bell that was to be rung by brides only. Florence and I each rung it but we could not induce Lucy or May to ring it. Later May said she was sorry that she had not rung it. From the Cabildo we went through the Washington Bld'g. then to the Michigan Bld'g. where we had a drink of ice-water, and while Florence sat there on the porch Lucy, May and I went through the Fisheries where I saw about the same as usual. When we joined Florence we told the girls they must not slight Missouri, so we went through the Bld'g. and registered,[45] and were just in time to hear the tail end of a concert by a female quartet, we went through the library where after identifying myself I received a copy of The State of Missouri from Mr. Walter Williams.[46] He said the books were to be given to married men only, but he would suspend the rules and give me one. Then we took the Intramural at No. 15 and rode to No. 7 where we crossed the bridge over arrow-head lake and entered the walled city of Manilla.[47] We visited the army exhibit and saw any amount of curious guns, canons, pistols, daggers and swords. In the Philippine Education Bld'g. we saw samples of compositions, doll dresses and hat making, as they were closing the building we had to leave a large amount unseen. We hurried as fast as possible to the parade grounds to see the scouts drill, and it was a very nice sight. They paraded and went through the manual of arms and then had a Calisthenic drill which looked very nice as

44. The Cabildo, or Town House, in New Orleans, was the site of the transfer of the Louisiana Territory from France to the United States in 1803.

45. Residents of various states were invited to register at their home state's pavilion. The lists of registrants were then published in the newspapers. For lists of Missouri registrants, see: *Missouri Republican*, 1904, passim.

46. Walter Williams served as Fair commissioner to the foreign press and as chief of publications for the Missouri Commission. He was editor and compiler of *The State of Missouri: An Autobiography* (Columbia, Mo., 1904), which told of the resources of Missouri. Eighty thousand copies were distributed free of charge to Missouri householders during the Fair. *WFB*, March 1904, pp. 21, 26, and Bennitt, ed., *History of the LPE*, p. 424.

47. Arrowhead Lake, so named for its shape, marked the entrance to the Philippine Exposition. The first feature one encountered upon crossing the bridge over Arrowhead Lake into the Philippine Exposition was a reproduction of the walls of Manila, which were built by the Spanish garrison to repel Chinese and Dutch invaders of the Philippines in the latter part of the sixteenth century. The Walled City enclosed an exhibit of war relics associated with Filipino history, furnished by the Philippine Constabulary, the United States War Department, and the Philippine Exposition Board. Newell, ed. and comp., *Philippine Exposition*, and *Official Catalogue Philippine Exhibits*, pp. 293-98.

A Bit of the Old World, from Moving Platform—Creation. *Halftone,* Creation, *by Henry Roltair, 1904. This rare interior view of a Pike concession shows one image of the history of the world as seen by visitors to "Creation."*

their hands encased in white gloves all moved together keeping time to the music of the band. After the drill we retraced our steps to No. 7 where we took the car to No. 12 then we went to the Colonnade of States and rested until the Cascades started, we enjoyed them awhile and after buying a souvenir book of Fair pictures for Lucy and May we headed for the Pike by way of the Bienville Bridge and the Plaza St. Anthony. We had a lunch at station No. 2. At first May was going to take milk but after tasting my coffee she decided to take some for herself. After lunch we took in some of the free shows then went into the glass blowers,[48] where we saw men and women putting glass heads on pins, blowing vases, spinning glass, which operation consisted of heating a bar of glass about the size of a lead pencil. An almost invisible thread like a cobweb was drawn from this heated bar and run over a wheel about six feet in diameter at the rate of a mile a minute. These fine threads are then mixed with silk, about one strand of silk to ten of glass, and woven into a cloth like fabric, from which very fine dresses, sofa cushions, table scarves etc. are made. In this building we all received a little glass bow as a souvenir. We walked down the Pike a little way to a souvenir machine where May and I made a souvenir for Angie with "A. A. Philibert Jonah"[49] on it, then we walked back on the other side and saw three or four little Chinese boys and girls from about five to eleven years of age, they sang in Chinese and English and one sang Yankee Doodle and told his age, he was right cute looking.[50] Then we went in to see Creation,[51] first we rode through the canal in a boat and saw different cities and scenes on the way, then we alighted from the boat and walked through a cavernous apartment where we saw a lady's head

48. Actually glass weaving and spinning, a Pike concession. "Popular Prices," p. 18.
49. It is unclear why the name on the souvenir would have been "A. A. Philibert Jonah," as there is no evidence that Angie was or had been married. She is listed in the St. Louis City Directories throughout the 1890s and early 1900s simply as "Angie Philibert," "Angela Philbert," or "Angela A. Philibert." There are no listings under "Jonah."
50. Possibly seen outside the "Chinese Village," a Pike concession operated by an association of Chinese merchants from Philadelphia that contained merchants' booths and a theater. MacMechen, "The Pike and Its Attractions," p. 21, and "Popular Prices," p. 20.
51. One of the illusion shows on the Pike. See: Henry Roltair, *Creation, the Formation of the Earth and Its Inhabitants: Evolved for the Benefit of All People Who Visit the World's Fair* (n.p., n.d.), printed booklet in the Missouri Historical Society Library.

resting on a table, and apparently could see right under the table, it is done by means of mirrors placed at an angle, then a boy's head on a pitchfork and a boy in a deep well, then we went up stairs and found ourselves in a moving boat passing scenery on each side, after leaving this boat we went in under the "Big Blue Dome" to see the finale. At first all was chaos, then the earth rolled slowly in, darkness fell, the sky became murky and overcast; light clouds, floating around, they gradually increased in density until a very bad storm was imminent, then the lightning began to flash and the thunder rolled, and as the storm increased the lightning became brighter until finally it came not in flashes but vivid forks as real as any natural lightning, then the storm gradually subsided and as the clouds dispersed a beautiful rainbow appeared in the sky and the sun sank below the horizon, only to rise again the next morning on an expanse of water, presently islands began to form, then vegetation appeared and Adam was seen seated on a rock, with Eve advancing from the opposite side. The next scene was four Angels, standing at the head of three flights of broad stairs, surrounded by flower beds and shrubs: all at once the flowers became illuminated, the whole was brilliantly lighted, the Angels opened their eyes and spread out their arms, and it made a very beautiful tableau which closed the scene.

Next we visited Jim Key the educated horse. He spelled, Hires Root Beer,[52] trust and several other words by picking up lettered blocks with his teeth. He also took letters from a numbered pigeon hole and put them into a lettered drawer, also done sums in arithmetic. Some one asked, How much is 3 x 6 + 5 - 9? and Jim picked out the block numbered 14. After the performance we went to see the stable. The man in charge said it took six years to train Jim and, he is being taught new tricks every day. Next we wended our way to the Administration Entrance and took a Page ave. car. We arrived home about 12 and not one of us seemed to be nearly tired as usual.

St. Louis Mo. Sept. 28th 1904

I visited the Fair to day for the fifteenth time. I arrived at the Louisiana Monument, where I was to meet Herman, at eleven o'clock. I waited until half past eleven but he did not come. While waiting for him I talked with a Chicago man. When I asked him how the St. Louis Fair compared with Chicago's, he hesitated, and I said, You don't want to go back on Chicago. Oh it isn't that, he said, Now you take this place right here, and you have Chicago beat to death, it's a beautiful sight at night. I went through the Education Bld'g. first and saw beautiful transparencies in the California University exhibit. They were large pictures, about sixteen by eighteen inches, of the moon, eclipse, meteors, buildings, trees etc. I saw boys from the St. Louis public schools doing bench work.[53] Each boy had a bench, saw, hammer, chisel, plane, square etc. and a drawing of the article on which he was working. Some of the boys were very neat and skillful with their work. The Chinese exhibit contained specimens of work in English grammar and composition, arithmetic, algebra etc. by Chinese sixteen and eighteen years of age. The composition was good and some of the writing was very fine, some of it was written in Chinese with the English translation under it. The police exhibit was also in this building, it contained photographs of noted criminals; gambling devices, and all kinds of instruments taken from criminals. In the Mines Bldg. was an exhibit from Idaho of a ram's horns embedded in a tree nine feet from the ground, they were supposed to be one hundred and thirty five years old. In the government bld'g. I saw a picture of the sun by the sun, and the solar spectrum. The Bolometer, an instrument which would register the one millionth part of a degree of heat. It was so sensitive that by placing the hand over an opening in the glass, the heat from the hand would cause the indicator to move.[54] I also saw one, two and ten thousand dollar notes, and saw them printing from engraved plates.

---

52. Hires Root Beer, a soft drink bottling company, had five booths and a laboratory at the Fair. Report of the Division of Works, 1905, p. 37, LPE Co. Records, Box 2/Series II/Folder 1.

53. One of the features of the Palace of Education was the conduct of actual classes. The St. Louis public schools established a series of actual schoolrooms at work. Focusing on forms of instruction that were less likely to be disturbed by the large number of visitors in attendance, the St. Louis schools demonstrated kindergarten, instruction in carpentry, sewing and cooking, music, and the education of the deaf on a rotating basis. See: "Plan for a World's Fair Exhibit of the Board of Education of the City of St. Louis," *Public School Messenger* 3 (March 14, 1904), p. 5, in Educational Museum of the St. Louis Public Schools Records, Missouri Historical Society Archives, St. Louis.

54. The bolometer is a resistance thermometer used in the detection and measurement of feeble thermal radiation and is especially adapted to the study of the infrared spectra.

Palace of Varied Industries and the Louisiana Monument. *Photograph, 1904. This view is one of many from the Plaza of St. Louis that a Chicagoan might have compared favorably with the scenes at the 1893 Chicago World's Fair.*

The design is engraved on a copper plate, this plate is then smeared with ink, then the surface is wiped and polished clean, leaving ink only in the engraved lines. A paper is then placed upon it, and it is put under a great pressure, which presses the paper into the grooves where it receives the impression from the ink. The plate is then cleaned and inked as before. In the Electricity Bld'g. I heard the notes of a bugle over the Radiophone.[55] There was a large electric search light at one side of the building, which was focused upon a receiving apparatus at the other side. A man in a booth near the light played the bugle and the sound was carried over the rays of light to the receiver.

The sound was clear and true but very faint. In the Machinery Bld'g. I saw moving pictures of the Westinghouse Co.'s employees and works. One picture was of the forging of a large piece of steel, and every time the electric hammer would strike the sparks would fly off like water. They also gave a demonstration of the Nernst lamp.[56] In the Transportation Bld'g. were two huge locomotives, one the Missouri and the other the St. Louis, they were an exhibit of the B. and O.R.R. There was what seemed to be an ordinary sized locomotive from Germany. It ran between Hamburg and Berlin at a speed of ninety miles an hour. There was an engine of the B. and O.R.R. which was built in eighteen

55. A transmitting and receiving station for radiotelephony made by American Telephone & Telegraph and General Electric. "The Radiophone," *WFB*, July 1904, p. 56.
56. The Nernst lamp, named for German physicist end chemist Walther H. Nernst, 1864-1941, is an electric incandescent lamp whose filament is comprised of a mixture of magnesia and the oxides of rare earth metals, which, when raised to a high temperature, become luminous and remain so with minimal current and without a vacuum. Mentioned in *Official Guide*, p. 75.

The History of the Engine. *Photograph, 1904. The B. & O. Railroad's exhibit of historic locomotives in the Palace of Transportation attracted the attention of Fair visitors struck by the remarkable development of rail travel from its origins in 1832 up to 1904.*

thirty two and had been in actual service for sixty years, until it was taken from the road in eighteen ninety three for exhibition purposes.[57] There was also a fine display of electric street cars, and the first grip car[58] used in the United States. I left early and taking a Delmar car arrived home about seven o'clock.

St. Louis Mo. October 8th 1904

I visited the Fair to day for the sixteenth time. I entered at the Lindell entrance about four o'clock and after listening to the Grenadier Guards band, from England, a little while proceeded to the Varied Industries Bld'g. On the way over I came across a Chinese procession.[59] First came the mounted police and Jefferson guards, the next I suppose was the Chinese orchestra. It consisted of Chinamen in jinrickashas,[60] playing all kinds of

musical instruments. Then came a large dragon about fifty feet long, then more Chinamen, and a couple of Japanese women in jinrickashas. In the Varied Industries I visited the German exhibit first, there were dining rooms, parlors, bed, music and reception rooms all beautifully furnished, one music room contained an inlaid piano, the first of the kind I ever saw. An ocean steamer's bedroom and bath was very complete and cozy looking. There was a very nice display of fine china, one center piece about three feet high and three wide at the base was valued at seven hundred and twenty dollars, and a Jardiniere[61] about two feet long with the figure of a woman at each end cost two hundred and seventy dollars. There was a collection of works of art by Carl Spindler,[62] at first glance you would take them for paintings, but on closer inspection, you could see that they

57. This locomotive was the *Atlantic*, and dated from 1831. Designed by Phineas Davis of York, Pennsylvania, it was in service for sixty-two years. Bennitt, ed., *History of the LPE*, p. 580.

58. A car equipped with a device for gripping the traction cable by which the car is moved, i.e. a cable car.

59. This Chinese procession was part of the festivities of Chicago Day at the Fair. *Daily Official Program*, October 8, 1904, pp. 1-2.

60. Commonly spelled "jinrikisha," this is a two-wheeled passenger cart drawn by one man, originally used in Japan and common to China, also known as a "ricksha."

61. An ornamental stand or vase for plants or flowers.

62. Karl Spindler, German artist from St. Leonhardt b. Boersch in lower Alsace, designed and executed the inlaid wood pictures, paneling, and furniture in the "Gentleman's Room," one of the rooms in the German section of the Palace of Varied Industries. He is not to be confused with the German novelist of the same name who lived 1796-1855. *Descriptive Catalogue of the German Arts and Crafts at the Universal Exposition, St. Louis, 1904* (n.p.: Imperial German Commission, 1904), p. 38.

Gentleman's Room, designed by Karl Spindler. *Halftone, in Descriptive Catalogue of the German Arts and Crafts at the Universal Exposition, St. Louis, 1904. One of many rooms in the Palace of Varied Industries designed by German craftsmen and artists, the "Gentleman's Room" was notable for its inlaid wood landscape pictures.*

were inlaid with different colored woods. There was one large woodland scene with a water way which looked very natural, the sky was a white wood with blue sap in one corner which very much resembled clouds. Shortly after leaving this display, I met Mrs. Sweeney, and Lulu and Blanche. After leaving them I saw a collection of eighty plates; each about the size of an ordinary dinner plate, the outer rim was gold with a picture in the center illustrating incidents in the life of Napoleon, the whole collection was valued at twelve thousand dollars. There was also a nice collection of silverware and tapestries in this section, and in another part of the building were three embroidered pictures about two and a half by four feet, made by Mrs. F. M. Hertel[63] of Chicago. The center picture was a copy of P. P. Rubens' celebrated painting The Descent from the Cross, it took two years and a half to complete it and was valued at eighteen hundred dollars.[64] There was also what was called a history of the United States, in the form of a blanket or quilt with the picture of each president embroidered on it with the date of birth and death. They ran from Washington to Roosevelt, the best part of fifteen years was taken up on this

quilt and its value was (No mention made of value). It was made by A. M. Paltinsky of N.Y. Mermod and Jaccard had a beautiful display of cut glass, one punch bowl and set of twenty five glasses with Fleur-De-Lis pattern was made specially for the Louisiana Exposition; the bowl including base was twenty five inches high by twenty four in diameter and weighed three hundred pounds before cutting. The set was valued at two thousand eight hundred and thirty five dollars. There was a cut glass table which they claimed was the first one ever made. It was about thirty two inches high by two feet in diameter and was made in three parts, and stoppered together; had no metal fastenings. They claim it cost twenty two hundred dollars to make it. I also saw them making steel pens. Each pen goes through four or five different machines operated by girls. First they are cut out, then bent, split, lettered and polished, closing time came before I had completed my round of this building so I left considerable unseen. I met Mr. Evans at the Art Wall Paper Co.'s exhibit. When the building was closed I strolled over to the Pike and left for home about half past six by way of the Easton ave. cars.

---

63. Mrs. Florence Hertel of Chicago won a gold medal for her hand-embroidered tapestry pictures. Department of Manufactures awards lists, p. 88, LPE Co. Records, Box 7/Series III/Subseries IV/Folder 2.
64. The piece Philibert describes is from *The Descent from the Cross*, painted 1610-11 by Flemish painter Peter Paul Rubens, 1577-1640. The original is in the Antwerp Cathedral in Belgium.

Brown Shoe Company Exhibit. *Photograph, 1904. One of many popular exhibits of St. Louis–based companies, this exhibit in the Palace of Manufactures included a working factory that demonstrated the manufacture of shoes.*

French Costume Exhibit. *Photograph, 1904. This exhibit of French gowns in the Department of Manufactures attracted the interest of many Fair visitors and provoked a variety of reactions. While Philibert admired the workmanship displayed, Schneiderhahn disapproved of the gowns' immodest cut.*

St. Louis Mo. October 15th 1904

I visited the Fair to day for the seventeenth time. I arrived at the Lindell entrance about half past three and went to the Manufacturers Bldg. About the first thing I saw was a Rose point lace dress in the Italian section, it was valued at fifteen hundred dollars. In this section there was some very odd furniture and any amount of marble statuary. The Mississippi fire proof glass Co. had a very nice exhibit booth, as also did the Winkle Terra Cotta Co. In the Mexican section was an onyx plate about eighteen [inches] in diameter, its value was forty five dollars. There was a fine art glass window which looked like a piece of transparent glass with vines painted on it in different colors. It was about the nicest thing of the kind I ever saw. The Hamilton Brown Shoe Co. had a working exhibit of the manufacture of shoes, which was very interesting to watch. There are quite a number of different machines used on each shoe, and the shoe is passed from one workman to another in different stages of completion. Near Hamilton Brown's was a working exhibit of some leather or kid firm. It showed how the kid was dressed and polished. The Austrian section contained cut glass and silverware, statues, watches, clocks, etc. One clock in particular was about eighteen inches high and represented a boy holding aloft a clock while at the base were five small fountains, with water running into five openings. The French section contained beautiful dresses, hats, uniforms, gloves, cloaks etc. also fine linen; one tablecloth in particular was lovely. While looking at the dresses I met Helen and John Woods, and after leaving them I saw an exhibit of trunks, one trunk which was dust and water proof was like the ones used in the Japanese war.[65] Farther on there was a representation of scenes from the life of Christ, in small figures, among others were, The birth of Christ, The scourging, Teaching in the temple, The sermon on the mount, The last supper and the crucifixion. In the French jewelry section there was the only pink diamond in the world, also red, blue and canary colored diamonds, and one Blue white one about as big around as a quarter of fifty two carats, valued at fifty two thousand dollars; also the smallest watch in the world, it was a plain gold open faced stem winder, about the diameter of a dime, it was valued at five hundred dollars, another one was about the thickness and diameter of a fifty cent piece, and it was valued at eight hundred dollars, there was still another which was a set on a ring at each end was a small cupid with a hammer, with which they struck the time on a golden bell, it took two and one half years to finish this watch, and the work was all done under a microscope, the value was twelve hundred dollars. There were a number of other odd and curious watches in this collection. There was also an odd clock; the figure of a boy was pointing at the top of an urn which revolved and showed the hour his finger was pointing at. There were working machines for making stockings, suspenders, and silk handkerchiefs, they were very complicated affairs, N. O. Nelson[66] had a display of very fine bath rooms. When closing time came I walked over to the Pike, and left for home about half past six by way of the Easton ave. cars.

St. Louis Mo. October 22nd 1904

I visited the Fair to day for the eighteenth time. I reached the grounds by way of the Lindell entrance about half past three and as I was walking across the Plaza St. Louis to see the kite flying contest, I heard a great clanking of bells

and saw the fire engines dashing towards the crowded Pike, and I followed them at a safe distance. They stopped in front of Mysterious Asia and carried a small stream in the front door, it was all over in ten or fifteen minutes and I hadn't even seen any smoke.[67] There was an engine house about two hundred yards from the fire, which was a fortunate thing as it was quite a windy day.

I went through Varied Industries Bld'g. to the Japanese section where I saw vases of all sizes and descriptions; some of them were five or six feet high, and one about two feet high was just covered with little monkeys, it was all hand made porcelain, valued at four hundred and fifty dollars. There was a large elephant's tusk about four feet long which was carved into eleven small elephants. First there was a large one, the next

Pictured Pottery and Vases, Japanese Section, Palace of Varied Industries. *Stereograph, Keystone View Company, 1905. This dense display revealed the skilled craftsmanship of the Japanese. The vase on the right is a "Monkey Vase" of the type Philibert described.*

---

65. Most likely a reference to the Russo-Japanese War of 1904-5, then underway.

66. Nelson Olsen Nelson, 1844-1922, manufacturer of building and plumbing supplies, pioneered the concept of profit-sharing. He was also known for his model company town at Leclaire, Illinois. See: Carl S. Lossau, "Leclaire, Illinois: A Model Industrial Village," *GH* (Spring 1988), pp. 20-31.

67. "Mysterious Asia," another of the Pike concessions, claimed to offer "a comprehensive entertainment of the life and manners of India, Ceylon, Burmah and Persia." "Popular Prices," p. 18. Fire was a real concern at the Fair, where wood construction and large crowds enhanced risk. Exhibitors and concessionaires were required to have fire insurance and to buy into two fire insurance protection pools, one for the Pike and one for exhibitors. For information on Pike fire protection, see: "Concessionaires' and Exhibitors' Pools for Fire Insurance Protection," *WFB*, April 1904, pp. 64-66, and *World's Fair Souvenir of the Engineer's Club of Saint Louis*, pp. 11-12.

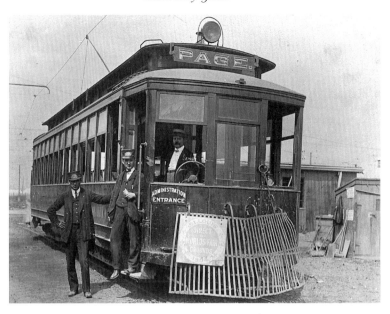

At the Street by Curve near Skinker Road, World's Fair Entrance.
Photograph, 1904. This Page Avenue Car often transported Edmund Philibert home from the Fair. It departed from the Administration Entrance near the intersection of Skinker and Lindell Boulevards.

was a little smaller and so on down all in one solid piece carved from one tusk, there were any number of other articles carved from ivory. I went through "A Country House" a part of the British exhibit, it represented the different rooms of a house all elegantly furnished. The dining room had a beautiful large table in it, the bed room and nursery were very nice. There was a model of some duchess's rooms on H.M. Ship "Ophir." They were nicely furnished and cozy looking, and there was a Roman plunge bath in connection with them. Loftis Bro.'s and Co. of Chicago had an exhibit of diamond cutting and polishing. The cutting consists in rounding the diamond into shape and is done by means of another diamond, after cutting it is clamped in an instrument with two short legs and a long arm, the legs are placed on a table and the diamond is set on the flat side of what appeared to be an emery wheel which made two thousand eight hundred revolutions a minute. Diamond dust and olive oil are poured on the wheel and in this manner the diamonds are polished. I went to the Transportation Bld'g. next and saw models of the methods of transportation

in Bolivia, Turkey, Cuba, South America etc. The Llamas were used in Peru, small donkeys in Constantinople, the dromedary for the deserts. There was a Palanquin[68] drawn by mules, ox carts etc. I went through the Pullman train, there were beautiful private cars, dining cars, chair cars, sleepers and compartment cars, some of them with lovely inlaid finishing. They were just grand and traveling in them must be a comfort. There was a small model of the steamship Deutschland showing the main dining room which seemed very large and must be so as it carries eleven hundred passengers besides its crew of five hundred men and officers. The Egyptian exhibit contained models of steamboats used on the Nile. The Japanese exhibit contained models of ships, maps, pictures and small models showing how the mail is distributed in Japan, in Formosa[69] the mail carrier is armed with a sword and rifle for his own protection. When the building was closed I walked over the Plaza St. Anthony to the Pike and up the Pike to the Administration entrance where I left on a Page ave. car at about a quarter after six o'clock.

---

68. A palanquin was a conveyance used primarily in east Asia, usually for the transport of one person. It consisted of an enclosed litter in the form of a box with wooden shutters that is borne on the shoulders of men by means of projecting poles. It is unlikely that what Philibert describes here was actually a palanquin.

69. Formosa, or Taiwan, was under Japanese rule in 1904, having been ceded to Japan by China at the end of the Sino-Japanese War of 1894-95.

Pennsylvania Railroad Exhibit of New York Central Station. *Photograph, 1904. This model in the Palace of Transportation illustrated the latest in rail and subway station design.*

St. Louis Mo. October 29th 1904

I made my nineteenth visit to the Fair to day. I arrived at the Lindell entrance at a quarter to three and heard the Mexican Artillery Band playing in the Plaza St. Louis band stand. Then I walked through the Varied Industries to Transportation Bld'g. where I went through a seventy seven foot long cruising yacht with eleven and a half foot beam, it was capable of a speed of twelve miles an hour with a sixty five horse power engine. The price of this yacht was twenty thousand dollars; it took first prize.[70] There was an automobile that had been run one hundred and thirty five thousand miles and was still in pretty good shape. There was the first grip car ever operated and used on the Clay st. line in San Francisco in eighteen seventy three. A type of horse car used in Louisville in eighteen seventy, with a brass conveyance at the side of the car to convey the fare to the box. A small horse car such as is used on large plantations in Cuba. Types of double deck street cars such as are used in London and Dublin. A car from the Northwestern Elevated in Chicago. A model of the first American and first Buenos Aires locomotive, and the "St. Louis," the largest locomotive in the world, an exhibit of the B. and O.R.R. The counterpart of the DeWitt Clinton train, the first train to make a regular trip in New York state.

In August eighteen thirty one this train left the Albany station on its first regular trip over the Mohawk and Hudson R.R. to Schenectady. It is said that the sparks from the engine were so thick that the passengers had to raise their umbrellas as shields, and naturally in a short while the umbrellas caught fire. The engine looked like a horizontal boiler on wheels, and with a smokestack on the front end, the tender resembled an ordinary open wagon, and the two coaches, very closely resembled stage coaches. On the next track to this train stood the Empire State express train, the fastest long distance train in the world, it makes regular trips between New York and Buffalo. The International Mercantile Marine Co. had models of State and apartment rooms on their steamships. The first class state rooms had two berths, an upper and a lower, a couch, electric push buttons, folding washstand, mirror, bottles, chairs etc. Those of the third class had four berths, two upper and two lower, and a washstand and looking glass, but no bowl, the floor space between the berths was about four by eight feet. Near Sickles Sadlery Co.'s exhibit was a five hundred dollar saddle of embossed leather with silver trimmings. The Pennsylvania R.R. had a very interesting model of their subway and station in New York City. I went to Machinery Bld'g. next and saw the large engine that operates

---

70. The term "first prize" is misleading. Grand prizes, gold medals, silver medals, and bronze medals were awarded to individual exhibitors within each exhibit classification. More than one grand prize was usually awarded. It is impossible to ascertain which exhibit Philibert is describing or which award was given (grand prize or gold medal), as the records of the awards given in the Department of Transportation have not survived in the LPE Co. Records.

the exposition's lighting system, in operation,[71] also a six hundred horse power Westinghouse steam turbine which made thirty six hundred revolutions a minute, there was one with the interior exposed, it looked like a big axle with any amount of small steel projections on it, there were corresponding projections on the inside of the covering, and it seemed as though there would be less than one half inch space between the two sets of teeth when closed, one set stationary, the other revolving at a terrific speed. The man in charge said, if one tooth was to fly out, it would make scrap iron of the machine in a minute, so I immediately proceeded on my way, and as it was about closing time I left the building and rested near machinery gardens for awhile, then took a light lunch at station No. two, and went to hear the Berlin band.[72] They played, Tombola March by E. Franke, Overture Egmont by Beethoven, Toreador Waltz by S. Bogle, and March of the Priests and chorus from The Magic Flute by W. A. Mozart. Of the four pieces I liked The Toreador Waltz best and Mozart's piece the least. As it was now about eight o'clock, I proceeded to the grand basin to see the fire works.[73] I took a position near the DeSoto bridge and had a tolerably good view of everything. There was a row of fiery fountains floating on the water and sending up showers of sparks, which made a very pretty effect, there were floating water lillies which changed color, and something darting in all directions on the water, which very closely resembled the movements of fish. There were five or six set pieces, a lot of red and green fire, and a number of aerial bombs. After the fire works I went on the Pike and spent a little while looking at some souvenirs and diamonds, and left the grounds at Lindell entrance about half past nine o'clock.

St. Louis Mo. Nov. 5th 1904

I made my twentieth visit to day. I arrived at the Administration entrance about half past two and visited the Chinese pavilion first. This building is a reproduction of Prince Pu Lun's[74] country residence. It consists of a house with openings on three sides, which face a central court. The walls and doors are carved and covered with inlaid work in ivory. The first thing I saw on entering the building was a large round table with a kind of marble center and a black wood border inlaid with mother of pearl. Some odd lanterns or chandeliers which were made of glass were very pretty. There were a lot of vases and carved ornaments, some fine embroidery, one embroidered table cloth with a crochet border and fringe about six inches long, was very nice, the fringe was in different colors, red, green, yellow, lavender, pink etc. a different color every two or three inches. In another room was Prince Pu Lun's bed made of ebony and inlaid with mother of pearl. On leaving this building I saw Chub but was not speaking to her. I went to the Forestry Bld'g. next and saw a model of a new building in Paris, showing the scaffolding used by stone masons, it was four or five stories high and all tied together with ropes. In the Ceylon section was a bookcase made from one log. It was about eight feet long and three feet in diameter, and one quarter section was cut out thus forming a shelf or desk, and the upright part was hollowed out to receive the books, which stood on edge behind a glass door. There was a machine for testing the strength of lumber and some beams about a foot by a foot and a half square were split under the pressure. A very pretty exhibit was of a forest scene in Minnesota, showing the different animals that inhabit the woods, they were stuffed but looked very natural looking. Near this exhibit was a hunter's lodge in the Adirondack Mts., live beavers and salt water fish, and some large transparencies about thirty by forty inches showing forest scenes in the big lumber districts. My next visit was to the Aeronautic Concourse where I saw the captive balloon make several

71. Among the exhibits in the Palace of Machinery were the power, lighting, and pumping plants of the entire exposition. With an aggregate 45,000 h.p., this power plant was reported to be third largest power plant then in operation in the United States. *Official Guide*, p. 79.

72. The Berlin Band played in Machinery Gardens on the evening of October 29, 1904, from 7:00 to 9:00 p.m. Philibert left in the middle of the program, as the pieces he describes were only the first four of eight played. *Daily Official Program*, October 29, 1904, p. 3.

73. Fireworks displays took place intermittently at the Fair. The October 29 program was staged by Paine's Fireworks. For a detailed program and description of this particular show, see: *Daily Official Program*, October 29, 1904, p. 16.

74. Prince Pu Lun of China, the grandson of the Tao Kuang Emperor of China who had reigned about sixty years previously, served as the head of the Chinese Commission to the World's Fair. "China's Display," *WFB*, April 1904, p. 56.

Inflating the François Airship. *Photograph, 1904. One of several airships at the Aeronautic Concourse, this dirigible, belonging to Hyppolite François of France, made only one tethered flight at the World's Fair.*

St. Louis Mo. Nov. 10th 1904

I made by twenty first visit to day. Florence, Norma,[76] Frank and I arrived at States entrance about half past eleven, and went at once to the Missouri Bldg. where we were to meet Ed[77] and his father, while waiting for them we went to the library where Frank received a book;[78] then to the Art gallery, in Missouri Bld'g. where we saw a life size picture of Pope Leo, and a lot of work done by the pupils of the Sisters of Loretto,[79] by this time it was half past twelve, and we thought Ed and John were hardly coming, so Frank and I went through Liberal Arts Bld'g. while Florence and Norma waited to meet them if they did come. In the Liberal Arts we saw nothing new except a machine which trimmed the edges of magazines. Four or five books about a half inch thick were placed in it end to end and at one stroke the blade cut them all as easily as if they were butter. We also saw a cheese cutter by means of which the cheese could be cut to the exact cent's worth. Say you have a twenty one pound cheese, the dial is regulated at twenty one pounds and another dial is set at the selling price per pound and if a customer calls for thirteen cents worth of cheese you just move the lever to thirteen and press it down and you have exactly thirteen cents worth cut off. We returned to meet Florence about two o'clock, during our absence she had met Mary, Clara, and Frank Clancy and Sid Whealen but had seen nothing of Ed and John so we gave them up, and all went to the Government Bld'g., and in a little while we separated to meet in Agricultural Bldg. at four o'clock. The two Franks, Florence, Norma and I went through Liberal Arts to Manufacturers Bld'g. where we saw a watch set in a ring. A row of diamonds in an ellipse runs around the exterior of the ring and at each end are two cupids with

flights, and in the Aerodrome I saw Benbow's and Francois's airships.[75] The Francois ship was one hundred and five feet long thirty five feet in diameter and the total weight was two tons. Next I went to the Alaska Bld'g., where there was fancy articles made by the Indians, school work etc. From there I went to Canada where I secured some literature and rested awhile, then went over to Ceylon where they had a great many curios and one carved ebony cabinet. I then took the Intramural at No. 9 and rode to the States Bld'g. entrance where I took a Taylor ave. car for home about six o'clock.

75. The Aeronautic Concourse, located at the northwestern corner of the fairgrounds on the present-day Washington University campus, was the staging and departure site of the Fair's balloon races and the display site for the airship exhibits. The facility, the grounds of which were surrounded by a windbreak, included a balloon shop for repairs and new construction of balloons and airships, a hydrogen manufacturing plant, pipes and valves for inflating up to ten balloons, a balloon testing building, and a large hangar for the housing of airships. "Aeronautic Concourse," *WFB*, March 1904, p. 28. There were a total of three airships on display at the Fair: *The Meteor*, belonging to T. C. Benbow of Butte, Montana; *La Ville de Saint Mande*, belonging to Hyppolyte François of France; and the *California Arrow*, belonging to T. S. Baldwin of Los Angeles. Of these airships, only Baldwin's made a successful flight. Benbow's airship made three flights on the end of a tether and two free flights, both deemed unsuccessful because of his inability to control his direction. Bennitt, ed., *History of the LPE*, pp. 606-10.

76. Edmund's niece, the daughter of his sister Sarah Catherine Philibert. Ortes-Barada family tree, Philibert Papers.

77. Possibly Ed Fitzwilliam.

78. Most likely a reference to the same book Edmund received on his visit of September 3, *The State of Missouri: An Autobiography*, edited by Walter Williams.

79. The Sisters of Loretto operated schools for the education phf girls in Florissant, Mo. (northwest St. Louis County) and in the City of St. Louis in 1904. St. Louis City Directory, 1904, and Sister M. Lilliana Owens, *The Florissant Heroines* (Florissant, Mo.: King Publishing Co., 1960).

Discovery of St. Anthony Falls by Father Hennepin, Modeled out of 1000 lbs. of Butter.
Photograph, 1904. This sculpture in the Palace of Agriculture's Minnesota exhibit was only one of many examples of statuary made of foodstuffs.

small hammers. When a secret spring is touched the cupids strike the hours on golden bells, with their little hammers, producing a distinct sound. Four years were consumed in making this watch, and the work was all done under a microscope. The watch itself is less than a half inch in diameter and costs twelve hundred and fifty dollars. Frank Clancy and I left the others in this building and went to the parcel room near Lindell entrance where Frank had his grip checked. Then we went through Varied Industries and Transportation Bld'gs., we went through the Pullman train, the Empire State Express train and a Chapel car of the A. Bap'st. Pub. Society[80] which had been in use for six years, it is run into a small town where there is no church and services are held there in it, it is hauled free of charge by the railroads. As it was getting late we took the Intramural at No. 3 and rode to the Agricultural Bld'g. and met the rest of the crowd at the butter display. This display consisted of a number of life size figures modeled in butter. There was a house, several cows, a woman milking a cow, a bust of President Roosevelt

glasses and all, and several others all very nicely modeled. We went to Machinery Hall next where we warmed up and viewed the large engines which furnished the power for the illumination, then we went to view the Cascades but they were not running, so we went to the Pike where I left the crowd at Fair Japan[81] and went to meet Angie at the St. Louis Statue. She came about a quarter after seven and we joined the others on the Pike, and while Angie was exchanging greetings with them Ferd and Ed came walking up, then we went to a restaurant opposite Creation and Ed treated us to a light lunch, after lunch Ferd took us all on the ocean wave,[82] I didn't want to go on at first as I thought it might make me sick, but it didn't and I enjoyed it. Next I took the crowd to the "Foolish House," and I nearly laughed myself sick, there was a sign outside which said "Souvenir rings given away to day." I asked Angie if she wanted a ring, at first she said yes, then as she thought it was a joke said no. We all assured her it was no joke, and the ticket seller asked what size ring she wore, she didn't know so he said hold up your hand please, How do you think this

---

80. American Baptist Publication Society.

81. Not to be confused with the Japanese Garden, "Fair Japan" was a Pike concession, one of the few depicting a foreign culture that was operated by foreign (Japanese) nationals. It was similar to the Japanese Garden in its efforts to re-create the architecture and landscape of the Japanese Imperial Gardens and contained a traditional teahouse staffed with Japanese women in traditional dress. It also boasted a Japanese fortune teller, a Japanese military band, and jinrikishas for hire. "The Creators of the Pike," p. 48, and MacMechen, "The Pike and Its Attractions," pp. 9, 12.

82. Possibly a reference to "Shoot the Chutes," otherwise known as the "Water Chutes," a ride similar to a log flume. Sam P. Hyde described this ride in his memoir, see p. 144.

Looking down the Pike. *Color lithograph, Continental Colortype Co., in* The World's Fair in Colortypes and Monotones, *1904. Looking east on the Pike, the "Battle Abbey" stands on the right and the "Scenic Railway" on the left.*

size would do? Taking up a couple of sleigh bells, and ringing them, while the crowd roared with laughter. On entering a man cheerfully invited us to be seated on a couple of chairs facing a looking glass. Thinking the trick was in the mirror I was just about to sit down but I remembered about the trick chairs just in time, later we had the satisfaction of seeing one of them collapse as a man sat on it and went sprawling on the floor. Farther on there were a number of mirrors which distorted the figure in the most comical way imaginable, a number of peep holes where upon putting your face against a small opening, you would be surprised to see it on the body of a monkey, convict, etc. Passing on we came to a maze of mirrors where you would see yourself advancing to meet yourself, and when turning aside to avoid a collision would bump into a mirror. At last we were all safely through and headed by Ferd and Ed we crossed a little bridge which had a sign reading, "Asleep at the switch; take a peep." Stepping on the bridge the floor would go down on one side and wobble at a great rate, and you would begin to think you

were "Asleep at the switch." Going up stairs we "Slid the Slide" and were leaving the place when Mary Clancy said, "Make Sid go down that slide, he is the only one that didn't go." So Ferd and I grabbed him and then he went willingly enough. Ferd and Frank Clancy took us to the Magic Whirlpool[83] next. Taking seats in a boat we were drawn up a steep incline, then we started down and kept circling around a waterfall, and into dark tunnels and out again into brilliantly lighted caverns, with fairy like scenes in them, and finally down a steep incline into the water again, where we drifted slowly through tropical groves and forests to the landing place. I led the way to the old plantation next.[84] We entered an open court where there were four or five typical log cabins in which the darkies[85] lived, then passed into a hall where there was a show of about a half hour's duration. It consisted of about twenty darkies singing, dancing, cakewalking etc. Some of them were very comical, and they put up a pretty good show. It was about ten o'clock by the time the show was over, so the eleven of us left for home on the Easton ave. cars.

83. One of the illusion rides of the Pike, the "Magic Whirlpool" projected fifty thousand gallons of water per minute. "Popular Prices," p. 19.
84. The "Old Plantation" claimed to "reproduce the actual olden life of the American negro and the charm of the Southern plantation home as it existed before the Civil War." The entertainments performed were promoted as a re-creation of slave entertainments. MacMechen, "The Pike and Its Attractions," p. 25.
85. For a discussion of the use of derogatory ethnic language by 1904 World's Fair visitors, see the Introduction to this volume, p. 24.

Government Building, Jerusalem Exhibit. *Photograph, 1904. This was one of many street scenes in the eleven-acre "Jerusalem" concession. Staffed by one thousand natives of Palestine, this "re-creation" of the city of Jerusalem contained three hundred structures, twenty-two streets, and six separate gates.*

Pumps in the Steam, Gas, and Fuel Building. *Photograph, 1904. Part of the physical plant of the World's Fair, the Steam, Gas, and Fuel Building was open to the public for inspection. With its pumps, valves, and boilers, it also offered a welcome respite to Fair visitors on cold days.*

St. Louis Mo. Nov. 12th 1904

I made my twenty second visit to the Fair to day. Florence and I arrived at the Lindell entrance about a quarter past three, and passed hastily through Manufacturers Bld'g. over Daniel Boone bridge, through Education Bld'g. across Napoleon bridge and up the East Cascade steps to the Virginia Bld'g. where we met Frank by appointment. Then the three of us went to Jerusalem[86] entering by the Jaffa gate. First we visited the birthplace of Christ, then the Mosque of Omar, at one side of the Mosque is a platform which is the property of the first merchant occupying it on that day, there he is permitted to sell his wares unmolested all day, but his right to the property ceases at midnight, and some one else takes it the next day and so on. Inside of the Mosque is a reproduction of the rock on which Mohamet stood when he ascended to heaven as the Mohammedans believe. They say the rock was so holy that it went up with Mohamet but was not quite holy enough to enter heaven, so it remained suspended in the air, with no connection whatever with the earth. The wailing wall was shown where the Jews go every morning to wail. Our next view was of a diorama of the Mount of Olives, showing the Garden of Gethsemane, Valley of Hebron, the dead sea and the Mohammedan minaret erected on the spot of the Ascension. The Mohammedans believe that on the judgment day the Valley of Hebron will be spanned by a keen edged sword about the width of a hair, across which all must walk, those who cross will be saved while those who fall off will go down to destruction, as a rule the Mohammedans will cross and all Jews and Christians will fall. Next we went along the Via Dolorosa or Way of Sorrow, a narrow street along which Christ bore the cross. The next stop was at the barracks where Christ was tried while His Mother waited with friends in a building on the opposite corner. The next I think was the Church of the Holy Sepulchre. Near this was a diorama of scenes attending the crucifixion, Judas with a rope going to a solitary place, The House of Joseph of Arametha, with the tomb of Christ in his garden, and lastly the crucifixion itself, with the Soldiers repulsing the crowd and shooting dice for Christ's garments. The figures stood out and

86. "Jerusalem," often described with the Pike entertainments, was actually more centrally located in a spot just west of Festival Hall and the Cascades. It was operated by the Jerusalem Exhibit Co. and could be visited at a cost of fifty cents, with an additional fee for its theater and for camel and donkey rides. "Popular Prices," p. 20, and MacMechen, "The Pike and Its Attractions," pp. 32, 41.

Theater in the Chinese Village. *Photograph, 1904. The "Chinese Village," with its multiple entertainments, was a favorite spot for Edmund Philibert and his family. The Chinese dragon already had attracted his attention when it paraded on the main grounds on Chicago Day.*

looked very natural. Next we saw a model of Solomon's temple and then went back to the Court of David. On one side of the street are two hotels, The Grand New Hotel and The Hotel Central, reproductions of those that were built in the Holy City for the benefit of tourists. Across the street from the hotels are the oldest and most interesting parts of Jerusalem. Down a steep stairway from the street is the courtyard of David, in front of the reproduction of the old Synagogue. At one side is the tower of David, the place where David is supposed to have written most of the Psalms, inside of the tower we saw a model of the tomb of Christ. In front of the hotels there were a long line of camels, the three of us got on one and had quite a ride up and down the street. Riding at a trot is nicer than at a walk. The camels kneel to receive their burden and as they rise you are thrown first one way and then another. We left the Holy City by the Jaffa gate and walked down past Japan[87] to the Boiler House.[88] The fires under the boilers were fed automatically here, and owing to so many fires the building was quite warm which

was quite a contrast to the cold air outside. We walked through slowly so as to get warmed up and at the West end we walked through a monster iron sewer or water pipe, standing up straight in it. I had to reach my arm almost to its full height above my head before I could touch the top of it. We went down the Pike next and Frank took us into the Chinese village where we saw a clever sleight of hand performance. A Chinaman took an empty shawl and spread it on the floor, then catching it in the middle he raised it up and there was a bowl of water underneath, taking another shawl he repeated the trick and brought out a still larger bowl, this time about the size of a china washbasin; another Chinaman ate fire, supposedly, then took a drink of water and put a lot of scrap paper in his mouth, and started to blow, in a few a thin stream of smoke came from his mouth which gradually increased in volume, and finally sparks and then flames came out. In another part was a game of rolling balls into holes. Florence and I tried it; she won a little mug and I won a little saucer. Leaving the village I led the way to Hereafter.[89] We walked in

---

87. Japanese Garden.

88. The Steam, Gas and Fuels Building, an annex to the Palace of Machinery, contained exhibits illustrating the generation of power. For the most part, its exhibits were in actual service, generating the Fair's power. *Official Guide*, pp. 76-79.

89. "Hereafter" was a Pike concession described as a "mammoth illusion of the realms to which the good and evil will be consigned after death." "Popular Prices," p. 18.

the entrance and all at once saw three familiar faces, which we recognized as our own, advancing towards us. Then we discovered that if we didn't make a turn we would go bumping into a large mirror. With a number of others we waited in an entry for a few minutes then were admitted to a hall where we took seats. In the center of the ceiling was a chandelier made of skull, arm and shin bones. The guide informed us that the large skull was that of Robert McCann a notorious murderer of England, and that the small skull above it was that of Robert McCann when he was a little boy. A man from the audience was then asked to step upon the stage. A man went up and sat on a chair by a table. The guide then ordered something for him to eat. A white robed figure brought in a turkey and put it on the table, but the man couldn't see it and running his hand around the top of the table would go right through the turkey but still couldn't see or catch hold of it. The same way with a bucket of water and a bottle of beer, and finally the ghost raised the bottle to strike him, and they all disappeared. Then the man appeared again and a young lady put her arms around his neck but he couldn't feel or see her. That concluded the first part of the performance, and amidst a great rattling of chains a door was opened and we were admitted to the lower regions. There was a scene from Faust and after viewing it we were asked to step back a little, when some skeletons dropped from the ceiling into the crowd amidst much shrieking by the women. The next scene was one of the boodlers, with barrels of money but nowhere to spend it, a man suspended by his nostrils, who, we were informed was continually poking his nose into other people's business. Next we were ushered into the throne room of his satanic majesty, where a skeleton jumped into the crowd again. From this room we passed through a beautiful grove to Paradise, where there were four or five scenes one blending into the other, the last one was angels floating in the clouds. This concluded the performance, and as this was Florence and Frank's last visit we went over the Plaza St. Anthony to the water way and down to the Plaza St. Louis where we took a good view of the Cascades, then left at the Lindell entrance about half past eight.

St. Louis Mo., November 19th 1904

I made my twenty third visit to the Fair to day. I arrived at the States entrance about half past three. I took the Intramural at No. 14 and rode to No. 7. I walked across the bridge of Spain to the walled city of Manilla. My first visit was to the Constabulary exhibit. There were all kinds of knives, bolos, guns and cannon that had been captured from the insurgents.[90] My next visit was to the Fisheries and Game Bld'g. There were snake skins twenty six feet long, stuffed reptiles and birds of all kinds, any number of shells, specimens of coral, fish traps, a stuffed water buffalo, etc. I went through the Agricultural Bld'g. next. This building contained a large display of hemp, one hundred varieties of rice, fruits, tobacco, models of agricultural implements etc. There were a number of models of houses, and I noticed nearly all of them had ladders instead of stairs. The Education and fine arts bld'g. was next. In the exhibit of St. Thomas University[91] was a photograph of a number of priests and cardinals with Archbishop Harty in the center. The writing and composition of the school children was good, and the drawing was very fine. The fancy work done by pupils of the girls' school was good and one handkerchief was grand, it was very fine linen and the border was all drawn or open work with a couple of very fine single threads running through it like cobwebs. There were a number of oil paintings which were good. I went to a typical Manilla House or Women's Bld'g. next. This building contained fine furniture, women's work, paintings etc. There was a red Narra[92] wood table about three and a half feet wide by eight feet long, another, round one nearly ten feet in diameter of the same wood. It is a red wood and very much resembles Mahogany. There was a bookcase made of black wood, with hollow carvings on it which must have been very difficult to make, a bedstead of the same wood with a cane bottom seemed as though it would be a cool bed to sleep on in a hot climate. In another part of the building were a number of hats. One white one was made of coconut fibre and looked like some very fine cloth goods, it was so closely and perfectly woven. I went to the Government Bld'g. next. It contained a number of statues and

---

90. "Insurgents" is a reference to those who participated in the Philippine Insurrection of 1899 in opposition to the American presence in the Philippines during the Spanish-American War.
91. The Catholic-supported University of Santo Tomas in the Philippines.
92. Also called Philippine Mahogany, narra is a hard wood that is noted for its ability to take a high polish.

Bridge Leading to the Philippine Exposition. *Photograph, 1904. The "Bridge of Spain" across Arrowhead Lake led the Fair visitor to the reproduction of the "Walled City of Manilla," which served as the entrance to the Philippine exhibits.*

paintings, a model of a house showing the different stages of completion from start to finish. A large silver coffee set, and a specimen of the work of some insect which gets in books and eats them destroying them completely. As it was getting late I took the intramural at No. 7 and rode to No. 15. While passing the Missouri Bld'g. I remarked to myself how pretty it looked when illuminated at night and thought I must visit it some time at night. Leaving the car at No. 15 I went to meet Mama and Norma at the DeForest Wireless Telegraph Tower.[93] I was to meet them at half past five, but was about fifteen minutes late. We went on the tower and viewed the illumination which showed to good advantage. I pointed out the dome of the Missouri Bld'g. to Mama. After leaving the top we stopped about half way down at the Wireless Telegraph Station. They could send messages to Chicago and several other places. On reaching the ground again we walked to the corner of Liberal Arts, then started

for the Model street, when we heard the fire department rushing towards us. We stopped to let it pass, but it went by Liberal Arts Bld'g. Then another one passed over the next street, and in a few minutes they were coming from all directions. By this time we could see the smoke and smell the wood burning, so we started back to see what was burning. On reaching the foot of the hill at the end of the Government Bld'g. the black smoke came pouring down so thickly that I was afraid to go farther. We found out that the Missouri Bld'g. was on fire so we turned back to meet Angie at the St. Louis statue. While waiting for her we saw a part of the fireworks, and when she came about seven o'clock, I started for the fire while the rest of them went to the Pike. I crossed the Plaza St. Louis and Joliet bridge, went along the water way to the Plaza of Orleans and crossing the DeSmet bridge went around the Mines and Fisheries Bld'gs. and up Government Hill to the Louisiana Bld'g. where I watched the fire awhile.

93. The two-hundred-and-fifty-foot high DeForest Wireless Telegraph Tower was brought to the Fair in sections from Buffalo. Operated by the American DeForest Wireless Co. of New York, it was a working wireless telegraph that was in communication with DeForest Company stations in several cities, including Chicago, Cleveland, and Kansas City. MacMechen, "The Pike and Its Attractions," p. 34, and "Wireless Telegraphy," *WFB*, March 1904, p. 35.

DeForest Wireless Telegraph Tower. *Photograph, 1904. The DeForest Tower, located at the head of the Plaza of Orleans southeast of the Palace of Liberal Arts (right) and the Palace of Manufactures, offered visitors the opportunity to both observe the operation of wireless telegraphy and view the fairgrounds from an elevated platform.*

On the West end of the building three flags were still floating although the fire was all around them, while I watched one of the flag poles took fire at the base and it must have burned the rope that held the flag, for a minute later it came fluttering to the ground unharmed. As I walked around the building I saw that the fire was doing the most damage in the South wing.[94] I returned to the East end of the Pike where I met the others about eight o'clock, we then took lunch at the restaurant near Creation. Mrs. Byrnes and her daughter Nellie came in while we were eating. After lunch we went to the Baby Incubators.[95] One baby was as small as a doll, its hand was about as big as my thumb. They have a number of Physicians and trained nurses in constant attendance on the babies. The gate receipts go towards keeping the babies, as there is no charge to the parents of the child. The babies are taken from their homes to the Fair in an incubator suspended on springs in an ambulance. We went to the Chinese village next and saw the fire eater perform the same tricks as usual, the sleight-of-hand performer took a large flower pot, two live rabbits and two bowls of water from under his magic shawl at different times, he also filled a cup with rice and placing another cup on it turned it over and he had two cups full, he then evened one cup till it was level full, placed an empty cup on it turned it over and jerked them apart, and showed an artificial flower growing in each cup. We tried our luck at fishing, Mama won a small basket, Angie a package of Joss sticks and I a small cup and saucer which I gave to Mama as a souvenir, she gave me a small red glass with my name on it. I also bought a couple of soap babies at the Baby incubators and gave Angie one as a souvenir. It was about eleven o'clock when we took the Easton ave. cars for home.

94. The fire Philibert describes partially destroyed the Missouri Building and badly damaged many of its furnishings. It started from an electric light wire located under the assembly room. *Missouri Republican*, November 20, 1904, and Bennitt, ed., *History of the LPE*, pp. 423-24.
95. The "Baby Incubators" was a Pike concession containing fourteen incubators for newborns and a nursery for incubator "graduates." A functioning exhibit, the Baby Incubators concession accommodated premature newborns from St. Louis. *The Greatest of Expositions* (St. Louis: Official Photographic Company, 1904), p. 249.

Minnesota State Building. *Photograph, 1904. Built among the trees and abutting graceful roadways, the state pavilions appeared as if they were set in a nicely appointed city rather than on the grounds of an exposition. The Massachusetts State Building is pictured to the left.*

St. Louis Mo. November 22nd 1904

I made my twenty fourth visit to the Fair to day. I arrived at the States entrance about half past ten and went to the Indiana Bld'g. first. Here I saw an inlaid table with a map of the United States as the top, Rhode Island was next. There was a piece of crochet or embroidered work here, that was done by an old sailor. It took him eight and one half years working ten hours a day to complete it. It was a chart of flags of all nations, and for the amount of time that was spent on it didn't amount to much. Nevada resembled a bargain sale, a pair of green portiers were marked three dollars, a palm two dollars and so on. Crossing the street I entered the Pennsylvania Bld'g. and found there an urn covered with four thousand rare coins, some of them dating as far back as three thousand B.C. the coins were all bolted to the urn, but could be detached separately at a moment's notice. This was the work of Edward Rausch the world's greatest coin collector. In Indiana I saw the original manuscript of the novel Fair God by Lew Wallace.[96] Passing

on to the Connecticut Bld'g. I saw a piano one hundred and seventy five years old it was a plain looking little thing about two wide by five long, there were also a number of clocks one hundred years old in this building. Arkansas had a clock made in Germany in 1763 for the Duke of Saxony. It was an old fashioned tall hall clock. Iowa was next, the building is prettier on the outside than it is on the inside. There was an organ on the stair landing, and a nice large reception room on the second floor, also an inlaid table with a top in which were inlaid cards, dice, dominoes, horse shoes, jockey whips, and other emblems of sport. Next I visited New York for the first time, I saw nothing in it to compare with the Missouri Bld'g. Crossing Commonwealth ave. I entered the Massachusetts Bld'g. where there was a photograph of the house in which Hancock and Adams were sleeping on the eve of the 19th of April 1775 when roused by Paul Revere. Minnesota contained nothing much except a large reading room. Arizona was a very small building, but it contained a lot of curios, among

---

96. Lewis Wallace, 1827-1905, author of *The Fair God* (1873), was the son of Indiana governor David Wallace.

Ruins of the Missouri State Building. *Snapshot, 1904. This view of the interior of the Missouri Building after its destruction by fire on the evening of November 19, 1904, shows the extent of the damage.*

Interior, Maryland State Building. *Photograph, 1904. This view shows the Maryland building as seen and described by Edmund Philibert. The portrait of Cardinal Gibbons, which he mentioned, hangs to the left.*

others picture frames made of Cacti wood, the wood resembles bone and the entire surface is perforated with holes. Indian territory contained a Seminole execution tree, it contained a number of bullet marks on the bark. There were two paintings of Thomas Jefferson and five generations of his descendants. New Jersey had a fine substantial frame building, which was a reproduction of the old Ford House at Morristown which was used by Washington as headquarters during one winter of the Revolutionary war. The big reception hall contained a large old fashioned fire place. Mississippi was represented by "Beauvoir" the last home of Jefferson Davis, I intended to visit this building but it was closed, so I went over to Oklahoma, where there were a number of hand carved mahogany tables made during the reign of Napoleon I and brought to this country one hundred years ago. Maryland had a painting of

The burning of the Peggy Stewart, a large painting of Cardinal Gibbons and a small square piano made in Baltimore in 1810 by James Stewart. I visited West Virginia next and from there went to Montana where there was a picture about eight by twelve feet of Custer's last battle, one of Lewis and Clark's expedition in 1804 when they discovered the first water flowing towards the West, and a pretty white onyx mantle. Crossing Constitution ave. I entered New Mexico's Bld'g. I guess it contained the oldest relic at the Fair; a bell that had been cast in Spain in 1355 and brought to America in the sixteenth century. The date showed plainly on the bell. Maine was represented by a log cabin. The reception room contained a large old fashioned stone fire place, with a rock shelf over it, and a cheery wood fire in it, I sat here awhile and warmed myself then went up stairs. The stairway was made of logs cut in two lengthwise and fitted into other logs which ran on an angle from one floor to another. Leaving the Maine Bld'g. I passed where the oil well drills were working, and went through the foundry to the Cement exhibit.[97] There were hollow blocks, and columns made of cement, and used for building purposes; they very closely resembled rock. I went to the T. P. A. Bld'g.[98] next but as they were breaking up

97. The exhibits Philibert describes here were part of the outdoor exhibits of the Department of Mines and Metallurgy, which included operating mines as well as oil wells, foundries, and the cement exhibit.

98. The Travelers' Protective Association building served as a headquarters, reception hall, and resting facility for members of that organization and their friends. *Official Guide*, p. 136. The T.P.A., founded in 1882, was primarily an association of commercial travelers. It lobbied to reduce or eliminate municipal and state license fees on commercial travel, reduce transportation rates, and assure moderately priced hotel accommodations. *St. Louis of '91: Progress and Prospects of the Magnificent Interior Commercial City* (n.p., Travelers' Protective Association of America, Missouri Division, 1891), pp. 51-65.

Par le Fer et Par le Feu (By Sword and By Fire), as exhibited in the Palace of Liberal Arts. *Photograph of painting by Polish artist Jan Styka, 1904.*

house keeping I didn't get any farther than just inside the entrance. I went to the ruins of the Missouri Bld'g. next. The outer walls were all standing but the interior and roof were entirely burned away with the exception of a portion of the East and West wings. Taking the car at Station No. 15 I rode to No. 2 where I secured a light lunch, then went through Varied Industries Bldg. to the German section, where I saw a reproduction of the Assembly room of the Saxon House of Deputies. It was a large room with paneled walls and ceiling, and contained an immense oval table with a doz. chairs around it. In another exhibit was an inlaid bed room set, and in still another was a fine inlaid table containing three thousand pieces and three hundred and fifty different kinds of rare woods. In Liberal Arts, I had often noticed an instrument which looked like an organ, with a snare drum on one side and a bass drum and pair of cymbals on the other, on a shelf in front were the figures of four dancing girls and a man with a baton in his hand. As I entered the building to day, this instrument was playing and it sounded like a full band playing, the man on the shelf would beat time and turn his head from side to side. There was a large picture, about twelve by twenty four feet, by Jan Styka[99] artist of

Paris. After leaving Liberal Arts Bldg. I walked around a little and left the grounds about half past five at the States entrance.

St. Louis Mo. November 24th 1904

I made my twenty fifth visit to the Fair to day. With Mama, Angie, Marie[100] and Norma I entered at the States entrance about half past one. We walked over to the rear entrance of the Art Palace, and I left them there and went over to the California Bld'g. It is a replica of the old Franciscan Mission of La Rabida, at Santa Barbara. Next I went to the Illinois Bld'g. it is situated on a hill and commands a good view of the grounds surrounding it, inside is a large hall with a mosaic floor, and a large vaulted dome above. A two story balcony runs around the outside, where it is very pleasant to sit in reasonable weather. I walked through the German R.R. exhibit[101] and went to the Forestry Bld'g. where I saw a house built entirely of yellow pine, furniture and all, the sides and ceilings of the rooms were paneled, one room was finished a kind of mahogany, another like Flemish oak, and the other, which was beautiful, was like a dark walnut, ebony, or rosewood, it was all beautifully polished and I never knew before that yellow pine could be

99. *Par le Fer et Par le Feu* (By Sword and By Fire), by Polish artist Jan Styka, had been exhibited in the Paris Salon in 1901. It depicted the Lithuanian Prince Witold swearing vengeance on the order of German Knights for the destruction of Kovno in 1362.

100. Edmund's niece Jeanne Marie, daughter of his sister Sarah Catherine. Ortes-Barada family tree, Philibert Papers.

101. This is a reference to the outdoor German Railroad exhibit located due north of the Palace of Forestry, Fish and Game.

Deutsches Haus, Weltausstellung St. Louis 1904 (German House, World Exposition, St. Louis, 1904). *Color lithograph by August Unger, 1904, Georg Buexenstein & Comp., repr. The German National Pavilion was a reproduction of the Charlottenburg Castle, erected by Frederick I, 1657-1713, the first King of Prussia, as a wedding present for his wife, Sophie Charlotte.*

finished so nicely. I visited the Distillery.[102] There were a number of large tubs about eight feet deep. In one was a lot of liquid which a man kept stirring. There was a metal moonshine still which had been captured in the mountains of Kentucky. It bore numerous bullet holes, in consequence of two moonshiners and three revenue officers losing their lives in its capture. I took the intramural next and rode to No. 12 and ascending the hill beside the Art Palace I met Mamma, Angie, and the children at the East side of festival hall, then we all went to the German Bld'g. It is a reproduction of The Charlottenburg castle, erected two hundred years ago by Frederick of Prussia.[103] The dome contains a chime of nicely toned bells, that sound the hours. Inside are reception rooms containing furniture that has been in the castle for two centuries. The German Emperor's wedding

presents, and many of his personal treasures. The walls are covered with rare tapestries, and from the ceilings of some of the rooms hung large chandeliers with wax candles in them. Some of the rooms were immense in size. Leaving this Bld'g. we crossed La Salle bridge and went to the Wireless Telegraph Tower, Angie, Marie and I went on top of it. We could see all over the Fair grounds, Forest Park and a part of the city. Half way down the Telegraph operator gave a demonstration. He said the messages are carried on ether at the rate of one hundred and eighty six miles a second. We walked through municipal street[104] and entered The correspondence school of languages, The Municipal museum and The Kansas City Casino, then we went to the Grand Basin to see the fireworks, and left for home by way of Lindell entrance about eight o'clock.

---

102. The Model Distillery of the Sunny Brook Distillery Co. of Louisville, Kentucky, was located south of the Palace of Forestry, Fish and Game and was an operating exhibit for the production of alcoholic liquors. A special U.S. Government permit had been taken out for its operation and an adjoining government bonded warehouse was established for the handling of the product. *Official Guide*, p. 147, and Bennitt, ed., *History of the LPE*, pp. 763-65.

103. The German Pavilion is described in *Official Catalogue of the Exhibition of the German Empire*, pp. 105-14.

104. The Municipal Street or Model Street, part of the exhibit of the Department of Social Economy, contained various "model" civic structures that housed the municipal exhibits of several cities. Among the buildings were a Model Town Hall, a Model Emergency Hospital actually used as the fairgrounds emergency hospital and clinic, and a Model Playground that served as a daycare center. Bennitt, ed., *History of the LPE*, pp. 553-54; "The Model Street: An Object Lesson"; "The Model City's Day Nursery and Home of Rest for Children," *WFB*, January 1904, p. 22.

President and Mrs. Roosevelt and D. R. Francis in Reviewing Stand on President's Day, Nov. 26. *Photograph, 1904. From this vantage point, President Theodore Roosevelt (seated left) and LPE Co. President David R. Francis (standing) reviewed the parade that included Filipino troops and both black and white American Cavalry units.*

St. Louis Mo. November 26th 1904

I made my twenty sixth visit to day. I entered at States entrance about ten o'clock, and visited Ohio, first, it contained life sized paintings of Mark Hanna[105] and President McKinley. Kansas contained rest rooms for ladies and reading and smoking rooms for gentlemen. Wisconsin is a pretty building, both inside and out in one parlor it had a nice hand carved piano that had been placed there by the manufacturers as an award for the building that came nearest to fulfilling the ideal of a state home. After leaving Wisconsin I went to the steps of the Government Bld'g. where I waited to see the military parade.[106] President Roosevelt was reviewing the parade from a platform opposite the Government Bld'g. The Filipino band played John Brown as they marched past the reviewing stand. The Cavalry, of which there were about three white and two Negro troops, came galloping past. The president's party then entered carriages and were driven away. I visited New Hampshire next. It is a reproduction of the house in which Daniel Webster was born. Vermont's Bld'g. was visited next. It is a reproduction of the house in which the Constitution was first written at Windsor. I next visited the pottery display where I saw some very beautiful vases. The Metal Pavilion[107] contained numerous articles made of aluminum, and a machine in operation which was drawing wire. The wire is drawn through a hole which is just too small for it to go through, it is therefore stretched until it is small enough to go through. It goes through one hole after another until it is reduced to the proper size. I went to South Dakota next. It contained a large room, with the walls and ceiling adorned with panels, made of different kinds of grain; corn, wheat, oats, barley etc. The Disciples of Christ Bld'g.[108] contained books, pamphlets and pictures of colleges. Oregon a reproduction of old Fort Clatsop[109] was next. It was built of logs with an old fashioned stone chimney and fire place. Across the street was the house of Hoo Hoo.[110] It was built by The lumberman's association, and contained tables made from slices of trees with the bark still on. A wooden obelisk highly polished showed the different ways of finishing the wood. I went through Grant's Cabin next and in the yard I saw a man cutting a splinter from one of the logs, for a souvenir I suppose. I spent a short time in the Art Palace, visiting the German, Austrian, British, International, and United States Sections. The German Section contained a good picture.[111]

105. Marcus Alonzo Hanna, 1837-1904, Ohio businessman and politician; supporter of fellow Ohioan President William McKinley; United States Senator, 1897-1904.

106. The central feature of the day, the military parade and salute consisted of several units of American military, including the Filipino Scouts and Constabulary under American command. *Daily Official Program*, November 26, 1904, pp. 3-4.

107. The Pottery display and the Metal Pavilion were both part of the outside exhibits of the Department of Mines and Metallurgy.

108. The Disciples of Christ Building was used as a place of worship and headquarters for members of the Disciples of Christ, reported as the third largest Christian congregation in the United States at that time. It was an enlarged replica of the original Disciples of Christ chapel, designed by Alexander Campbell, founder of the denomination. The original chapel was located near Bethany, West Virginia, and had been built in 1840. *Official Guide*, p. 136, and *Daily Official Program*, June 3, 1904, p. 23.

109. Fort Clatsop on the Pacific Coast was where Meriwether Lewis and William Clark wintered over in 1805-6 on their exploration of the Louisiana Territory and search for a route to the Pacific Ocean.

110. The House of Hoo Hoo was the gathering place of members of the Concatenated Order of Hoo Hoo, the lumbermen's mutual benefit organization. *Official Guide*, p. 136.

111. *The Son*, by Hans Koberstein of Germany, won a bronze medal in the Department of Art. It is pictured in Bennitt, ed., *History of the LPE*, p. 519.

There was a picture of a man lying on a bed with a soldier's coat thrown over him, and in the room were two soldiers in sorrowful attitudes, while on the table was a crucifix between two lighted candles. The international section contained a bit of Chinese art in the shape of a figure supporting a column on which was a ball, inside of the outer ball was another, inside of that another, and so on, there were eighteen balls in all, each one delicately carved, and the wonder is how it was done, as they are entirely too large to be carved separately and put through the small opening which is in each ball. This piece was all carved in ivory. Descending the Cascade steps I crossed Jefferson and Lewis and Clark bridges and crossed the Plaza St. Anthony to Station No. 2 where I had lunch, and then went to the Siam Bld'g. It contained a model of a temple and house, an ancient war drum, a large pair of elephant's tusks, Hodah's or elephant saddles, articles inlaid with mother of pearl, drawings and school text books, and portraits of the King, Queen & Prince of Siam. Nicaragua contained specimens of woods, pictures, furniture etc. There was a very pretty bed room set, made of wood resembling, mahogany. The bed was a single one and had a canopy over the head. The Argentine Republic, contained views and pictures, one picture showed a very novel fire escape, it was a canvas chute, held on the upper floor by firemen and running on an angle to the ground where it was held in place by more firemen, there was no danger of falling out as it was closed on all sides and only open at the top and bottom. Guatemala contained specimens of wood and coffee. In the Anthropology Bld'g. the Daughters of the American Revolution had on exhibition a pistol that was taken by General George Washington at the surrender of Cornwallis.[112] I walked through the Indian reservation until I came to the Patagonians.[113]

Ainu Carver. Photograph, 1904. Caucasoid in appearance and heavily bearded, the Ainu from Japan were a great mystery for anthropologists at the Fair. Fair visitors, however, were often more interested in their activities and handwork. Philibert was simply impressed that the Ainu did not appear "dirty" or "lazy."

There was a man and a woman sitting in a dirty looking tent, near a fire on the ground. They were very lazy looking. There was a piece of black looking meat on a stick near the fire. The Ainus[114] were next, they were not as dirty nor nearly as lazy looking as the Patagonians. Two women were preparing some grain, cleaning it and pounding it in a mortar, made from the stump of a tree, while two of the men were carving knives and spoons out of wood. I visited the U.S. Life saving station[115] next. It contained a self bailing life boat, guns and rockets for carrying ropes to shipwrecked vessels, life cars which run between the wreck and shore on ropes, a number of statistics etc. The Refrigerating Plant was next visited, but there

---

112. The surrender of Lord Charles Cornwallis at Yorktown on October 19, 1781, effectively ended the American Revolution.

113. Also called the Tehuelche Indians of Patagonia, this group, consisting of five men, one woman, and a girl aged ten, was a Native American group brought to the Fair from extreme southern Argentina. Quite tall—the men averaged six feet—the Patagonians were accomplished horsemen. Bennitt, ed., *History of the LPE*, pp. 676-77, and Hanson, *Official History*, p. 101.

114. The Ainu were aboriginal people from the island of Hokkaido in Japan. Their group consisted of four men, three women and two children. More Caucasian than Asian in appearance, they were thought to be related perhaps to the Cossacks of Siberia. In one of the Fair's "official histories," they were described as "the most cleanly and courteous, most gentle and refined folk on the grounds." Bennitt, ed., *History of the LPE*, pp. 674-75. For an account of how the Ainu were brought to St. Louis, see: Starr, *The Ainu Group*.

115. One of the U.S. Government Treasury Department's exhibits, the U.S. Life Saving Station attempted to replicate a life saving station for the aid of offshore ships in distress and the rescue of shipwrecked crews. Daily demonstrations took place in the U.S. Life-Saving Lake, located just northeast of the Palace of Agriculture. Hanson, *Official History*, pp. 75-80.

was nothing much to see in it, so I ascended the hill to Morocco, there seemed to be nothing much there either, except a lot of booths with articles for sale, so I went to the Temple of Fraternity.[116] It was a very large building with wide hallways running its entire length, and a large reception room in the center. On either side of the hallways were rooms for the use of the different fraternal societies of Missouri. Idaho was the next on the list but owing to sickness of the host it was closed to visitors so I went to the Hermitage, a building erected for Tennessee by private subscriptions of the people. It is a reproduction of the home of Andrew Jackson, and is said to be a faithful copy, even to the wall paper in the reception hall. The reception hall contains a circular stairway with a very light balustrade, and in the side hall is another stairway with a large landing midway up. From the landing to the second floor the stairs are the width of the hall with the exception of about one foot of space between the balusters and wall. The Hostess of this building was born at the Hermitage and is the grand daughter of General Jackson. All of the rooms were large with high ceilings, and it looked as though it would make a comfortable home. The next building I visited was Georgia, it is a reproduction of "Southerland," the country home of General John B. Gordon. Every piece of material used in this building is a product of the State of Georgia. Like Tennessee it was built with funds collected by popular subscription. Virginia was represented by "Monticello" the home of Thomas Jefferson. The building was constructed from the original plans which were made by Jefferson himself. On a mantle in one of the rooms was a clock which had been in the Jefferson family prior to the revolution. I went around near Festival Hall next and heard the Great Organ,[117] then crossed Napoleon bridge, and went through Education Bld'g. and around to the front of the Grand Basin where I viewed the Cascades and illumination awhile and left the grounds about five o'clock at Lindell Entrance.

St. Louis Mo. November 30th 1904
I made my twenty seventh visit to day. I entered at Administration entrance about ten o'clock, and visited the Austrian Bld'g. for the second time. While examining a fine lace handkerchief a gentleman and lady came up beside me. She said; Look at that handkerchief, one dollar and sixty cents; Then he looked and said, Sixty dollars you mean. She said, Well what is that one in front of it for, then he looked again and said, It's a hundred and sixty dollars; and so it was. In the same case with it was a collar for sixty dollars. There were also beautiful fans with ivory and tortoise shell ribs, and a lot of fine vases and glassware. Crossing the street I went through Belgium again. There I saw patent sliding doors which operated without any tracks either above or below, the levers which operated them were concealed in pockets, into which the doors would slide. I think the parquetry and inlaid borders in this building, were the prettiest I ever saw. There was an old Flemish dining room of the early part of the sixteenth century. The walls and ceiling were nicely paneled and carved, and the floor which was inlaid was covered with rugs. The furniture was of antique pattern. In the Brazilian Bld'g. I received a half pound box of some new kind of tea. I walked through the Forestry Bld'g. and saw nothing new, except a choke attachment for shot guns. I went to the Agricultural Bld'g. next, in the California exhibit were a couple of radishes weighing twenty nine and thirty one pounds respectively. The Colorado exhibit contained the largest potatoes I ever saw, some of them were about a foot long. North Dakota's exhibit contained the log cabin which President Roosevelt occupied when he was a ranchman in Dakota. California also had a reproduction of the great seal of the state, made of beans of various colors. The Missouri exhibit contained corn and grain of all kinds, and some large pictures of Missouri farm scenes, also statues of an Indian and white women, with dresses made of corn shucks. The Indian women were adorned with strings of beads made from grains of corn. The figures had nice faces, and I thought the dresses were very artistic. In another part of the building

116. The Temple of Fraternity was a pavilion dedicated to the various fraternal organizations and served as the Exposition reception hall and headquarters for fraternal organizations and associations that met on the fairgrounds. *Official Guide*, p. 136.
117. The Great Organ in Festival Hall was reported to be the largest organ in the world, constructed by Murray M. Harris Organ Company, of Los Angeles, California. Daily concerts were performed on the organ. On this date, November 26, Philibert heard Frank Wilbur Chace play selections that included works by Meyerbeer, Bach, Elgar, and St. Louis composer Ernst Kroeger. *Official Guide*, p. 42; *Daily Official Program*, November 26, 1904, p. 5; Hanson, *Official History*, p. 178.

Missouri Corn Palace. *Photograph, 1904. The exhibit of the State of Missouri in the Palace of Agriculture included this dome, made entirely of corn and erected at a cost of $10,000.*

was the figure of a man dressed in a full dress suit that was made of binder twine. Missouri had a special corn exhibit.[118] It consisted of a large booth with the interior lined and paneled with corn of different colors, there were also a number of pictures and emblems made of corn. Passing the wind mill exhibit, I crossed the bamboo bridge and entered the Philippine reservation. As cold as the day was; (and there were icicles on a bush on which the sun had been shining for a couple of hours) I saw an Igorotte with nothing on him but a coat and sash, he didn't seem to mind the cold at all. I went to the Forestry Bld'g.

first. It contained, a large slab, about 5 ft. wide by 20 ft. long, from a Philippine cedar tree. Some kind of a black wood like ebony, which was very beautiful, a number of specimens of Narra wood, tables and other furniture including a dresser a century old and inlaid with ivory, baskets, wood fibre, large coils of rattan,[119] rattan furniture, gutta percha,[120] rosins, gums etc. The Ethnology Bld'g. contained pictures of the different tribes, shields, arms, cannon, musical instruments, specimens of native weaving and in a court in front of the building, a small house built up in a tree, a model of the houses of the tree dwelling Moros.[121]

---

118. Missouri's corn exhibit included a six-sided domed structure built entirely out of corn. Called the "Missouri Corn Palace" or the "Missouri Corn Temple," even the structure's interior was decorated with corn, corn husks, and corn stalks. Inside were several easy chairs for the relaxation of visitors. Much was made of the fact that in 1904 Missouri was the largest grower of corn in the United States, producing 10 percent of the nation's supply. See: Bennitt, ed., *History of the LPE*, pp. 425-26.

119. Made from climbing palms noted for the great length of their stems.

120. A grey to brown tough plastic substance obtained from the latex of Malaysian sapotaceous trees, gutta-percha is used primarily for electrical insulation.

121. A reference to the Islamic Llanao Moros, who inhabited the inland regions of Mindanao. Not to be confused with the Samal Moros, fishermen who lived on the shores or bayous of Mindanao and built their houses on pylons over the water. Tribal groupings of both the Llanao and Samal Moros were on display at Arrowhead Lake on the grounds of the Philippine Exposition. Newell, ed. and comp., *Philippine Exposition*; Francis, *Universal Exposition*, vol. 1, p. 571.

Igorots in "European Dress." *Photograph, 1904. This view illustrates the Philippine Igorots as Secretary of War Taft might have wished them to be clad, with short trousers and coats rather than simple loincloths. Such coats might have been all that the Igorots had to keep the cold out when Philibert saw them at the end of November.*

Clothing the Igorots

One of the Filipino tribal groups exhibited at the Fair was the Igorots, whose native clothing generally consisted simply of a loin cloth. This skimpy dress stimulated one of the more humorous debates that emerged during the course of the Fair. In June, Secretary of War and former Governor of the Philippines William Howard Taft suggested that the Igorot men wear short trousers, at least, in order to avoid "any possible impression that the Philippine Government is seeking to make prominent the savageness and barbarism of the wild tribes either for show purposes or to depreciate the popular estimate of the general civilization of the island." Rather than assuaging post-Victorian sensibilities, Taft's suggestion provoked a great deal of mirth from the public, while stimulating an outcry from the anthropologists. The *St. Louis Post-Dispatch* published a cartoon depicting Taft chasing a loincloth-clad Igorot with a pair of trousers clutched in his hands, while the Fair's director of exhibits, Frederick Skiff, taking up the anthropologists' case, argued that the scientific value of the Igorot exhibit "would be completely lost by dressing these people in a way unlike that to which they are accustomed." The

ultimate by-product of the dispute was to increase the popularity of the exhibit. The conflict was ultimately resolved when the Board of Lady Managers sided with the anthropologists.

An interesting outgrowth of this has been the emergence of a popular myth that it was the prudishness of the Lady Managers that led to efforts to clothe the Igorots. One image in the Missouri Historical Society's Photographs and Prints Collections (reproduced above) shows Igorots clothed in European style jackets or coats with the caption: "As the Lady Managers wanted to have them." This was, in fact, not the case, as the research of historian Robert Rydell has demonstrated. See: Rydell, *All the World's a Fair*, pp. 172-74. The foregoing quotations are as cited by Rydell.

In the autumn, as cold weather approached, the clothing issue again resurfaced. W. P. Wilson, chairman of the Philippine Exposition Board, held the opinion that the Igorots should continue to wear their traditional loincloths despite the weather. The board opted to heat and insulate the Igorots' huts instead of issuing sufficiently warm clothing. See: Vostral, "Imperialism on Display," p. 24.

The Life Saving Drill. *Photograph, 1904. This demonstration, held at the U.S. Life Saving Station, shows one of the techniques that could be used to aid offshore ships in distress or rescue shipwrecked crews.*

Crossing Arrow Head Lake I walked down to the Life Saving Lake; where I was just in time to see them rescue two men from the mast in the middle of the lake; which act concluded the afternoon's exhibition, so I went on to the Transportation Bld'g. where I went through the day train between St. Louis and Kansas City. It consisted of an Engine, Mail, Baggage, Dining and Chair car with one or two day coaches, and I think it was much nicer than the Empire State Express. By this time I was feeling rather hungry so I made for my old stand Station No. 2 where I took lunch. Here the girls were laughing and joking and having a gay time, but nevertheless it seemed to me they were sorry, that the ending of the Fair was so near. After lunch I went through Varied Industries Bld'g. for the last time, but I saw nothing new except a number of church windows and statues. I went through Manufacturers Bld'g. where I saw an Ermine cloak trimmed in Russian Sable, in the French Section. There was no price marked on it but I was told it cost $12 000.00. In this section there was also a red court gown. The organ recital was going on when I entered Liberal Arts Bld'g. and I listened to a couple of pieces, then strolled through the Bld'g. to the Chinese section, where I saw a tree with eighty birds on it. It was made entirely of silver, and the birds were of all species. There were vases about ten inches high worth ten and twelve hundred dollars, and one vase about six inches high three inches in diameter at its widest and one inch at its narrowest part, on an ivory stand, about two inches high was worth $10 000.00. At least that is the information I heard one lady give a number of others, she said it was a genuine peach blow vase, and a lost art among the Chinese, they have never been able to get that exact shade, I don't know whether she was right or not. The vase was a kind of Terra Cotta color and perfectly plain. I went through Mines, Education and Electricity Bld'gs. next. In the latter building I saw the first electric car used by Thomas Edison.[122] Ascending to the Terrace of States, I viewed the Cascades and general surroundings awhile then went to see the Cascade pumps in operation[123] There are three pumps but they only use one at a time, they are rather small common looking things and the wonder is how they can raise such a tremendous amount of water to such a height. Leaving the pump house I took the Intramural at No. 16 and rode to No. 3 where I entered the Pike and walked to the East end, and left the grounds at the Lindell Entrance.

St. Louis Mo. December 1st 1904

I made my twenty eighth and last visit to the Fair to day. I entered at the Lindell entrance about a quarter to five and as this is the last day of the Fair I proceeded to get a last view of the Pike. I entered at the East end and it was just jammed. Everybody was in a jovial mood and seemed determined to have a good time. There were horns, cow bells, rooster calls, feather ticklers, confetti and any number of other things very much in evidence to help make things lively. Most of the shows were running at reduced prices, and Hereafter was taking them in pretty lively at fifteen cents per head.[124] There were a great many policemen and Jefferson guards on duty, besides some mounted policemen stationed along at intervals. As I neared the center of the Pike the crowd became denser, then thinned out a little as I got farther along and at the West end they were pouring in in a steady stream. There was an old darky watching them shoot the chutes,[125] and every time a boat would strike the water she would let out a hearty laugh. Leaving the Pike, I went through Machinery Hall, and then walked down Louisiana way. As I crossed Davy Crockett bridge a tally ho[126] preceded and followed by mounted police came along and I recognized Pres. Francis on it with thirty or forty others, whom I took to be the board of directors. As the coach passed the people cheered and Francis raised his hat in acknowledgement, as this was Francis Day.[127] Continuing on I walked through the sunken garden and along the Government Terrace and over the Plateau of States to Station No. 14 where I took the intramural alighting at No. 1, I walked up to the Grand Basin and sat watching the Cascades awhile, then I ascended to the Terrace of States and as this was my last opportunity I spent some time in viewing the Cascades and illumination in all directions, then descending the East steps I walked along by the Grand Basin and Plaza of St. Louis taking a farewell look at everything as I went, and it made me feel a little sad to think that it would soon be all over forever for I had spent many pleasant days there, but everything must come to an end sometime, so I left Lindell entrance for the last time at about half past seven.

---

122. Thomas Edison's personal exhibit in the Department of Electricity included the "storage battery he [had] designed for automobile use." *Official Guide*, p. 76.

123. Located in a grotto at the eastern approach to the Terrace of States were three centrifugal pumps supplying water for the Cascades, each with the capacity to deliver thirty thousand gallons of water per minute. The pumps were powerful enough that as of mid-August no more than a single pump had had to be utilized at one time. The Cascade pumps were open to the public and considered to be an exhibit of the Department of Machinery. *Official Guide*, p. 80.

124. The "Hereafter" normally charged twenty-five cents admission. "Popular Prices," p. 18.

125. A reference to the Pike water ride, "Shoot the Chutes."

126. A coach drawn by four horses.

127. Closing day of the Fair was set aside as "Francis Day" to honor Louisiana Purchase Exposition Company President David R. Francis. *Daily Official Program*, December 1, 1904.

Edmund Philibert

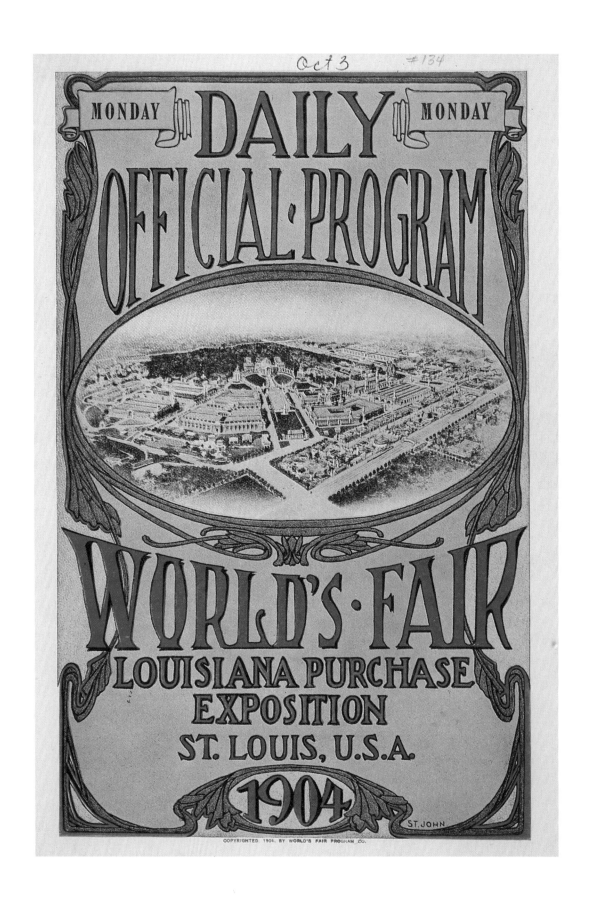

List of World's Fair Expenses

St Louis Mo. April 30th 1904[1]

1st visit: Car fare .20 Admission 1.00 Souvenir .06 Needle threaders .25 Soda .15 Intramural .20 Total 1.86 April 30th[2]

2nd visit: Car fare .10 Admission .50 Soda .15 Intramural .10 Total .85 May 21st

3rd visit: Car fare .10 Admission .50 Lemonade .30 Alps .25 Total 1.15 May 28th

4th visit: Car fare .10 Admission .50 Souvenir .06 Hagenbeck's .10 Intramural .20 Total .96 May 30th

5th visit: Car fare .10 Admission .50 Total .60 May 31st

6th visit: Car fare .10 Admission .50 Intramural .10 Lemonade .05 Total .75 June 19th

7th visit: Car fare .10 Admission .50 Intramural .10 Total .70 July 9th

8th visit: Car fare .35 Admission 1.00 Soda .35 Orangeade .20 Total 1.90 July 16th

9th visit: Car fare .20 Admission .50 Intramural .30 Tea Set .40 Total 1.40 July 23rd[3]

10th visit: Car fare .30 Admission 1.50 Intramural .90 Root Beer .10 Sandwich .10 Program .05 Chinese Coin .05 Total 3.00 July 30th

11th visit: Car fare .20 Admission .50 Total .70 Aug. 13th

12th visit: Car fare .50 Admission 2.50 Ferris Wheel 2.50 Launch 1.25 Refreshments .50 Parcel .15 Souvenirs .20 Intramural 1.50 Lost .01 Total 9.11 Aug. 20th[4]

13th visit: Car fare .30 Admission 1.00 Programme .05 Supper .95 Lung Tester[5] .10 Glass Bottle .10 Total 2.50[6]

14th visit: Car fare .40 Admission 2.00 Programme .05 Lemonade .20 Intramural .80 Souvenirs .55 Lunch .85 Glass-Blowers .40 Creation 2.00 Jim Key 1.00 Total 8.25[7]

15th visit: Car fare .05 Admission .50 Programme .05 Total .60[8]

16th visit: Car fare .10 Admission .50 Fountain Pen .25 Programme .05 Total .90 Oct. 8th

17th visit: Car fare .10 Admission .50 Programme .05 Total .65 Oct. 15th

---

1. Philibert Papers.
2. Trip to Fair with Angie; carfare or streetcar fare for two, to Fair and back, at five cents per trip; admission for two at fifty cents apiece; one intramural trip for two at ten cents per trip; souvenir unknown.
3. The tea set was purchased for Florence McCallion at the Japanese Garden.
4. Ferris Wheel trips cost fifty cents. The lost cent was the penny that Philibert had dropped into the pot of quicksilver (mercury) in the Texas exhibit in the Palace of Mines and Metallurgy. The cost for the "launch" was for a twenty-five-minute ride in an electric launch on the lagoon, at twenty-five cents apiece for five people. "Popular Prices," p. 20, and Ferris Wheel advertisement in *Daily Official Program*, October 18, 1904, p.14.
5. Efforts to identify the "lung tester" have been unsuccessful. On this date, however, Philibert did spend the evening on the Pike. The "lung tester" may have been a feature of one of the many Pike entertainments.
6. This visit took place on August 27, 1904.
7. Souvenirs include a souvenir book of Fair pictures purchased for Lucy and May Byrne, and a souvenir made for Angie at a souvenir machine. This visit took place on September 3, 1904.
8. This visit took place on September 28, 1904.

18th visit: Car fare .10 Admission .50 Programme .05 Total .65 Oct. 22nd

19th visit: Car fare .10 Admission .50 Programme .05 Supper .20 Total .85 Oct. 29th

20th visit: Car fare .10 Admission .50 Programme .05 Aeronautic Concourse .25 Intramural .10 Total 1.00 Nov. 5th

21st visit: Admission 1.75 Programme .05 Intramural .20 Temple of Mirth 1.10 Old Plantation 1.10 Angie's Pictures .50 Total 4.70 Nov. 10th[9]

22nd visit: Car fare .25 Admission 1.00 Programme .05 Lecture Book .10 Camel ride .35 Chinese Pool .20 Hereafter 1.50 Total 3.45 Nov. 12th[10]

Visits of Katie,[11] Florence, Mama, Norma and Marie Total 11.50[12]

23rd visit: Car fare .25 Admission .50 Program .05 Intramural .10 Lunch .40 Baby incubator .50 Soap Babies .20 Fish Pond .30 Total 2.30 Nov. 19th[13]

24th visit: Car fare .10 Admission .50 Program .05 Intramural .10 Lunch .20 Total .95 Nov. 22nd

25th visit: Car fare .40 Admission 1.00 Program .05 Intramural .20 Wireless Telegraph Tower .75 Total 2.40 Nov. 24th[14]

26th visit: Car fare .10 Admission .50 Program .05 Lunch .20 Total .85 Nov. 26th

27th visit: Car fare .10 Admission .50 Lunch .20 Intramural .10 Total .90 Nov. 30th

28th visit: Car fare .10 Admission .50 Intramural .10 Total .70 Dec. 1st

---

9. The admission cost was for three adults and one child, the fee for a child's admission being twenty-five cents.

10. The camel ride was a feature of the "Jerusalem" concession. The "Chinese Pool" is most likely a reference to the arcade game that Philibert and his sister Florence played in the "Chinese Village."

11. Possibly Sarah Catherine Philibert, Edmund's sister and the mother of Norma and Marie. Ortes-Barada family tree, Philibert Papers.

12. Probably a reference to expenses borne by Edmund Philibert when he was unable to join his family at the Fair. For an account of one such Fair visit paid for by Philibert, see Florence McCallion's letter to her husband, October 6, 1904, on p. 124 of this volume.

13. "Soap Babies" were purchased at the "Baby Incubator" concession; "Fish Pond" is a reference to an arcade game at the "Chinese Village."

14. The Wireless Telegraph cost twenty-five cents per person to visit. *Official Guide*, p. 136.

Festival Hall. *Photograph, 1904. The ornately decorated Festival Hall, positioned atop "Art Hill," was the focal point of the Fair's Main Picture.*

Florence McCallion

Florence McCallion was Edmund Philibert's sister. During the summer and fall of 1904, she spent an extended period in St. Louis with her family and frequently accompanied her brother Edmund to the fair. The following text consists of a handful of letters written by McCallion to her husband Frank, a farmer in Cadet, Missouri. These letters indicate that she was better educated than her brother—not uncommon among artisan families, where male children left school early to enter apprenticeships. Written to an intimate for whom she clearly felt immense affection, McCallion's letters reflect a great desire on her part to include her husband in the Fair experience.

Night View from the Wireless Telegraph Tower. *Photograph, 1904. This view, west-northwest from atop the DeForest Wireless Telegraph Tower, across the Plaza of Orleans, pictures Festival Hall and the Colonnade of States in the distance.*

Japanese Tea Party. *Photograph, 1904. Florence McCallion and her brother Edmund Philibert may have been served tea in a setting such as this in the Japanese Garden.*

World's Fair Letters

St. Louis Mo. July 24th 1904[1]

My Dear Husband,

I did wish that you were with me yesterday. I had such a lovely time at the Fair. There was only one thing that marred my pleasure, and, that was your absence.

I thought about you all day and evening. I wish you could come up and stay at least a month and go to the Fair every day. I know you would enjoy it.

Edmund[2] had to work in the morning, so Angie and I went out early and met Edmund in the afternoon.

We went through the Indian Territory, Indiana, Iowa, Arkansas, Kansas, Utah, Rhode Island, Connecticut, and Pennsylvania State Buildings.

We also went through the Agriculture and Horticulture Buildings, and the Japanese Garden and Bazaar. At the Japanese Garden we had green Japan tea made by the Japanese, and served by Japanese girls in native costume. They served little Japanese cakes with the tea. Some of the girls were as white as we are. They all wear white stockings and sandals. They have a studio and two men painting pictures.

In the Horticulture Building at the California display, they had the State Capitol at Sacramento made of almonds, and an elephant made of english walnuts. At the Mississippi exhibit there was a horse made of pecans. We saw some persimmons as large as an orange. In the Agriculture Bld'g. there was a plow that I wish

---

1. Florence McCallion's letters to her husband, Frank McCallion, Philibert Papers.
2. Florence's brother Edmund Philibert. See p. 80 for Edmund's description of this same visit.

you had one like, then you wouldn't have to walk so much and get so tired. In the Indiana B'ld'g. we saw the original copy of Lew Wallace's Fair God. Also numerous other manuscripts of different writers. There was one by Mrs. Lew Wallace. Lew Wallace's was beautiful, so even and neat, and the writing was lovely. In Iowa there was an inlaid table with a piece of wood from the battleships Maine and Oregon. Pennsylvania has [the] Liberty Bell,[3] and an urn covered with 4,000 coins. Every known coin is represented. Some of them date as far back as 3,000 B.C. One piece had a figure of St. Aloysius[4] stamped on it. Another had a Pope's head (at least it looked like it). In Connecticut we saw the bed Oliver Ellsworth died in.[5] The chair George Washington sat in during the first Congress,[6] and afterwards owned by Andrew Jackson. A spinnet (sort of a piano) over 150 years old. Chippendale furniture, Washington mirrors, Martha Washington's tea table. Another table that came over from France in a ship load of beautiful furniture supposed to be for a bride, but it was rumored that it belonged to Marie Antoinette and that there was a plot to rescue her, so she didn't get away but the furniture did.[7] There was an inlaid clock in the Agriculture Building with 50,000 pieces of wood in it. Some of them were almost like a pin head. In Indian Ter. there were some beautiful paintings by a Cherokee Indian, Mrs. Narcissa Owen, 72 years old. A young man, he had one sixteenth Indian blood (cherokee) in him, gave Angie and me a sheet of this paper and an envelope as a souvenir.[8]

We saw the floral clock, but I, and Angie also, were disappointed in it. Edmund bought me the cutest little Japanese waiter, just about four inches long, with a sweet little tea pot, sugar and cream and two cups and saucers.

Of course your baby has to have some thing to play with.

We got home about half past nine.

We rode on the intramural at the Fair. If the buildings are very far apart you know it is too much of a walk for me.

I do hope and pray that my baby can come up soon. I want to see him so badly, and kiss him and hug him too—My lips are homesick for those kisses you promised them.

How is your wheat? I hope all right. Of course I know that it is not *all* good, but I hope it is not as bad as you thought. Is it?

With lots of love and kisses from your loving wife

Florence

St. Louis Mo. Sept. 24th 1904

My Dearest

I hope you are well and not working too hard: I am so lonely and homesick for *you*. I wish you were here right now.

Yesterday Helen treated Katie[9] and I to a most enjoyable afternoon and evening at the Fair. We took the Easton Avenue car and and entered the grounds at the Pike. Then we took the Intramural and rode to the Virginia B'ld'g. The Richmond Va. guards were drilling;[10] we watched them awhile, then went through the building. There was nothing of special interest there. There was some old furniture and a large painting of Thomas Jefferson.

From there we went to the Boer War.[11] I was wishing you were with us. It was fine. The horses

---

3. The Liberty Bell was brought to the Fair by the state of Pennsylvania and exhibited in the Pennsylvania State Pavilion in response to a petition of seventy-five thousand St. Louis school children. It arrived on June 8, 1904. The bell had previously been exhibited at fairs in New Orleans (1885), Chicago (1893), and Atlanta (1895). *Official Guide*, pp. 48-49, and *Daily Official Program*, June 8, 1904, pp. 4-5.

4. St. Aloysius Gonzaga, Italian Jesuit, 1568-1591, canonized 1726.

5. Oliver Ellsworth, 1745-1807, jurist and statesman and prominent in Connecticut's activities in the Revolutionary War.

6. A reference to the First Continental Congress, which sat in Philadelphia in 1774 just prior to the American Revolution.

7. Marie Antoinette, wife of Louis XVI of France, was executed by guillotine in 1793 during the French Revolution.

8. This letter was written on the letterhead of the Indian Territory Building.

9. Possibly Helen Woods and Florence's sister, Sarah Catherine.

10. September 23, 1904, was Virginia Day at the Fair. Among other activities was a morning military parade ending at the Virginia Building, which included the Richmond Blues, a Virginia National Guard unit. *Daily Official Program*, September 23, 1904, p. 2.

11. The Boer War, 1899-1902, was fought between Great Britain and the two Boer Republics (the South African Republic, or Transvaal, and the Orange Free State) over the future status of South Africa. In 1904 a group of South African and British Boer veterans, including Boer generals Piet Cronje and Benjamin Johannes Viljoen, were brought to the 1904 World's Fair, with the backing of St. Louis businessmen, by Captain Arthur W. Lewis, a Missourian by birth and British officer during the Boer War. In a twelve-acre amphitheater, the Boer veterans re-created the battle of Colenso, fought on the Tugela River on December 15, 1899, and the battle of Paardeburg, fought on February 27, 1900. They were accompanied by about fifty South African natives of the Swazie, Zulu, and Basuto tribes, whose presence on the concession grounds gave the setting an added air of authenticity and a source of often mistreated labor. See: MacMechen, "The Pike and Its Attractions," p. 33; "The Boer War Exhibition," *WFB*, March 1904, p. 39; Ted C. Hinckley, "When the Boer War Came to St. Louis," *MHR* 61 (April 1967), pp. 285-302.

The Boer War. *Photograph, 1904. This snapshot of the Boer War Exhibition demonstrates the realism of the re-enaction and shows the horses playing dead, just as McCallion describes.*

would fall down as if shot and lie down a long time perfectly motionless just like they were dead. Others would stand, walk and run around with saddles but no riders. One horse and soldier was wounded. The horse was shot in the leg, he limped around just exactly like he was really hurt. Oh it was fine.

Then we went through Agricultural and Horticultural Buildings. I enjoyed it just the same as if I had never been there. In the Nebraska exhibit in the Agriculture Bldg. we saw biograph views,[12] farmers in the fields etc.

Then we went up in the Ferris Wheel. We went around twice. After that we went to the Cascades and I enjoyed it as much as ever.

Then we had some lunch and hot coffee. Went to the Pike to the Baby Incubators.[13] They were in little glass cases lying on snow white cotton and dressed in sweet little white dresses. The girls with blue ribbon and the boys with pink. Some of them looked like dolls. One was such a tiny little delicate doll like baby, it seems almost impossible that it could live. We saw the nursery. There were little white and gold beds and babies that had graduated from the incubator. It was very interesting.

After that we went to the Temple of Mirth ("Foolish House"). We laughed all the time we were in there. There were looking glasses that made us look tall and thin, little and fat, long waisted and short legged, longed faced, and every ridiculous way imaginable. We looked through peep holes and saw our faces on a monkey's body. Also on a convict, on a girl in a low cut dress and worst of all, on a girl in a bath tub. You could only see the head, & arms; and legs thrown out side of tub. When a man looks in it will answer for him just the same.

Then we went home and arrived about eleven o'clock. What do you think of that? Don't you think we enjoyed ourselves. Helen stood all of the expense.

Edmund invited Katie, the children (Marie and Norma) and myself to the Fair today. We were all ready when it clouded up and looked like we would have a big storm, but it passed around and only rained here. It rained all afternoon, and quite heavy. We were very much disappointed. . . .[14]

---

12. Described in the *Daily Official Programs* as "biograph pictures in motion."
13. Cf. Philibert Diary, November 19, 1904, p. 104.
14. The letter ends here, as the last pages are missing.

Kiralfy's Louisiana Purchase Spectacle Libretto. *Program, 1904, LPE Co. Records. Florence McCallion attended this allegorical pageant. In its last scene, the character of "Civilization" triumphs over the chained "Spirit of Mississippi," and "Columbia" pays homage to the "New Louisiana."*

St. Louis Mo. Oct. 6th 1904

"My Honey Boy"

I am having such a lovely time. Saturday Edmund treated Katie and I to the Fair.[15] I got you a map at the Government building. We went in several places that I had been in but there is always some thing I hadn't seen before.

We went through the Palace of Fine Arts. It was grand. What do you think, we went to see the Igorots. They look like bronze statues. A great many women were weaving and some men were blacksmithing. One of the women gave me her autograph. I had my white shawl on my arm. She said, "puty, puty," meaning pretty. Just think they charge fifty cents a person now to go in there.[16]

My foot is better but still hurts a little.

Yesterday, Helen treated Katie and I to "Louisiana," a play at the Odeon. It was fine. We saw the death of DeSoto. He and two monks and another man were in a little skiff or canoe on the Mississippi River. When DeSoto is dying, the monk holds the crucifix and DeSoto kisses it.[17]

The scene is beautiful. It looks exactly like moonlight. I was wishing you could have seen it. . . .

With best love, hugs, and kisses from yours only

Florence

Palace of Art. *Photograph, 1904. Of the major exhibit palaces, the Palace of Art at the Fair was the only permanent structure. Today it is the home of the Saint Louis Art Museum.*

15. The previous Saturday was October 1, 1904. Edmund Philibert, Florence's brother, probably just stood the expense of this outing, as his diary does not indicate a visit to the Fair on this particular date. See Philibert's list of World's Fair expenses for his account of money spent on visits by Florence and other family members, p. 118.

16. The fifty-cent charge was most likely a fee to view programmed activities at the ethnological villages in the Philippine Exposition. Francis, *Universal Exposition,* vol. 1, pp. 571-72.

17. Hernando DeSoto, 1500?-1542, Spanish explorer, credited with the discovery of the Mississippi, actually did die on the banks of that river.

St. Louis Mo. May 7th 1905

My Dear Husband

I hope you are well. How is your eye and your leg? I hope all right . . .

This afternoon Edmund and I went out to the Fair Grounds. When we entered it made me heart sick to see the ruin and desolation. They charge twenty-five cents admission. All there is left of the Pike is Blarney Castle,[18] a part of Fair Japan, Helter Skelter,[19] and the cabins in Old Plantation. We saw a part of the Japanese Temple and two of their idols. The idols are hideous looking things. The Temple is four hundred years old. It is put together without a nail.[20]

We saw a couple of statues from the Baby Incubators. Italy, France, Austria, and mostly all of the Foreign and state buildings are blotted off of the map. There is not a *stone* left or in fact the least sign of France, Cuba, Italy, Forestry, Fish and Game, Texas, Kentucky and a great many other buildings. All around that part of the grounds would make you feel home sick for the Fair. Edmund and I were both wishing the Fair was going on.

A man by the name of Brookings[21] bought Great Britain. It is standing just exactly as we saw it at the Fair. The grounds are just the same also.

Demolition of the Pike. *Photograph, c. 1905. Looking east down the Pike after the close of the Fair, the partially destroyed "Streets of Cairo" is on the right, and the "Magic Whirlpool" is pictured on the left.*

18. Blarney Castle, or the Old Parliament House, was a restaurant in the Irish Industrial Exposition at the east end of the Pike.

19. Not mentioned in the official histories of the Fair or the various publicity materials promoting it, reference to "Helter Skelter" is found only in the official records of the Fair. The Report of the Department of Works lists a "Helter Skelter" building that cost one thousand dollars to build. Given that figure, it could not have been much more than a booth; the parcel-checking booth, for example, cost five hundred dollars to build. Report of the Department of Works, 1905, p. 38, LPE Co. Records, Box 2/Series II/Folder 1.

20. The reference is probably to the original gateway of the three-hundred-year-old Temple of Nio Mon that was brought from Japan for the "Fair Japan" concession. MacMechen, "The Pike and Its Attractions," pp. 9, 12.

21. Robert S. Brookings, 1850-1932, financier and philanthropist, was president of the Washington University Corporation from 1897 until 1928. He purchased some of the paneling from the British Pavilion for his home on Lindell Boulevard in St. Louis. The pavilion itself, an exact copy of Queen Anne's Orangery at Kensington Gardens, originally designed by Christopher Wren, was purchased by Washington University and served as its art school until 1926. The offices of the pavilion were redecorated with the wood carvings and inlaid panels from the Chinese Pavilion at the Fair. Frank O'Brien, "Meet Me in St. Louis," *Washington University Magazine* 44 (Spring 1974), p. 11; Mary Powell, "Public Art in St. Louis: Sculpture, Architecture, Mural Decorations, Stained Glass," *St. Louis Public Library Monthly Bulletin* (July-August 1925), pp. 188-89, offprint in the Missouri Historical Society Library; Missouri Historical Society Information Files: "Louisiana Purchase Exposition—Britain."

Festival Hall after the Fair. *Photograph, c. 1905. This snapshot shows the desolation of the Fairgrounds as Florence McCallion might have seen it. The spectacular Grand Basin has been drained, although Festival Hall is still largely intact.*

Canada, Ceylon and Brazil are still standing. As we passed Brazil I thought of the times we were there and had coffee. There is only the steel frame work of Belgium left. "Mexico is out of sight." All there is left of the Agricultural B'ld'g. is the skeleton of the first floor, except on the side near the Boer War, the brick wall is still standing as high as the second floor.[22] The lagoons are nothing but a rocky waste. In some parts a railroad track is laid, and the bridges partly gone. One of the paved streets is partly torn up. The Louisiana monument is still safe except the front tablet which has been removed. The St. Louis, LaSalle and Joliet statues are the same as ever. You remember they were all near each other. The Manufactures, Liberal Arts, Varied Industries, Mines & Metallurgy, Machinery, Transportation, Educational, Electricity, Government and U.S. Fisheries are almost the same as when we saw them. They have started to take the staff[23] off of Manufactures B'ld'g. near the top, but it is not very noticeable yet. We could almost imagine we were at the Fair right around there. Some of the gardens are very pretty. A great deal of the statuary still remains. Lewis & Clark, also Father Marquette's and Jefferson's are gone. Festival Hall and the colonnade of states are very much the same, but oh! how we missed the splashing, roaring, tumbling of the cascades.

There was one lone lemonade stand occupied, so Edmund treated just for "old times sake."

It would take me all night to tell you every thing and I am just as tired as if I had been at the Fair. . . .

All send love to you. Love and kisses to you from your loving and affectionate wife

Florence

---

22. Contrary to McCallion's recollections, the Palace of Agriculture was a single-story structure. Efforts to make it two story or to add a second-floor gallery or balcony were turned down by Isaac S. Taylor, Director of Works, and by the Committee on Grounds and Buildings. Experience at Chicago's World Columbian Exposition in 1893 had shown that exhibitors would not agree to have their displays relegated to a second-story location. Isaac S. Taylor to Frederick Skiff, October 6, 1902, in Minutes of the Committee on Grounds and Buildings, October 11, 1902, LPE Co. Records, Box 2/Series II/Subseries I/Folder 3.

23. Staff was a mixture of plaster of paris and fiber (jute, burlap, or wood excelsior) that formed the covering of the exhibit palaces and the statuary. Inexpensive and easily made as well as durable and easy to cast or mold, staff made the building of the temporary exhibit palaces and statuary affordable and practical. *Official Guide*, pp. 152-53. For a discussion of how the staff statuary was created, see: Robert T. Paine, "How the Sculptor's Model Is Enlarged," *Brush and Pencil* 13 (December 1903), pp. 184-89.

Sam P. Hyde

Sam P. Hyde was a bookkeeper from Belleville, Illinois. Born in 1850, he was active in the First Presbyterian Church and a collector of art objects, war relics, and coins. In 1909—five years after the Fair—Hyde assembled a memoir of his World's Fair visits. Written in calligraphy and illustrated by his own sketches and snapshots, Hyde's multi-dimensional presentation of his Fair visits reflects his artistic temperament. The narrative that follows is illustrated exclusively with snapshots and illustrations from the original volume.

The St. Louis statue, titled The Apotheosis of St. Louis, *stood in the Plaza St. Louis near the Main Entrance to the fairgrounds.*

SAM. P. HYDE
BELLEVILLE ILLS.
1909

My original intention was simply the preservation of some views taken by myself and friends and my effort to present them in attractive form has led me into reminiscences of some personal experiences.[1]

But the fair has passed into history. The vast buildings have vanished like things of air, the sights and sounds of the great show are growing dim in the vista of passing years, and it is meet that we record some of the impressions that remain. Coming generations may want to see a world's fair and be able to pay for it but they come high and there will certainly not be another in our day.

Realizing the magnitude of the enterprise and the extremely interesting nature of the work, Ben[2] and I wanted to watch the progress of it from the start. We visited the grounds many times during the two years preceding the opening.

Our first visit was just after the surveyors had finished their preliminary work and the hills and valleys bristled with their stakes. I am told that much annoyance was caused by some of these stakes being carried off by souvenir fiends. We did not get one. Many

1. Hyde Memoir. Photocopy in Journals and Diaries Collection, 1909, Missouri Historical Society Archives. Original in Missouri Historical Society Photographs and Prints Collection.
2. Either a close friend or relative, "Ben" often accompanied Sam Hyde to the Fair. Efforts to identify him further have proven unsuccessful.

trees were tagged—some for felling and others for transplanting.

We went again when the hills and valleys were disappearing before the dredge and scraper and the face of the landscape was changing every day. And again when the sights of the vast buildings had been marked and long trains of cars were unloading lumber and iron and sewer pipe and rock and sand and cinders. And we were there when the skeletons of the buildings began to rise from the broad acres that had been leveled by the hand of man.

We went in the winter when the molding of the statuary and decorations in staff was going on in enclosed buildings and finished sections of the work set out to dry—here a group of goddesses, there a regiment of plaster horses and over yonder a half acre of cupids. We amused ourselves criticizing the figures and wondering where they would all roost when the time came.

We saw the palaces rise in grandeur and beauty like visions of the night. Columns, cap and cornice came into place and the gods took their places to look down for six months[3] on the passing throng from every nation under heaven. Savage and civilized, Polock, Siberian, Scandinavian and Hottentot. We went as long as we could go in free and when they closed the gate we paid the fare and went for we knew it was once for all and the chance of a lifetime.

To us it was a sad sight to see the beauties of nature marred, and forest trees that had been fifty years in growing, cut down in an hour. The very idea of restoring the park was a farce on its face though stipulated in a heavy bond, restored but how?

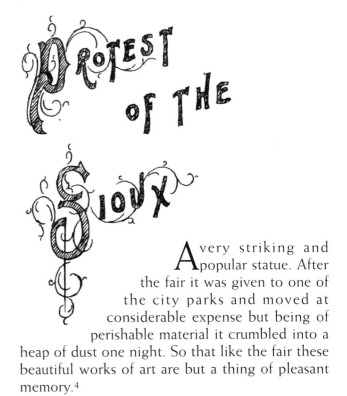

A very striking and popular statue. After the fair it was given to one of the city parks and moved at considerable expense but being of perishable material it crumbled into a heap of dust one night. So that like the fair these beautiful works of art are but a thing of pleasant memory.[4]

---

3. The Fair actually lasted for seven months, April 30 to December 1, 1904.

4. According to John C. Ewers, "Cyrus E. Dallin: Sculptor of Indians," *Montana: The Magazine of Western History* 18 (January 1968), p. 39, the sculpture was titled simply *The Protest*. Efforts to verify the post-Fair disposition of this statue have been unsuccessful. However, there were several Fair statues, in staff, that went to St. Louis area parks, among them one titled *Cherokee Chief*, which was placed in Compton Heights Park in St. Louis. David R. Francis, *Universal Exposition*, vol. 1, p. 660, and Iglauer, "The Demolition of the Louisiana Purchase Exposition," pp. 458-59.

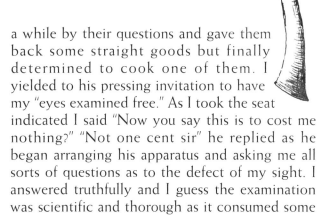

Liberal prizes were offered for the best drilled body of woodmen and companies came from all over the country. The uniforms [were] of great variety, the drills occupied several days. Regular army officers were the judges. The axes with which they drill are made of aluminum. Twenty four men drilled in a company.

Quite a familiar sight in the early days of the fair, and something of a nuisance with all was a well dressed man standing at the entrance to an optical instrument display[5] with a hunk of green glass in one hand and chunk of clear glass in the other. Any one wearing spectacles was sure to encounter him for such was his prey. He would tell you that your glasses were made of the green glass, that the other was Brazilian pebble out of which they would make you a pair at trifling cost, that they had right there a celebrated optician who would examine your eyes without charge and would consider it a favor if you would come in and take a seat. These booths were numerous, it seemed as if I was always running up against the man with a chunk of glass but I judge the business was not profitable as these "pullers in" became more obtrusive and impertinent and towards the last the "barker" was discontinued. I was annoyed for

a while by their questions and gave them back some straight goods but finally determined to cook one of them. I yielded to his pressing invitation to have my "eyes examined free." As I took the seat indicated I said "Now you say this is to cost me nothing?" "Not one cent sir" he replied as he began arranging his apparatus and asking me all sorts of questions as to the defect of my sight. I answered truthfully and I guess the examination was scientific and thorough as it consumed some time, resulting at last in his mounting two pair and handing them to me, one was to wear on the street—the other at my desk. "How much" I asked. "Three dollars and a half please." I arose from the chair and laid them on the table with the remark "Well I will call on you when I desire to change my glasses. I will get along with the old ones for the present" and having taken the precaution to hold on to them I placed them on my nose and walked out.

I will not attempt to describe the expression on the face of the professor. But he said never a word. The profession doubtless suffered many such disappointments as they soon became less importunate with their offers of gratuitous service. My man got the experience for his pains all right. And I some information on optics. I had taken him at his word.

---

5. This probably was a concession of A. S. Aloe Instrument Co., a St. Louis optical firm. "Official List of Concessionaires," *WFB*, May 1904, p. 42.

This is my prize picture. I had carried the Kodak about all the morning and not done much business, when on descending the steps from the government building I spied this old savage[6] in all his glory of bead and feather, striding along with the step of a king. "There's my game" said I "I'll shoot him if I lose my scalp for it." I well knew the antipathy of the Indian to having his picture taken and that there was some danger attending the enterprise, but this was such a fine specimen I determined to take the chances.

Calculating quickly the distance I wanted, the direction of the light, and at what point I could catch him with a good background, I followed him a few paces and running quickly ahead, passed him and touched the button at the supreme moment.

My next thought was to get away, for the old fellow had seen my camera and heard the shutter snap. It was not a wholesome place for me to remain. As he stopped in his tracks with a savage grunt I shot across the lawn. He stood there for a moment glaring at me and uttering grunts like a hog. As I headed for the Liberal Arts Building where I could lose myself in the crowd and render pursuit difficult, I yelled back at him "O you will die sure."[7] But he resumed his path and I escaped with my prize. He had his feather head dress on when I spotted him and I did not know that he had taken it off till I developed the film, such was the excitement of the moment, and such the vicissitudes of Kodaking. However I doubt if he would have put it on again if I had asked him.

There is a Witchery in Kodakery, and the enthusiast is as proud of a good picture as the artist who has sat down with palette and brush and worked out the detail by hand, albeit he has only touched a button. The study of light, grouping, pose and setting are the same in either case, and to compass them all in a moment and touch the button in the nick of time when your subject is an unwilling one, is an achievement to be proud of.

---

6. For a discussion of the use of derogatory ethnic language by 1904 World's Fair visitors, see the Introduction to this volume, p. 24; cf. also pp. 10-11 for a discussion of the Fair planners' presentation of Native Americans at the Fair.
7. A reference to the popular notion that Indians believed that photography robbed them of their souls.

The Fair was not open on Sunday so we made it the occasion of one of our Sunday strolls to go all around it on the outside. We reached the grounds by the Taylor Av. cars and struck west on the turnpike. Coming to the entrance to the Inside Inn, we went inside of the Inside Inn and on through the Inside Inn to the outside of the Inside Inn but inside of the fence enclosing the Inside Inn and sat on the porch for some time looking through the barred gates in to promised land. Resuming our journey we skirted the enclosure on the west by a country road and saw miles of highboard fence and some pretty country. It was an experiment of course and we found it a good long walk but Ben is good company and the time was not ill spent.

Arriving at the north east corner we hit a lunch stand and braced up with a cup of coffee. I challenged Ben to walk on to our starting point just to complete the circuit but he had had enough of tramping and would not walk another mile simply for sentiment. I remember that walk with much pleasure for we saw much of interest. The Inside Inn cost $400,000. It was well patronized.[8]

I did not visit the Igorrots. I could see nothing interesting. . . . But they seemed to have a tremendous attraction for the ladies.

The Tyrolean Alps from outside the gates. This was surely a wonderful show.

8. The Taylor Avenue line would have let Hyde off at the States Buildings Entrance, at the southeast corner of the fairgrounds. Just to the west, along Oakland Avenue, was the Inside Inn. The Inside Inn, built by E. M. Statler, was a twenty-five-hundred room, three-story hotel erected inside the southeastern corner of the Exposition grounds, able to accommodate up to six thousand guests. The county road on the west was Pennsylvania Avenue and the land there was yet undeveloped. The northeast corner, the end of Hyde's hike, placed him at the Main Entrance to the fairgrounds at Lindell Boulevard. *Official Guide*, p. 16, and "The Inside Inn," *WFB*, November 1903, p. 33.

SIX INCH SIEGE GUN
THE LARGEST PORTABLE
GUN IN THE US SERVICE

ONE of the excellent features of the great fair was the military display.[9] Militia from the different states took turns about camping in the grounds and you were sure of seeing a good drill every day. Early every morning there was a regiment drill on the plaza Saint Louis and Ida and I were early enough one morning to see it and catch the bugler as the troops withdrew.[10]

It was somewhat inspiring on entering the grounds to feel that the whole world was there and every nation showing its best products and doing its best to please. Every civilized nation had its sailors, its soldiers and its military band. And there were uniforms as varied and as brilliant as the kaleidoscope. And music to charm the senses or split the ears (according to your taste) at every turn. Perhaps the most popular music was the Filipino military band of sixty pieces.[11] Wonderful tales were told of the extraordinary talent of those little brown fellows. They surely did make fine music, but of all the music that I heard on the grounds from start to finish nothing hit my ear like the three or four Italians at the gondola landing from twilight well into the night. Between them they had some six or eight little wind and string instruments and they would sing in foreign tongue and play the most beautiful airs I ever heard. It may be that the surroundings had something to do with heightening the effects. The balmy breeze of summer, the splash of water as the gondolas landed and departed with their passengers. The picturesque figures of the gondoliers and the general good feeling of the rest and pleasure seeking crowd on which the moon vied with a million electric lights in casting a mellow glow. Oh it was so sweet to sit there and look and listen, why could it not last forever? Who wanted to think of going home? Home was a fool.

I was alone as usual when the best things were going on, or at least I was in a frame of mind to get the most pleasure out of the sublime when there was no one yanking at my sleeve and

9. Written inside the letter O: "Ida remarked as the regiment filed off of the grounds that day 'I don't wonder that a man likes to be a soldier.'" Ida was Hyde's wife.

10. Throughout the Fair, units of the regular army, West Point cadets, and National Guard units from a number of states encamped on the fairgrounds. Barracks were located and parades were held on the present-day campus of Washington University just south of the Aeronautic Concourse and east of the Athletic Field. *Official Guide*, p. 144.

11. There were two Filipino Bands; the Philippine Scouts Band numbered forty-one pieces, and the Constabulary Band numbered eighty pieces. *Official Catalogue Philippine Exhibits*, pp. 269-71.

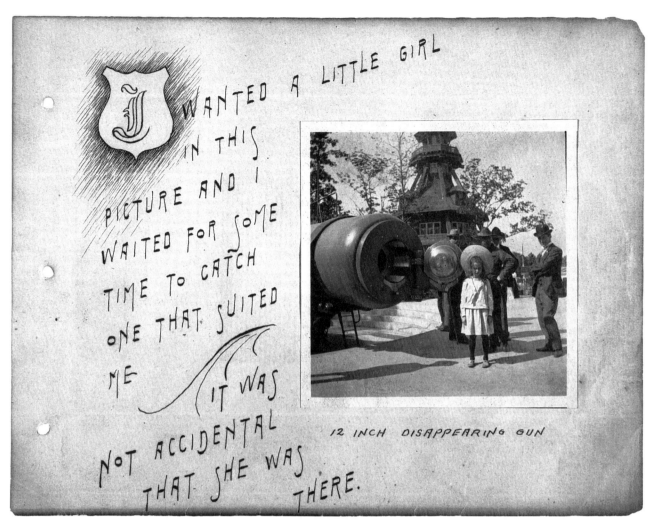

I WANTED A LITTLE GIRL IN THIS PICTURE AND I WAITED FOR SOME TIME TO CATCH ONE THAT SUITED ME. IT WAS NOT ACCIDENTAL THAT SHE WAS THERE.

12 INCH DISAPPEARING GUN

The big guns were located on Government Hill behind the U.S. Government Building. The Washington State Pavillion is pictured in the background.

saying "O come on." So I "paid the fare there of" and went down into the ship. For I was determined not to miss a boat ride under the moonlight. I saw the lagoons by night all right but I didn't enjoy it quite as much as the young fellow who sat next to me with his arm around his girl.

It was painful amidst such scenes to contemplate the long tedious car ride of seventeen miles before me and I tried to forget it but it would not down. So I stayed as long as I dared and pulled myself away with a sigh.

IT WAS MOONLIGHT ON THE LAKE

Ben and I had laid ourselves out for a big time on the nation's birthday and were early on the grounds with Kodak and lunch box, but although Jonathan and David[12] were not better friends than we, the morning was not half spent till it was demonstrated that two persons of such dissimilar tastes should not go sightseeing together.

I wore his patience out lingering at some art treasure, and at the next turn Ben would fasten on to a chunk of old sand stone and I could not pull him off. But science and art should not quarrel and longsuffering is one of Ben's virtues.

It was an incessant "Oh come on" but I confess that I saw much of interest and beauty among the geological specimens by virtue of my stony hearted friend, and when noon arrived and we tapped the lunch we found ourselves extremely congenial along that line.

There are doubtless exceptions to the rule of rain on the Fourth, but this was not one of them, it caught us unfortunately in a Japanese pagoda high up on the hillside from whence we had a fine view of the pools and flooded walks and the bedraggled crowds wading about in them. It rained to beat the band.

It was a cold day for the camera though I obtained one good one by getting a friend to touch the button while Ben and I sat on the railing at the Illinois Building. I had thought to take in some of the shows with Ben but the

---

12. A Biblical reference to King David and Jonathan, the son of Saul. Cf. I Samuel 18:1-4.

Sam P. Hyde and Ben. *Pausing for a picture, as they sat on the railing of the Illinois Building, "Just before the rain."*

Pike had no attractions for him. I could not prevail upon him to "Shoot the Chutes" nor would he go "to the North Pole" nor descend "into the depths of the sea." He cared nothing for "the creation of the world" and as for "the Hereafter" he said we would see that soon enough without charge.[13] So we took a trip on the "intramural" and as evening drew on we lunched near the entrance and sat on the steps under shelter to watch the countless thousands streaming towards the gates. It was still raining and pools of water stood in all the walks. Maids and matrons young, old, and so so trying to save their skirts presented a display of hosiery worthy of the great fair and we had found another subject on which we were congenial—tell it not in gath.—

My recollections of that day savor much of disappointment but its closing hours still linger as a pleasant memory, (seeing Ben enjoy the show.)

THE IRISH VILLAGE blocked the eastern end of the Pike. I never heard the show spoken of and did not visit it. Taken by Pieksen.[14]

GETTYSBURG. This cyclorama with other war pictures and the large collection of war relics was well worth the price of admission 50¢.[15]

---

13. Reference to several rides on the Pike: "Shoot the Chutes," "Trip to the North Pole," "Under and Over the Sea," "Creation," and "Hereafter."
14. The Irish Village was a Pike attraction titled "The Irish Industrial Exhibition." It consisted of a village of several buildings containing an exhibit of "Irish national industries," more accurately described perhaps as Irish historical sites, and a theater where performances of plays by Yeats were undertaken by Celtic players. "Popular Prices," p. 18. "Pieksen" is possibly John W. Pieksen, a traveling salesman with Cupples Wooden Ware Company in St. Louis. St. Louis City Directory, 1904.
15. The cyclorama of Gettysburg was one of several cycloramas in the Battle Abbey. Its admission price was actually twenty-five cents. "Popular Prices," p. 19.

Of all the foreign nations that participated in the fair, none made so good a showing and won such universal praise as Japan. There must have been many more of the Japs at the fair than were in attendance at their displays for we met them at every turn and never saw one in a bad humor, they were always pleasant when you spoke to them. They are a nation of homely men but the women were fairly goodlooking. The Japanese government appropriated four hundred thousand dollars for their displays and other enterprises raised it to half a million. A good round sum when we remember that their war with Russia was hardly over.[16] They were represented in most of the great buildings and their displays were of especial interest from the fact that unlike the other civilized nations, their civilization was about on a par with our own though it had developed on different lines and entirely independent of us. We watched them at work on their building. The material had come across the sea in great bundles and crates and was piled up on their grounds. We examined their curious tools—the saws having the teeth pointed the wrong way, so that they drew the saw instead of shoving it. But we observed that they made good joints and finished their work well.

I was particularly struck with their display in the Forestry, Fish and Game Building, and amazed at the variety and fine appearance of the preserved and canned fish, pearl buttons from shells, various products of the sea and models of their boats and tackle. Truly they had little to learn from us about catching fish and curing them. Their display of straw goods was something marvelous. Their trimmings and lace and fancy work in straw baffles description.

I never tired of looking at their wonderful art work in bronze and porcelain and ivory—the vases and

bricabrac were a source of endless delight, and the feather work silk embroidery and fabrics, lanterns & fans were simply of fabulous delicacy and beauty.

But if I must say what article of all their displays impressed me most I would take you to the art gallery where the whole side of one room was given to a painting of two Bengal tigers life size walking through the snow. So perfectly natural was the fur that you could hardly believe it was a painting but were seized with a desire to feel it with your hand.

I had never seen a pelt painted like that and determined to see what was the secret of such marvelous effect. A close inspection showed that each individual hair had been stroked on with a brush finer than a thread. It was difficult to even estimate the time consumed in such a work. The American artist will daub the paint on with a sweep of the hand and be satisfied with general effects at long range. I will never forget that picture.[17]

I have said that the Japanese women were fairly good looking. I remember one in particular, she was in attendance in a booth decorated with large boughs of (paper) apple blossoms, far removed from the other Jap displays, and was selling pictures and translated Jap story books. She was dressed in the bewitching costume of Tokio. All rich soft delicate silk with a pillow bound to her back with an elegant sash. A picture of feminine loveliness and one that for delicate beauty would rank above par under any flag. I talked with her considerable, and on my next visit sought her again but found her in the garb of a well dressed American girl. I asked her which dress she preferred, she said, "O the other is so much more comfortable." I told her that the costume of Tokio was much the most becoming. She was a beautiful girl however in either and I should have liked to get better acquainted, but though I haunted that little booth I never

---

16. In fact, the Russo-Japanese War was not yet over as the Fair took place. The fighting, which had begun in February 1904, continued until March 1905. The peace treaty was not signed until September 5, 1905. On the Fair visitors' reaction to the Japanese, see the introduction to this volume, pp. 24-26.

17. Painted on a screen, this work, titled *Tiger*, was by Japanese artist Suiseki Ohashi and won a gold medal in the Department of Art. It is pictured in Bennitt, ed., *History of the LPE*, p. 531.

This is the Japanese girl whose picture on fans and lanterns we were familiar with in our youth but it is not as we saw her at the fair. How an artist that can paint a tiger so well should make such a botch of a woman is a mystery. Doubtless Tokio has its Gibson and this is the only face he knows

Hyde is alluding here to Charles Dana Gibson, 1867-1944, contributor of illustrations to magazines (Life, Schriber's, Harpers, et al.) and creator of the "Gibson girl" look.

found her there again. I think it was her that I passed one day as she was hurrying towards the gates with a suit case but our acquaintance did not permit me to speak. I would take no chances of having one of those ugly little Japs jump on my neck.

This incident happened towards fall when by chance I was quarantined from Belleville[18] and spent three successive days at the fair and I saw more in those three days than in all my other trips put together barring Thanks Giving Day, because I was alone and free to follow up any adventure and take my time where I most enjoyed the sights. The fact is I was handicapped when ever I had company. Nothing knocks all the sentiment and enterprise out of a man like an eternal "O come on."

We would like to have purchased some of the beautiful things we saw but the prices on every thing were simply fabulous. It looked as if the

rule was to estimate a fair price for an article, multiply it by two, add fifty per cent for tariff, another fifty per-cent for freight, twenty five more upon general principals and ten and two fives for Francis.[19]

Little vases such as I had bought at the Chicago fair for two dollars were marked six and eight dollars. The Austrian display of decorated and cut glass was a place in which my soul delighted, I sought it often and lingered long, I priced many pieces that I fancied but had to content myself with looking at them.

There was a vase among the rookwood goods[20] that I wanted—one hundred dollars— the Japs had a bronze vase as big as a nail keg that I wanted bad—one hundred and seventy five dollars. (Three months' wages.)

18. Given the crowded conditions on the fairgrounds, Fair officials were continually concerned about the risk of disease. Keefer, "Dirty Water Clean Toilets."
19. David R. Francis, President of the Louisiana Purchase Exposition Company.
20. Pottery of the Rookwood Pottery Company of Cincinatti, Ohio. "The Craft of Rookwood Potters," *WW*, August 1904, n.p.

One of the wonders and conspicuous attractions of the World's Fair at Chicago was the Ferris Wheel. It compared favorably as an engineering achievement with the Eiffel Tower of Paris. Its original cost was about $380,000. It is said to have paid a fortune the year of that fair. From there it was removed to a lot north of Lincoln Park where it stood at a heavy loss to the owners 'til it was again taken down and set up at the St. Louis fair where it proved a disastrous enterprise. At the close of this fair they could not give it away as no one would wreck it for the old iron. Dynamite was applied and the noble structure was reduced to a tangled mass of steel bars. It measured 250 feet in diameter and gave its passengers a fine view of the grounds. Having taken a ride in it with sister Sue in 1893 I did not patronize it again.

This wonderful picture was taken by cousin Sally close from one of the cars, when just starting on the decent.

It was the only one of its kind and truly wonderful. The experiment was satisfactory but too expensive ever to be repeated.

The Ferris Wheel is a thing of delightful memory to those who took a ride but painful to those who took stock.

The axle upon which it turned was 45 feet long and 32 inches thick weighing seventy tons. The largest piece of steel ever forged.

The steel towers on which it rested were one hundred and forty feet high. It loaded thirty six freight cars coming from Chicago.[21]

Up in the Ferris Wheel, *snapshot by Sam P. Hyde's cousin Sally.*

The Luxurious Way. *The roller chair or push chair could be rented, either with or without a guide, by Fair visitors from the Clarkson Concession Company and was marketed as an alternative to walking about the fairgrounds rather than as an aid to the disabled.*

---

21. Hyde's facts appear to be accurate. According to *The Greatest of Expositions*, p. 31, the Ferris Wheel measured 250 feet high and contained 4,200 tons of metal. The axle did weigh 70 tons. It had 36 gondolas or cars, each with an attendant, and could carry 2,000 persons. It made 4 revolutions per hour. An advertisement in the *Daily Official Program*, October 18, 1904, p. 14, claimed the Ferris Wheel was 264 feet high and made 6 stops per revolution. According to the Report of the Department of Works, 1905, p. 38, it cost $170,000 to erect the Ferris Wheel at the St. Louis Fair. LPE Co. Records, Box 2/Series II/Folder 1.

It was delightful when we were tired, to sit down and watch the people pass.

Thanksgiving being a general holiday again, we supposed that every body would go to the fair, and we wanted to get an early start. In a spirit of charity I had asked a certain poor boy to be my guest for the day and expected to spend two or three dollars on him (though I could hardly afford it). He agreed to meet me on the square at six o'clock but was not there and I let one car go waiting for the kid to show up. Still he did not come so I went that day alone. He told me the next day that the folks did not wake him up in time. I am glad they did not for the weather was fine and I made a record day of it and spent the three dollars on souvenirs which I now value above price.

I had watched with great interest the wonderful skill of the man at the turning lathe in the machinery building[22] and admired the little vases he made with loose rings around the stem all made out of a block of Georgia gum four inches long and two inches square. I asked him how many rings he could turn on one of those blocks. After a moment's thought he said "I think I could make one like a spool with fifty rings, but no one would want to pay what it was worth." "How much would you want" said I. "Two dollars" he replied. I was too poor to invest that amount so I asked "How many rings will you put on for a dollar." After a moment's pause he said "Twenty

five." "Let her go" said I. He sharpened his chisels and picked out a good block. It was an exceedingly interesting performance and quite a crowd gathered to watch it.

He had evidently seen it all in his mind's eye before he began and had laid it out for thirty one rings expecting to break some in the turning. But one by one they were formed and cut loose to the last ring without a break and I had six rings more than I had bargained for. It had taken him just fifteen minutes and I gladly handed him the dollar.

It certainly is a master piece of turning. The rings are of four sizes, being turned in four layers.

I would give him two dollars now to see him put fifty rings on a spool of that size. But it's the only one of its kind, made to order and a fine specimen of the possibilities of the lathe.

I had noticed in the East India Building (when Ida and I took some ice tea one day) the delicate china ware they used, each piece bearing a little picture of an elephant with a palm tree and some other figures. It occurred to me that a few pieces of this ware would be nice for our china closet so I dropped in there and negotiated with the Hindoo for a cup saucer and plate. In the Jap display there was a little vase that my heart coveted, I went into a corner and counted my available cash. It was marked $3.75—not a high price I thought as things were going at the Fair. But I could not see

---

22. Souvenirs were readily available for purchase throughout the fairgrounds, even in the exhibit palaces. The Department of Manufactures, for example, set aside several sections in the palaces of Manufactures and Varied Industries for exhibiters who wished to demonstrate and sell wares at retail to individual Fair visitors, while the balance of the buildings was set aside for the larger booths of manufacturers who were devoted to increasing their connections for the wholesale trade. *WFB*, April 1904, p. 34, and *Official Guide*, p. 71.

how I could buy that vase and ride home. I went back and looked at it again and it seemed prettier than before, then back to my corner to balance cash again and see if there was not another nickel to be found, mislaid or overlooked in some odd pocket, but rake and scrape and delve as I would, I had so much hard cash and no more, and it was ten cents short of getting home by rail with the vase. Not less than four times did [I] repair to that secluded corner to go over my assets and try to resurrect another coin of the realm. But I could not cough it up, so with a sigh I pulled myself away and tried to forget it.

I looked again for the beautiful Jap girl in a little booth covered with apple blossoms but she was not in attendance that day and when evening drew on and the big buildings were about to close I turned my foot steps towards the Pike to watch the revelers by gaslight. "Good things of day begin to droop and drouse and night's black agents to their prey do rouse."[23]

Trouble had begun early on the Pike. A thousand pedestrians thronged the great thoroughfare beneath ten thousand electric lights, whilst the din of cow bells, whistles, megaphones, the infernal yelling of the barkers mingled with the boom of cannon in the sham battle shows,[24] and every body making all the noise they could with every conceivable device that would produce discord upon general principles rendered a pandemonium that I don't expect to hear again this side of Hades. Troops of young men joining hands would worm through the crowd in a string and coming on to some poor fellow walking sweetly with his girl they would quickly encircle the unsuspecting couple, dance around them yelling like fiends incarnate and close in till all were involved in a human maelstrom and indescribable confusion. Then they would break away and scatter as quickly as they came, leaving the bewildered swain to pull themselves together, pick up their hats and their dignity, shake out their ruffled garments, take their bearings and move on. Serpentine[25] shot through the air like meteors of varied hue and confetti rained in torrents. Every stiff hat was a target for the inflated bladder.[26] No respect was shown to age or dignity, no mercy to starch and feathers, it was an all round go as you please and if you didn't like it you could get off of the Pike.

One of the most popular noise-making schemes and perhaps the most effective in results was the dragging of several tin cans by a string over the cobblestones. The carnival spirit prevailed however and no body got mad however severe the punishment. But it was getting late in the season and many of the shows had resorted to showing some of their best stock on a platform at the door between the performances. Females were conspicuous of course. Spanish, French and Russian dancing girls. Esquimos, Scandinavians and Hottentots. And the shorter their skirts the bigger the crowd that gathered to hear the barker tell what wonderful stunts they would do.

Performance to begin "right away." I was taking in these free shows and studying the faces from a scientific point of view. Repulsively vile, most of them and I thought it would take no prophet to detect "the mark of the beast" on their foreheads.

---

23. The correct quotation is: "Good things of day begin to droop and drowse, / Whiles night's black agents to their preys do rouse." William Shakespeare, *Macbeth*, Act III, scene ii.

24. Sham battle shows included "Cummin's Wild West, Indian Congress and Rough Riders of the World" on the north side of the Pike, which claimed to re-create Wild West scenarios, and the "U.S. Naval Exhibition" at the west the end of the Pike, which re-created naval battles using miniature reproductions of warships. The sounds of the "Boer War" re-creation of the battles of Colenso and Paardenberg are less likely to have been heard on the Pike as that concession was located some distance south of the Pike beyond the Ferris Wheel and opposite the Palace of Horticulture. "Popular Prices," p. 19; "The Boer War Exhibition"; and MacMechen, "The Pike and Its Attractions," pp. 18, 20.

25. Long narrow strips of rolled colored paper thrown so as to unroll as streamers.

26. Water balloon.

Poor girls perhaps it was rather their misfortune than their fault that they were there. I noticed the disappointment on the face of the professor sometimes when the crowd instead of thronging to the ticket box after his talk would all march off to the next free show. "The Great Creation" "Under and Over the Sea" "Mysterious Asia" "The Girls of Madrid" were ringing on the ear, whilst ever and anon rose a deep voice "Hagenback Hagenback"[27] and here would come a great camel down the crowded thoroughfare with a girl in oriental costume on its back.

I drew up at last in front of a platform on which sat some half dozen of as vile looking creatures as ever bore the name of woman.

A well dressed young man mounted the box and presented the merits of his show in something like these words. Remember however that this speech is not as I recall it after four years, but copied verbatim from a memorandum I made the next day. I have not drawn on my imagination nor substituted expressions. These are his words not mine.

"Now gentlemen we have a hot show in here and I would not advise spinsters from the church sewing societies to come in, it is no place for prudes and old maid missionaries. I am candid with you when I say it's a warm entertainment, and boys if you bring your sweethearts in here you can call their attention to the fresco on the ceiling when the temperature gets too high and while they are looking aloft you watch the stage and you'll catch it all.

"Some people go out of here saying 'it's awful, it ought not to be allowed' others say 'it's fine and it's all right.' Now as I say we have an all round warm show but you are not obliged to remain if it's uncomfortably warm. Some people think it has been bad before this, but these are lively girls and it's hard to hold them down. And as this is Thanksgiving night we have turned the girls loose and it's hotter than ever. Now come right in the performance begins right away. Some folks say it is going too far while others would like to see it carried further, but we will admit it is the limit. We have put the price down to one dime, only ten cents pass right in and get your money's worth one dime pays the bill."

You might suppose that after hearing this statement in plain English that the show was not decent, the crowd would have turned away with one accord. On the contrary there was a rush for the ticket window. Men and women and young fellows with nice looking girls on their arms bought their tickets and passed in. If this was the spirit of the Pike it was an unclean spirit. But they were on a lark and had some curiosity to see what "the limit" was. And yet it was a holiday and my last chance, I had spent very little on Pike shows, why should not I be a little bad just for once. No said I, when I want to be bad I won't be bad that way, and I put the dime back in my pocket and dropped out of line. I believe if the Pike had been a mile longer it would have led to hell.

Everybody wanted to see the Sunken Gardens and some very curious notions prevailed concerning them. Some people actually thought they were in a cave, and others expected to see them under water. Long after the Fair had closed a keeper at one of the gates had a corn stalk stuck in an old iron pot filled with earth and labeled "the sunken garden." It had gotten to be a joke. It was certainly the finest display of artistic effects in foliage plants I had ever seen. It was a picture literally.[28]

_____

27. A reference to "Hagenbeck's Trained and Wild Animal Show."
28. The Sunken Garden was so named because it was depressed three feet below the surrounding ground. Bennitt, ed., *History of the LPE*, p. 167. The Sunken Garden is pictured on p. 57 of this volume.

The grand organ built in Festival Hall was the largest in the world. There were one hundred and forty stops and ten thousand pipes. The largest pipe was 27 inches by thirty six feet. The smallest could not be seen with the naked eye (without permission).[29] This picture gives some idea of the wonderful achievements in landscape gardening. Taken by Pieksen.

And yet I had a desire to imbibe a little of the spirit of the Pike. I wanted to be a boy again. Be a little bit bad perhaps. Get as drunk as lemonade would make me, spend a little money and have an all round good time. So "I said in mine heart. Go to now I will prove thee with mirth." I had tried in vain to get Ben to do the Pike with me on the Fourth and now having Roger[30] along I thought surely this is my time. But I found Roger no more of a fool than Ben. I

was determined to shoot the chutes but could not prevail upon him to follow. "Here then" I said "hold my bundles and wait for me for I am going to shoot the chutes if it takes the hair off."

I paid my dime and ascended to the dizzy platform. A number of young people crowded into the car and the signal was given. "Now yell as loud as you can" said I "for that is part of the fun." I set them the key as we started. And they yelled all right. I will not attempt to describe the sensation, but no native born American will shoot the chutes and not yell.

We struck the water and shot into the air again and then were towed to the landing. I did not notice till I got out that I had lost my glasses in the shock. Returning I fished in the water and dirt in the bottom of the boat till I found them. I discovered also that my head was aching. I did not care to shoot again but I have been glad ever since that I did, and have regretted that I did not ride on the scenic railway for I heard it was fine.

---

29. The organ in Festival Hall, according to the *Official Guide*, p. 42, was indeed the largest in the world, and it did contain 140 stops, 239 movements, and 10,059 pipes. It measured 33 feet wide by 62 feet long and 40 feet high, and required a train of 14 cars to transport it. According to Hanson, *History of the LPE*, pp. 178-79, its largest pipe was 32 feet long.

30. Presumably another friend of Hyde's, efforts to further identify "Roger" have been unsuccessful.

Palace of Education from the West.

For these beautiful views I am indebted to my friend—Pieksen—

Same looking down from the Terrace.

Festival Hall and the Colonnade of States at night. *Snapshot, 1904.*

Many an hour I sat watching these lights as one who hates to be awakened from a pleasant dream.

"Were such thing here as we do speak about, or have we eaten of the insane root that takes the reason prisoner?"[31]

---

31. The actual quotation is "Were such things here as we do speak about? / Or have we eaten of the insane root / That takes the reason prisoner?" Shakespeare, *Macbeth*, Act I, scene iii.

Bibliography

Unpublished Primary Sources—Missouri Historical Society Archives, St. Louis

Corbett, Katharine T. Survey of popular attitudes toward St. Louis history, undertaken in preparation for the Missouri Historical Society's exhibit *Meet Me at the Fair: Memory, History, and the 1904 World's Fair*, 1994.

Educational Museum of the St. Louis Public Schools Records.

Francis, David R., Papers.

Hyde, Sam P., Photograph Album and World's Fair Memoir, 1909, photocopy in Journals and Diaries Collection, 1909. Original in Missouri Historical Society Photographs and Prints Collection.

Kessler, George E., Papers.

Louisiana Purchase Exposition Company Records.

Philibert Family Papers.

Schneiderhahn, Edward V. P., Diaries, 7 vols.

Newspapers

Missouri Republican
Belleville Advocate

Published Primary Sources

Barrows, Samuel J. *Tour of the Interparliamentary Union Tendered by the Government of the United States.* Washington, D.C.: Government Printing Office, 1905.

Bennitt, Mark, ed. *History of the Louisiana Purchase Exposition.* St. Louis: Universal Exposition Publishing Company, 1905.

Bitter, Karl Theodore. "Sculpture for the St. Louis World's Fair." *Brush and Pencil* 13 (December 1903), pp. 165-83.

Buel, J. W., ed. *Louisiana and the Fair: An Exposition of the World, Its People and Their Achievements.* 10 vols. St. Louis: World's Progress Publishing Co., 1904-1905.

Crunden, Frederick M. "The Louisiana Purchase Exposition." *American Monthly Review of Reviews* 27 (May 1903), pp. 547-56.

Daily Official Program, World's Fair, St. Louis. Published daily (except Sunday) for the duration of the Fair, April 30-December 1, 1904.

Descriptive Catalogue of the German Arts and Crafts at the University Exposition, St. Louis, 1904. N.p.: Imperial German Commission, 1904.

Ellis, DeLancey M., comp. *New York at the Louisiana Purchase Exposition, St. Louis, 1904: Report of the New York State Commission.* Albany, N.Y.: J. B. Lyon Company, 1907.

The Forest City. St. Louis: n.p., 1904. Appeared as a weekly serial from April 14 through November 3, 1904.

Francis, David R. "The Greatest World's Fair." *Everybody's Magazine* 10 (April 1904), pp. 437-51.

————. *The Universal Exposition of 1904.* 2 vols. St. Louis: Louisiana Purchase Exposition Company, 1913.

The Greatest of Expositions. St. Louis: Official Photographic Company, 1904.

Hanson, John Wesley. *The Official History of the Fair, St. Louis, 1904.* St. Louis: n.p., 1904.

Hoch, Edmund S. "A Fifty-Million-Dollar Exposition." *National Magazine* 18 (May 1903), pp. 165-81.

International Exposition St. Louis 1904: Official Catalogue of the Exhibition of the German Empire. Berlin: Georg Silke, [1904].

Lane, Michael A. "New Dawns of Knowledge: III—Man: Individual and Race." *National Magazine* 20 (July 1904), pp. 416-22.

Memorial Volume of the Diamond Jubilee of St. Louis University, 1829-1904. St. Louis: Press of Little & Becker Printing Co., 1904?.

Newell, A. C., ed. and comp. *Philippine Exposition, World's Fair, St. Louis, 1904.* St. Louis?: n.p., 1904?.

Official Catalogue of Exhibitors, Universal Exposition, St. Louis, U.S.A. 1904: Department N, Anthropology, rev. ed. St. Louis: The Official Catalogue Company (Inc.), 1904.

Official Catalogue Philippine Exhibits, Universal Exposition, St. Louis, U.S.A. 1904. St. Louis: The Official Catalogue Company (Inc.), 1904.

Official Guide to the Louisiana Purchase Exposition. St. Louis: The Official Guide Co., 1904.

Paine, Robert T. "How the Sculptor's Model Is Enlarged." *Brush and Pencil* 13 (December 1903), pp. 184-89.

Reed, John B., ed. *Montana, The Treasure State: Its Resources and Attractions for the Homeseeker, Prospector and Investor.* St. Louis: Con. P. Curran Printing Co., 1904.

Rogers, Howard J., ed. *Congress of Arts and Science: Universal Exposition, St. Louis, 1904.* 8 vols. Boston: Houghton, Mifflin and Company, 1905-1907.

Roltair, Henry. *Creation, the Formation of the Earth and its Inhabitants: Evolved for the Benefit of All People Who Visit the World's Fair.* N.p., n.d. Printed booklet in the Missouri Historical Society Library.

Rossiter, Johnson, ed. *A History of the World's Columbian Exposition.* 4 vols. New York: D. Appleton & Co., 1897.

St. Louis Car Co. at the Universal Exposition, St. Louis, U.S.A., 1904. St. Louis?: n.p., 1904?.

St. Louis City Directories.

St. Louis County Directories.

St. Louis of '91: Progress and Prospects of the Magnificent Interior Commerical City. N.p., Travelers' Protective Association of America, Missouri Division, 1891.

Starr, Frederick. *The Ainu Group at the Saint Louis Exposition.* Chicago: The Open Court Publishing Company, 1904.

Steffens, Lincoln. "The Shamelessness of St. Louis: Something New in the History of American Municipal Democracy." *McClure's Magazine,* March 1903, pp. 546-60.

Turner, Frederick J. "The Significance of the Louisiana Purchase." *American Monthly Review of Reviews* 27 (May 1903), pp. 578-84.

Wetmore, Claude W., and Lincoln Steffens. "Tweed Days in St. Louis: Joseph W. Folk's Single-handed Exposure of Corruption, High and Low." *McClure's Magazine,* October 1902, pp. 577-86.

World's Fair. St. Louis 1903: Official Classification of Exhibit Departments. St. Louis?: n.p., 1902?.

World's Fair Bulletin. Vols. 1-6, November 1899-December 1904.

World's Fair Souvenir of the Engineer's Club of Saint Louis. St. Louis?: n.p., 1904.

Zum Andenken an die Neunundvierzigste Generalversammlung des Deutschen Roemisch-Katholischen Central-Vereins gehalten in St. Louis, Mo., den 11., 12., 13., und 14. September 1904. St. Louis: n.p., 1904.

World's Fair Bulletin (WFB) Articles Cited in Notes

"Aeronautic Concourse." March 1904, p. 28.

"The Boer War Exhibition." March 1904, p. 39.

"China's Display." April 1904, p. 56.

"Colossus of Vulcan." May 1904, p. 15.

"Concessionaires' and Exhibitors' Pools for Fire Insurance Protection." April 1904, pp. 64-66.

"The Creators of the Pike." April 1904, pp. 46-51.

Early, James F. "The Sculpture of the U.S. Government Building." January 1904, p. 40.

"German and Tyrolean Alps." April 1904, pp. 52-53.

"The Inside Inn." November 1903, p. 33.

"Interesting Exhibits in the Palaces of Agriculture, Art, Mines and Metallurgy, and Forestry Fish and Game." November 1904, pp. 2-8.

"Italy's Pavilion." July 1904, p. 48.

McGee, W. J. "Anthropology." February 1904, pp. 4-9.

MacMechen, Thomas R. "The City of St. Louis, The Best Governed Municipality in the United States." March, 1904, pp. 12-16.

————. "The True and Complete Story of the Pike and Its Attractions." April 1904, pp. 4-34.

"The Model City's Day Nursery and Home of Rest for Children." January 1904, p. 22.

"The Model Street: An Object Lesson in Municipal Government at the World's Fair, St. Louis, U.S.A." August 1904, pp. 16-18.

"Musical Attractions at the Exposition." February 1904, p. 36.

"Official List of Concessionaires." April 1904, pp. 41-43.

"Official List of Special Days and Events." May 1904, pp. 49-57.

"Official Report of Admissions from April 30th to December 1st, 1904." December 1904, pp. 44-45.

"The Opening Ceremonies of the Louisiana Purchase Exposition, St. Louis, U.S.A., April 30th, 1904." June 1904, pp. 4-24.

"The Pike Parade." May 1904, pp. 68-69.

"Popular Prices of Admission Will Prevail to Shows on the Ten Million Dollar Pike." May 1904, pp. 18-20.

"Push or Roller Chairs." March 1904, p. 35.

"The Radiophone." August 1904, p. 56.

Rogers, Howard J. "Educational Exhibit." December 1903, pp. 4-6.

————. "Social Economy." February 1904, pp. 10-13.

Skiff, Frederick J. V. "The Universal Exposition, An Encyclopedia of Society." December 1903, pp. 2-3.

Swarthout, William N. "A Descriptive Story of the Philippine Exhibit, World's Fair. St. Louis, U.S.A." June 1904, pp. 48-58.

"Wireless Telegraphy." March 1904, p. 35.

World's Work (WW) Articles Cited in Notes

"The Craft of the Rookwood Potters." August 1904, n.p.

"The March of Events—An Editorial Interpretation." August 1904, pp. 5203-10.

Marcosson, Isaac F. "Transportation as a Measure of Progress." August 1904, pp. 5095-109.

Secondary Sources

Bachhuber, Claire Marie. "The German-Catholic Elite: Contributions of a Catholic Intellectual and Cultural Elite of German-American Background in Early Twentieth-Century Saint Louis." Ph.D. diss., St. Louis University, 1984.

Badger, Reid. *The Great American Fair: The World's Columbia Exposition and American Culture.* Chicago: N. Hall, 1979.

Benedict, Burton. *The Anthropology of World's Fairs: San Francisco's Panama Pacific International Exposition of 1915.* Berkeley, Calif.: Scholar Press, 1983.

Birk, Dorothy Daniels. *The World Came to St. Louis: A Visit to the 1904 World's Fair.* St. Louis: The Bethany Press, 1979.

Blodgett, Geoffrey. "Cass Gilbert, Architect: Conservative at Bay." *Journal of American History* 72 (December 1985), pp. 615-36.

———. "Frederick Law Olmsted: Landscape Architecture as Conservative Reform." *Journal of American History* 62 (March 1976), pp. 869-89.

Bodnar, John. "Power and Memory in Oral History: Workers and Managers at Studebaker." *Journal of American History* 75 (March 1989), pp. 1201-21.

Bradford, Phillips Verner, and Harvey Blume. *Ota Benga: The Pygmy in the Zoo*. New York: St. Martin's Press, 1992.

Brueggemann, Martin Rudolph. "St. Louis' 1904 World's Fair: A 'Thick' Exposition." Bachelor of Arts thesis, Reed College, 1987.

Coleman, William. "Science and Symbol in the Turner Frontier Hypothesis." *American Historical Review* 62 (October 1966), pp. 22-49.

Cornfeld, Richard. "The Poetic Vision: The Design of the St. Louis World's Fair." *Classical America*, 1973, pp. 56-66.

Cortinovis, Irene E. "China at the St. Louis World's Fair." *Missouri Historical Review* 72 (October 1977), pp. 59-66.

DeConde, Alexander. *This Affair of Louisiana*. New York: Charles Scribner's Sons, 1976.

Ebert, Carl S. *A Story of St. Louis World's Fair Spoons*. St. Louis?: n.p., 1982?.

Ewers, John C. "Cyrus E. Dallin: Sculptor of Indians." *Montana: The Magazine of Western History* 18 (January 1968), pp. 34-43.

Finkelston, Theodore. "The Apotheosis of St. Louis: Politics, Ego and High Ideals in the Making of a Civic Symbol." *Gateway Heritage* 9 (Summer 1988), pp. 2-11.

Flanagan, John T. "Reedy of the *Mirror*." *Missouri Historical Review* 43 (January 1949), pp. 128-44.

Frisch, Michael. "American History and the Structures of Collective Memory: A Modest Exercise in Empirical Iconography." *Journal of American History* 75 (March 1989), pp. 1130-55.

Gilbert, James B. *Perfect Cities: Chicago's Utopia of 1893*. Chicago: University of Chicago Press, 1991.

Glassberg, David. "History and the Public: Legacies of the Progressive Era." *Journal of American History* 73 (March 1987), pp. 957-80.

Gleason, Philip. "An Immigrant Group's Interest in Progressive Reform: The Case of the German-American Catholics." *American Historical Review* 73 (December 1967), pp. 367-79.

Greenhalgh, Paul. *Ephemeral Vistas: The Expositions Universelles, Great Exhibitions and World's Fairs, 1851-1939*. Studies in Imperialism, gen. ed. John M. MacKenzie. Manchester, U.K.: Manchester University Press, 1988.

Harris, Neil. *Cultural Excursions: Marketing Appetites and Cultural Tastes in Modern America*. Chicago: University of Chicago Press, 1990.

Harris, Neil, et al. *Grand Illusions: Chicago's World's Fair of 1893*. Chicago: Chicago Historical Society, 1993.

Hendershot, Robert L. *The 1904 St. Louis World's Fair: The Louisiana Purchase Exposition Mementos and Memorabilia*. Iola, Wisc.: Kurt R. Krueger Publishing, 1994.

Hinckley, Ted C. "When the Boer War Came to St. Louis." *Missouri Historical Review* 61 (April 1967), pp. 285-302.

Historic Buildings in St. Louis County. Clayton, Mo.: St. Louis County Historic Buildings Commission, et al., 1983.

Horgan, James J. "Aeronautics at the World's Fair of 1904." *Missouri Historical Society Bulletin* 24 (April 1968), pp. 214-40.

Hoxie, Frederick E. "Exploring a Cultural Borderland: Native American Journeys of Discovery in the Early Twentieth Century." *Journal of American History* 79 (December 1992), pp. 969-95.

Iglauer, Henry S. "The Demolition of the Louisiana Purchase Exposition of 1904." *Missouri Historical Society Bulletin* 22 (July 1966), pp. 457-67.

Keefer, Karen M. "Dirty Water and Clean Toilets: Medical Aspects of the 1904 Louisiana Purchase Exposition." *Gateway Heritage* 9 (Summer 1988), pp. 32-37.

Lears, T. J. Jackson. "Making Fun of Popular Culture." *American Historical Review* 97 (December 1992), pp. 1417-26.

Leighton, George R. "World's Fairs: From Little Egypt to Robert Moses." *Harper's Magazine* 221 (July 1960), pp. 27-37.

———. "The Year St. Louis Enchanted the World." *Harper's Magazine* 221 (August 1960), pp. 38-47.

Levine, Lawrence W. "The Folklore of Industrial Society: Popular Culture and Its Audiences." *American Historical Review* 97 (December 1992), pp. 1369-99.

Liebenguth, Jane Anne. "Music at the Louisiana Purchase Exposition." *Missouri Historical Society Bulletin* 36 (October 1979), pp. 27-34.

Lossau, Carl S. "Leclaire, Illinois: A Model Industrial Village." *Gateway Heritage* 8 (Spring 1988), pp. 20-31.

Loughlin, Caroline, and Catherine Anderson. *Forest Park*. Columbia, Mo.: The Junior League of St. Louis and University of Missouri Press, 1986.

McConachie, Alexander Scot. "The 'Big Cinch': A Business Elite in the Life of a City, St. Louis, 1895-1915." Ph.D. diss., Washington University, 1976.

McCormick, Richard L. "The Discovery that Business Corrupts Politics: A Reappraisal of the Origins of Progressivism." *American Historical Review* 86 (April 1981), pp. 247-74.

McNaught, Kenneth. "American Progressives and the Great Society." *Journal of American History* 53 (December 1966), pp. 504-20.

Magnaghi, Russell M. "America Views Her Indians at the 1904 World's Fair in St. Louis." *Gateway Heritage* 4 (Winter 1983-1984), pp. 21-29.

Malone, Dumas. *Jefferson the President: First Term, 1801-1805*, vol. 4 of *Jefferson and His Time*. Boston: Little, Brown & Co., 1970.

Mandell, Richard D. *Paris 1900: The Great World's Fair.* Toronto: University of Toronto Press, 1967.

Muccigrosso, Robert. *Celebrating the New World: Chicago's Columbian Exposition of 1893.* Chicago: Ivan R. Dee, 1993.

Mutschnick, Clara Rose. "St. Louis Prepares for a World's Fair, 1898-1904." Master's thesis, St. Louis University, 1945.

Nasaw, David. *Going Out: The Rise and Fall of Public Amusements.* New York: Basic Books, 1993.

O'Brien, Frank. "Meet Me in St. Louis." *Washington University Magazine* 44 (Spring 1974), pp. 7-13.

Owens, Sister M. Lilliana. *The Florissant Heroines.* Florissant, Mo.: King Publishing Co., 1960.

Piott, Steven L. "Modernization and the Anti-Monopoly Issue: The St. Louis Transit Strike of 1900." *Missouri Historical Society Bulletin* 35 (October 1978), pp. 3-16.

Powell, Mary. "Public Art in St. Louis: Sculpture, Architecture, Mural Decorations, Stained Glass." *St. Louis Public Library Monthly Bulletin* (July-August 1925). Offprint in the Missouri Historical Society Library.

Primm, James Neal. *Lion of the Valley: St. Louis, Missouri.* 2d ed. Boulder, Colo.: Pruett Publishing Company, 1990.

Provenzo, Eugene F., Jr. "Education and the Louisiana Purchase Exposition." *Missouri Historical Society Bulletin* 32 (January 1976), pp. 99-109.

Rafferty, Edward C. "George Edward Kessler." *Gateway Heritage* 11 (Spring 1991), pp. 63-65.

———. "Orderly City, Orderly Lives: The City Beautiful Movement in St. Louis." *Gateway Heritage* 11 (Spring 1991), pp. 40-62.

Raiche, Stephen J. "The World's Fair and the New St. Louis, 1896-1904." *Missouri Historical Review* 67 (October 1972), pp. 98-121.

Rosenstone, Robert A. "Learning from Those 'Imitative' Japanese: Another Side of the American Experience in the Mikado's Empire." *American Historical Review* 85 (June 1980), pp. 572-95.

Rydell, Robert W. *All the World's a Fair: Visions of Empire at American International Expositions, 1876-1916.* Chicago: University of Chicago Press, 1984.

Rydell, Robert W. *World of Fairs: The Century-of-Progress Expositions.* Chicago: University of Chicago Press, 1993.

"St. Louis Celebrates: The World's Fair of 1904." *Missouri Historical Society Bulletin* 11 (October 1954), pp. 54-72.

Schultz, Stanley K., and Clay McShane. "To Engineer the Metropolis: Sewers, Sanitation, and City Planning in Late-Nineteenth-Century America." *Journal of American History* 65 (September 1978), pp. 389-411.

Sprague, Stuart Seely. "Meet Me in St. Louis on the Ten-Million-Dollar Pike." *Missouri Historical Society Bulletin* 32 (October 1975), pp. 26-32.

Takada, Hiroko. "Images of A Modern Nation: Meiji Japan and the Expositions, 1903-1904." Senior seminar paper, school unknown, 1992.

Thelen, David. "Memory and American History." *Journal of American History* 75 (March 1989), pp. 1117-29.

———. "Social Tensions and the Origins of Progressivism." *Journal of American History* 56 (September 1969), pp. 323-41.

Tompkins, Jane P., ed. *Reader-Response Criticism: From Formalism to Post-Structuralism.* Baltimore: The Johns Hopkins University Press, 1980.

Trennert, Robert A. "A Resurrection of Native Arts and Crafts: The St. Louis World's Fair, 1904." *Missouri Historical Review* 87 (April 1993), pp. 274-92.

Vostral, Sharra L. "Imperialism on Display: The Philippine Exhibition at the 1904 World's Fair." *Gateway Heritage* 13 (Spring 1993), pp. 18-31.

Willett, Julie A. "'The Prudes, the Public, and the Motion Pictures': The Movie Censorship Campaign in St. Louis, 1913-1917." *Gateway Heritage* 15 (Spring 1995), pp. 42-55.

Williams, Walter L. "United States Indian Policy and the Debate over Philippine Annexation: Implications for the Origins of American Imperialism." *Journal of American History* 66 (March 1980), pp. 810-31.

Wilson, William H. *The City Beautiful Movement.* Baltimore: The Johns Hopkins University Press, 1989.

Witherspoon, Margaret Johanson. *Remembering the St. Louis World's Fair.* St. Louis: Comfort Printing Co., 1973.

Young, Dina M. "The St. Louis Streetcar Strike of 1900: Pivotal Politics at the Century's Dawn." *Gateway Heritage* 12 (Summer 1991), pp. 4-17.

Index